**Work Incentives
and Income Guarantees**

Brookings Studies in

SOCIAL EXPERIMENTATION

TITLES PUBLISHED

Educational Performance Contracting:
An Evaluation of an Experiment
Edward M. Gramlich and Patricia P. Koshel

Work Incentives and Income Guarantees:
The New Jersey Negative Income Tax Experiment
Joseph A. Pechman and P. Michael Timpane, Editors

Editors: JOSEPH A. PECHMAN

P. MICHAEL TIMPANE

Work Incentives and Income Guarantees: The New Jersey Negative Income Tax Experiment

Contributors: Joseph A. Pechman and P. Michael Timpane

Robert A. Levine

Felicity Skidmore

Albert Rees and Harold W. Watts

Henry J. Aaron

Robert E. Hall

Peter H. Rossi

Bette S. Mahoney and W. Michael Mahoney

Michael C. Barth, Larry L. Orr, and John L. Palmer

The Brookings Institution

Washington, D.C.

Library of Congress Cataloging in Publication Data:
Main entry under title:
Work incentives and income guarantees.

(Studies in social experimentation)
Papers and comments presented at the conference at
Brookings Institution, Apr. 29–30, 1974, sponsored by the
Brookings Panel on Social Experimentation.
Includes index.
1. Negative income tax—New Jersey—Congresses.
2. Labor supply—New Jersey—Congresses.   3. Guaranteed
annual income—New Jersey—Congresses.   I. Pechman,
Joseph A., 1918– ed.   II. Timpane, P. Michael,
1934– ed.   III. Brookings Institution, Washington,
D.C. Panel on Social Experimentation.   IV. Series.
HC107.N53I58   361.6'2'09749   75-2321
ISBN 0-8157-6976-8
ISBN 0-8157-6975-X pbk.

9 8 7 6 5 4 3 2 1

THE BROOKINGS INSTITUTION is an independent organization devoted to nonpartisan research, education, and publication in economics, government, foreign policy, and the social sciences generally. Its principal purposes are to aid in the development of sound public policies and to promote public understanding of issues of national importance.

The Institution was founded on December 8, 1927, to merge the activities of the Institute for Government Research, founded in 1916, the Institute of Economics, founded in 1922, and the Robert Brookings Graduate School of Economics and Government, founded in 1924.

The Board of Trustees is responsible for the general administration of the Institution, while the immediate direction of the policies, program, and staff is vested in the President, assisted by an advisory committee of the officers and staff. The by-laws of the Institution state, "It is the function of the Trustees to make possible the conduct of scientific research, and publication, under the most favorable conditions, and to safeguard the independence of the research staff in the pursuit of their studies and in the publication of the results of such studies. It is not a part of their function to determine, control, or influence the conduct of particular investigations or the conclusions reached."

The President bears final responsibility for the decision to publish a manuscript as a Brookings book or staff paper. In reaching his judgment on the competence, accuracy, and objectivity of each study, the President is advised by the director of the appropriate research program and weighs the views of a panel of expert outside readers who report to him in confidence on the quality of the work. Publication of a work signifies that it is deemed to be a competent treatment worthy of public consideration; such publication does not imply endorsement of conclusions or recommendations contained in the study.

The Institution maintains its position of neutrality on issues of public policy in order to safeguard the intellectual freedom of the staff. Hence interpretations or conclusions in Brookings publications should be understood to be solely those of the author or authors and should not be attributed to the Institution, to its trustees, officers, or other staff members, or to the organizations that support its research.

Foreword

The issue of work incentives has been central to the debate in recent years about ways of improving public programs directed at alleviating poverty. Many observers—among them politicians, welfare administrators, and social scientists—believe that financial assistance given to poor but able-bodied recipients encourages them to drop out of the labor market and that much of the money is spent for harmful or frivolous things. Such beliefs have long impeded efforts to reform the federal welfare system, the patchwork of decades, and they contributed heavily to the failure of Congress to enact the family assistance plan proposed by President Richard M. Nixon in 1969.

Recognizing the centrality of the incentives question, the U.S. Office of Economic Opportunity in 1967 proposed a large-scale experiment to investigate the effect of income guarantees on work incentives. The investigation, officially designated the New Jersey Graduated Work Incentive Experiment, was conducted from 1968 to 1972 by the Institute for Research on Poverty of the University of Wisconsin and Mathematica, Inc., of Princeton, New Jersey. Four localities ultimately were involved: Trenton, Paterson-Passaic, and Jersey City, New Jersey; and Scranton, Pennsylvania.

Involving more than 1,300 intact husband-and-wife families assigned to either experimental or control groups, the experiment provided guaranteed cash payments of from 50 to 125 percent of poverty line income but imposed a tax of from 30 to 70 percent of family income. A great quantity of statistical information—sociological as well as economic—also was collected from both groups of families. A four-volume report containing analyses of the data from many perspectives was issued by the Institute for Research on Poverty and Mathematica in late 1973 and early 1974, and other studies of the experiment have appeared elsewhere in the literature of the social sciences.

Because of the importance of the issues in negative income taxation, the Brookings Panel on Social Experimentation (a list of whose members appears on page xiii) held a conference of economists, sociologists, political scientists, and research administrators at the Brookings Institution on April 29 and 30, 1974, to review the findings of the official report and to draw lessons from it for income maintenance policy and for social experimentation in the future. Both the Institute for Research on Poverty and Mathematica endorsed the idea of such a conference, and several of their staff members participated in it. This book is a record of the papers and invited comments that were presented at the conference—introduced, summarized, and edited by Joseph A. Pechman, director of the Brookings Economic Studies program, and P. Michael Timpane, who was a Brookings senior fellow until September 1974. The conference participants and their affiliations are listed on pages 225–26.

Among the contributors, Robert A. Levine wishes to thank Robinson Hollister, Joseph Kershaw, James Lyday, and Heather Ross for their collective memories and comments. Felicity Skidmore acknowledges her debt to David Kershaw, James Lyday, Thomas Skidmore, and Harold Watts for their constructive criticisms of an earlier draft of her paper. Henry J. Aaron acknowledges his debt to Philip Spevak for programming assistance; to Charles Mallar for comments on a draft of his paper; and to Irwin Garfinkel for information on the New Jersey and Pennsylvania welfare systems. Robert E. Hall is grateful to Dennis Bindley for data supplied; to Bronwyn Hall for computer aid; to Wynetta McNeill for editorial help; and to the National Science Foundation for research support.

This is the second book in the Brookings series of Studies in Social Experimentation. The series, which is under the guidance of the Brookings Panel on Social Experimentation and is supported by a grant from the Edna McConnell Clark Foundation, assesses the usefulness of experiments as a way of increasing knowledge about the effects of domestic social policies and programs of the federal government. Goddard W. Winterbottom prepared the manuscript for publication, Evelyn P. Fisher verified its factual content, Mary B. Hevener and Nancy Kandoian provided research assistance, and Helen B. Eisenhart prepared the index.

The views expressed in this book are those of its contributors, and should not be ascribed to the staff members, officers, or trustees of the Brookings Institution or to the Edna McConnell Clark Foundation.

January 1975 KERMIT GORDON
Washington, D.C. *President*

Contents

Tables

Figures

xiii

JOSEPH A. PECHMAN

P. MICHAEL TIMPANE

Introduction and Summary

The New Jersey experiment in income maintenance was unique in several respects. First, it was the forerunner of numerous other large-scale, controlled social experiments testing the effects and feasibility of new social programs by observing how they operate in practice. Second, it was concerned with a live policy issue that could not be resolved satisfactorily on the basis of available data: whether cash allowances, whose net benefits decline as work income increases, significantly reduce work by the recipients. Third, the data to be collected would provide an unusually rich source of information for analysis by economists and other social scientists. This information was the basis for an exhaustive report that was submitted to the U.S. Department of Health, Education, and Welfare in late 1973 and early 1974.[1]

The experiment was conducted at a time when the public and policymakers alike increasingly were concerned about the cost of growing welfare rolls and the alleged impact of the welfare system on the incentives of the poor to lift themselves out of poverty. The traditional welfare system was designed to assist those who were not able to support themselves because of age, disability, or special family circumstances. Families headed by able-bodied men generally are excluded from such programs on the presumption that the head should support his family by working. In addition, the income of welfare recipients was taxed, often substantially, so that they were able

1. Harold W. Watts and Albert Rees (eds.), *Final Report of the New Jersey Graduated Work Incentive Experiment*, vols. 1, 2, 3, and David N. Kershaw and Jerilyn Fair (eds.), vol. 4 (University of Wisconsin—Madison, Institute for Research on Poverty, and Mathematica, 1973, 1974) (referred to later as *Final Report of the New Jersey Experiment*).

For a summary of the major findings by several of the authors of the report, see *Journal of Human Resources*, vol. 9 (Spring 1974), pp. 156–278. The term "New Jersey experiment" used throughout this book, in keeping with the title of the final report, includes the Pennsylvania experiment, as do the data in the report.

to keep little if any of their income. Before 1967 the nominal tax rate of the federally financed assistance program was 100 percent of such income; thereafter, federal law allowed recipients to keep the first $30 per month plus one-third of any additional earnings, but supplementary benefit programs enacted by some state legislatures produced considerable variation in actual tax rates.

The negative income tax idea was advanced, first, to improve the traditional welfare system by providing a minimum, nontaxable allowance to all families; and, second, to maintain the work incentives of the poor who were able to work by permitting them to keep a significant fraction of their earnings. For example, the basic allowance might be $1,500 for each adult and $500 for each child, so that a family of four would receive a total of $4,000. Another possibility would be $1,000 for each person in the family regardless of age, which also would provide a total of $4,000 for a four-person family. As well as receiving the basic allowance, the family would pay tax on each dollar of its income.[2] The rate of this tax might be 30 percent, 50 percent, 75 percent, or even 100 percent. Thus, with a basic allowance of $4,000 and a tax rate of 50 percent, a family with an income of $2,000 would have a disposable income of $5,000: $4,000 of the basic allowance and $1,000 of its own income left after the payment of taxes. With an income of $4,000, the family would have a disposable income of $6,000: the $4,000 basic allowance plus $2,000 of its own income after taxes. With an income of $8,000, a family would break even—the $4,000 basic allowance would exactly equal the tax of $4,000—and its disposable income would be $8,000.

The idea of a negative income tax met with considerable resistance, partly because of costs but primarily because many people believed that the guarantee of a minimum level of living would provide an irresistible inducement for a significant number of persons, especially able-bodied males, to reduce their hours of work or to stop working entirely. Although economists had been making econometric estimates of the effect of a negative income tax on work effort, the results had proved inconclusive.[3]

Aside from labor response, several other questions about the operation of a system of cash allowances could be answered by such an experiment.

2. Deductions might be allowed for such items as medical expenses, work clothes, union dues, and the like, but no personal exemptions would be allowed as in the positive income tax system.

3. See Glen G. Cain and Harold W. Watts (eds.), *Income Maintenance and Labor Supply: Econometric Studies* (Markham, 1973). The econometric studies generally found income and substitution effects of the predicted positive sign, but the magnitude of the effects varied considerably.

Of primary concern were the administrative problems of paying cash allowances. How should income be defined? Over what period should it be measured? Are there unusual problems of enforcement and compliance? Although these questions seem to be caught up in minor details, they are crucial to an evaluation of the workability and cost of a negative income tax.

Another set of questions concerned the effect of cash allowances on the life style of the recipient families. Will the families use the cash allowances for such frivolities as gambling, drinking, excessive entertainment, and other nonessential or harmful forms of consumption, or will they use the allowances to buy more or better qualities of such essentials as food, clothing, and shelter? What effect, if any, would the allowances have on the education of the children, the physical and mental health of the family members, and leisure activity?

The conference sponsored by the Brookings Panel on Social Experimentation on April 29 and 30, 1974, focused on these and related issues of importance to national policy. The remainder of this chapter summarizes the formal papers presented at the conference, as well as portions of the discussion that followed.

Planning the Experiment

The opening paper, by Robert A. Levine, who was assistant director for research, plans, programs, and evaluation of the Office of Economic Opportunity (OEO) when the experiment was funded, traces the development within the government of the idea of commissioning a negative income tax experiment. To some, the major objective was experimental—to observe the labor-supply response of adult males, which they hoped would be slight—whereas to others it was mostly to demonstrate the administrative feasibility of a negative income tax. Levine's paper makes clear that the experiment was conceived by the OEO as part of a broad strategy to obtain administrative and congressional approval of a negative income tax.

The next paper, by Felicity Skidmore, describes the general design features of the experiment and the important decisions that were made in designing and carrying it out after the OEO agreed to fund the experiment and approved it in general terms. Skidmore's paper gives a detailed account of the problems that were encountered and of the administrative and analytical skill that was needed to overcome them. It was generally agreed at the conference that the experiment was carried out efficiently and that the analysis was done objectively and competently.

Skidmore's discussion reveals shortcomings as well as strengths in the experiment's design. The experiment benefited from important advances in techniques of field experimentation, notably the Conlisk-Watts design,[4] which enabled the experimenters to obtain for the same cost a significantly larger sample of relevant data than would have been possible with a simple random design. Despite problems of sample attrition and occasional disturbing influences of outside events, the basic design enabled the experimenters to collect a body of high-quality longitudinal data on the economic and social behavior of the working poor. At the same time, it was necessary to make some hard choices that limit the analytical uses of the data. These included choices with respect to the selection of the sample, the guarantees and tax rates, the site of the experiment, and the duration of the experiment.

The experiment concentrated on poor and near poor—that is, 125 percent or less of poverty income—male-headed families. This decision was based on a careful assessment of the policy significance of the behavior of this group under a negative income tax, but it excluded from study another policy-significant group, poor families headed by females; it led to an underrepresentation of families with full-time working wives; it excluded working families slightly above the eligibility line whose labor force participation also would be discouraged by a negative income tax; and it concentrated on intact families who differed in both known (for example, more children) and unknown (for example, emotional stability) ways from fractured families.

The experiment examined eight combinations of guarantees and tax rates. This design afforded an opportunity to observe the distinct effects of these two variables, but it also increased the required sample size and costs and thus limited alternatives concerning, for example, duration and number of sites. The samples for each treatment group, however, were all quite small.

The experiment operated at three urban sites in New Jersey and one in

---

4. The full model is described in John Conlisk and Harold Watts, "A Model for Optimizing Experimental Designs for Estimating Response Surfaces," in American Statistical Association, *Proceedings of the Social Statistics Section, 1969*, pp. 150–56. Its application is discussed further in Charles E. Metcalf, "Sample Design and the Use of Experimental Data," *Final Report of the New Jersey Experiment*, vol. 2, pt. C, chap. 5. The design basically called for eligible families to be stratified by previous income; a predetermined number from each stratum was then assigned to the various experimental plans and the control group, with individual assignments achieved randomly.

Pennsylvania. The sample is a reasonable representation of the eligible population, with balanced social and ethnic characteristics, in the urban Northeast, but it is not representative of the entire country. Clearly, any limited site experiment reflects only imperfectly the conditions that a universal program would introduce.

The experiment was conducted for only three years in each site. A major drawback of the experiment is that the effects of a permanent negative income tax program remain unknown.

Labor Supply Response

The paper by Albert Rees and Harold W. Watts, who were codirectors of the experiment, summarizes the labor supply findings of the experiment. The major finding is that there was only a small (5 to 6 percent) reduction in average hours worked by the male heads of the families who received negative income tax payments. For reasons that are still not understood, this occurred entirely among white men; for black men, the response was insignificant but (surprisingly) positive, whereas for Spanish-speaking men, the response was also insignificant but negative. For white and Spanish-speaking working wives, who had a low participation rate to begin with, the negative reaction was greater—about one-third of previous work effort for whites and more than one-half for those who are Spanish speaking. The behavior of black working wives was not affected.

These results are evaluated in two papers by economists who had no connection with the experiment. Henry J. Aaron focuses much of his attention on the difficulties of interpretation arising from the fact that the welfare system of New Jersey was altered while the experiment was under way. He suggests that this change in the welfare system created complex and shifting incentives for individual families that are virtually impossible to quantify for purposes of analysis. Aaron also suggests other measurement problems that might lead to an underestimate of labor supply response. On the other hand, Robert E. Hall, who develops a model to evaluate the data on labor supply response obtained from the experiment, argues that the results are consistent with theoretical expectations and are statistically significant.

Nevertheless, a number of the conferees were not persuaded that the experimental data can be regarded as definitive on this score. Three major problems accounted for most of this skepticism. First, the effects noted by

Aaron and others of changes in the New Jersey welfare system after the experiment was under way altered the net guarantees and tax rates in a haphazard way. Second, the limited time period covered by the experiment makes it difficult to draw conclusions about the effect of a permanent negative income tax. Third, the results for the nonwhite families included in the experiment, which are puzzling, may be unreliable because of high attrition rates.

Effect of the Changes in the New Jersey Welfare System

At the outset, it was considered essential to conduct the experiment in a state in which male-headed families were not eligible for any welfare assistance. Only in such a situation would the difference between the families in the experimental and control groups reflect the effect of the negative income tax alone. New Jersey was chosen as the major site partly because it had no plan under the unemployed parent part of the federally supported Aid to Families with Dependent Children (AFDC-UP) program, which extended aid to unemployed fathers. (Male heads were eligible for the locally financed general assistance program, but the benefits under this program were extremely low.) On January 1, 1969, however, New Jersey introduced a generous AFDC-UP plan for which most of the families in the experimental sample were eligible. Such families were kept in the sample, but they were required every payment period to choose between payments from welfare or the experiment.[5]

The change in the New Jersey welfare system had two effects on the results of the experiment. First, most of the families who originally were

5. The Aid to Dependent Children (ADC) program was established by the Social Security Act of 1935 to provide income-related transfer payments to families whose father had deserted or divorced the mother. Therefore, it was a program restricted to families with female heads. The name of the program was changed later—with no implications for the functioning of the program itself—to Aid to Families with Dependent Children (AFDC). An amendment to the Social Security Act in 1961 expanded the program to cover certain categories of two-parent families by adding an "unemployed parent" segment to the AFDC program, thereafter called AFDC-UP. Because the unemployed parent invariably is a father, this program is also referred to as AFDC-UF.

The AFDC-UP (or AFDC-UF) program is at state option regarding decisions as to whether it will sponsor a program at all and as to the level of benefits and the eligibility criteria. New Jersey chose not to have such a program until January 1, 1969, when it instituted one of the most generous in the country. The state treasury could not support the program at that level, however, and its generosity was cut substantially in July 1971.

placed in two of the least generous experimental plans—those with a minimum guarantee of 50 percent of the poverty line income and a 50 percent
tax rate (the 50–50 plan) and a 75 percent guarantee and a 70 percent tax
rate (the 75–70 plan)—either chose to receive welfare payments or had incomes that exceeded the breakeven levels (see the explanation above). The
few families that chose the experimental payments under these plans were
dropped from the analysis of the labor supply responses because their number was so small. In addition, relatively few of the families assigned to the
somewhat more generous 100–70 plan had incomes below the breakeven
level and thus most received no payments. The experiment therefore provides little basis for judging the amount of labor that might be supplied by
families under a 70 percent negative income tax plan. Moreover, the information from the remaining plans is not sufficient to measure the effects of
different guarantees and tax rates.

Second, the availability of the welfare option meant that families in the
experiment who were eligible for welfare faced very different guarantees and
tax rates under each negative income tax plan from those faced by families
ineligible for welfare. The result is that the observed differences between the
experimental and control families cannot be related unambiguously to the
stated guarantees and tax rates even for tax rates below 70 percent. As
Aaron explains in his paper, the net guarantees and tax rates after taking
into account the welfare option are very much lower—but not in the same
proportion—for each of the plans than the stated guarantees and tax rates
suggest.

The implications of this point were discussed at length by the conferees.
One group pointed out that, because of the existence of other government
assistance programs (in kind as well as in cash), it would have been impossible to arrange an experiment in which the net guarantees and tax rates for
each experimental family were known with certainty. Under the circumstances, the experimental results should not be interpreted as providing
estimates of the labor-supply response to any particular guarantee or tax
rate, but rather of the response to the *difference* between the guarantees or
tax rates among various plans. Such estimates still could be regarded as
significant because any negative income tax plan probably will be superimposed on other existing programs, creating a complex environment that
inevitably will alter the marginal rate that would actually apply to particular families.

Another group felt that, for the reasons mentioned by Aaron, it is virtually impossible to infer anything about the marginal effects of the different guarantee levels or tax rates on labor supply. Because the net guarantees and tax rates are lower than the stated guarantees and tax rates, the calculations from the experimental data may understate the labor supply response to the type of negative income tax plans that are offered as policy alternatives in the United States. The combination of uncertainties as to the effect of different plans also makes it impossible to estimate the costs of various national negative income tax plans on the basis of the experimental results.

Short-term versus Long-term Effects

Although the objective of the experiment was to estimate the labor supply response of a permanent negative income tax, to simulate the effect of a permanent plan obviously was impossible in an experiment lasting only three years. Early in the experiment, the study designers urged the OEO to cover some families for a period of three years and others for a period of five years, which would have permitted them to build a duration variable into the statistical analysis. But because of budget constraints, the OEO did not provide the necessary funds for a five-year period.

The temporary nature of the experiment is important because the work behavior of individuals may depend not only on their current needs and economic circumstances, but also on their future expectations. Whether the labor supply response in the experiment was greater or smaller than the response would be in a permanent plan is not clear. Some workers—particularly women who work to supplement their husbands' income—might be induced by the negative income tax payment to stop working temporarily or to reduce their hours of work with the expectation that they could go back to work or work longer hours after the negative income tax arrangement ceased. This factor would lead to an exaggeration of the labor supply response in an experiment of short duration. On the other hand, the enactment of a permanent negative income tax might bring on effects—for example, early retirement or less inhibition in quitting jobs—that a temporary experiment would be unable to capture.

Michael Boskin and Jacob Mincer, two of the formal discussants, as well as a number of other conferees, expressed the opinion that the temporary nature of the experiment probably led to an understatement of the labor supply response by male heads of families to a permanent negative income tax. Such workers usually are attached to a job that requires them to work a fixed number of hours a week. It is unrealistic to expect many of these workers to seek another job with shorter hours in the interest of obtaining a cash assistance payment for a three-year period, although over a longer period of time, employment structures might well change to make such decisions feasible. Moreover, the fact that the experimental families purchased relatively more durable goods than control families suggests that the former did not react to the additional income provided by the experiment in the same way that they would respond to a permanent change in income. Such behavior is consistent with the hypothesis that workers consider longer time horizons than three years in making economic decisions.

Although admitting that the experiment could not reproduce the conditions that would prevail under a permanent negative income tax, other conferees took the position that the results are not necessarily biased in one direction or the other. Furthermore, it is not at all certain that the three-year duration was too brief to capture most of the labor supply effects of a permanent negative income tax. Whether the time period that controls economic behavior is three years, ten years, or a lifetime is still not known. In any event, the results of the experiment were considered to be important to the policymaker, at least as an indication of the short-run consequences of a negative income tax decision. Although the long-run effects remain uncertain, the experiment suggests that there would be sufficient time to readjust the terms of any plan that is actually adopted before the full consequences of the long-run effects become evident.

The Racial and Ethnic Puzzle

A major problem mentioned by both the experimental analysts and their critics was the unexpected behavior of the black (and, to some extent, the Spanish-speaking) workers in the experiment. On the average, little change occurred in the work effort of these participants in the experiment; in fact, as compared with the control groups, the work effort of black males actually increased during the experimental period. This difference in behavior may stem from some unobserved characteristics of the experimental and control groups, from economic differences among sites (in which racial and ethnic compositions differed), from the bias of differential attrition rates, or simply from difficulties in data collection unique for these populations. These findings need to be explained or, as Hall suggests, dismissed as unreliable.

Other Behavioral Responses

The income maintenance project sought information about responses other than work effort to the experimental treatments and to income changes in general. These responses, such as consumption and employment behavior, education, and health status, were useful not only as control variables to explain variations in labor supply, but also as a basis for interpreting the social significance of a negative income tax. These measures were reviewed and evaluated for the conference by Peter H. Rossi, the lone sociologist among the writers.

As already indicated, the experimental families made larger investments in housing and durable goods than the control families. There also was evidence that less job turnover occurred under the more generous plans, and that turnover which did occur was mainly among younger workers shifting to better jobs. It was reported at the conference that analysis now in progress will show significant increases in educational attainment among experimental family members. But the data for health status, family composition, and individual well-being revealed few consistent and interpretable patterns among experimental families.

According to Rossi, these negative findings may reflect poor design and analysis; but to some extent, they may be the result also of the dominance of economists in the decisions on experimental design and analytical priorities. He points out, for example, that the relatively homogeneous nature of the sample population, which was considered an advantage from the economists' standpoint, made it virtually impossible to detect significant experimentally induced changes in such variables as family composition and individual well-being. He also pointed out that there has been a persistent absence of analysis that would systematically explain economic effects in social psychological and sociological terms. In particular, the small but significant reduction in hours worked and the changes in hours of job search, in job quality, and in worker satisfaction have begged for analysis, little of which has yet been done.

The conferees did not dispute Rossi's observations regarding the experimental design, nor was there disagreement that further analysis of the nonlabor supply response would be useful. But several conferees challenged

Rossi's contention that the experiment was dominated by economists. Other social scientists were heavily involved from the beginning and substantial resources were devoted to the noneconomic questions. On the other hand, some believed that it was right to emphasize the labor supply response as the dominant focus of the experiment—if only because the state of the experimental art was rudimentary at the time the experiment began.

In any event, given recent advances in experimentation and analysis, a much more productive combination of the disciplinary techniques ought to be possible in future experiments. Such a combination of talent could help to develop more of the richness of individual responses to experimental treatments; and the number and variety of the observations needed to obtain statistically significant results for a broad range of issues would require a much larger sample than was used in the New Jersey experiment.[6]

Policy Implications

The policy implications of the New Jersey experiment doubtless will be debated for a long time. Opinions will differ, not only because of doubts about the methodological problems that are reviewed in this volume, but also because of the changes that have occurred in U.S. social policy during the last few years. Many advances have been made in related areas of labor-market research since the mid-1960s, and the numerous changes in income support programs—reforms in AFDC itself, the creation of supplemental security income for the aged, and the expansion of the food stamp program—have created a very different environment for income maintenance policies.

Nevertheless, many of the conferees feel that the experiment will have a significant effect on attitudes toward negative income taxation. As Rees and Watts point out in their paper in this volume: "The burden of proof would now appear to be on those who assert that income maintenance programs for intact families will have very large effects on labor supply." Michael Barth, Larry Orr, and John Palmer note that the finding that the labor-supply response of male family heads usually takes the form of a reduction in hours of work rather than complete withdrawal from the labor force should moderate the pressure for a strict work test and shift more

---

6. Robert Hall contended that the labor supply results could have been replicated with a much smaller sample (see his paper in this volume), but he did not address himself to the question of sample size for determining other types of responses.

attention to distributive equity in decisions about guarantees and tax rates. They also emphasize that the experiment demonstrated the administrative feasibility of a negative income tax, including practical solutions for such problems as the definition of income and the establishment of accounting periods for determining eligibility. Various anecdotes concerning the impact already observed in executive and legislative deliberations were cited by them and others at the conference as confirming these claims of policy relevance.

Others are skeptical about these claims. Bette and Michael Mahoney argue in their paper that the experiment's design was biased toward moderate tax rates in the belief that such rates would mean greater work effort. This bias was compounded by the absence (for analysis) of several guarantees at the 70 percent tax rate. But, the Mahoneys point out, the major effect of a moderate tax rate is to extend the work disincentive farther up the income distribution. They also believe that, because the price of moderate tax rates is a lessened alleviation of poverty, the emphasis on them is unfortunate.

Other reservations were expressed. The temporary nature of the experiment, combined with the intrusions of New Jersey welfare law and some of the decisions on sample composition and on guarantees and tax rates, introduces considerable uncertainty regarding the implications of the experiment for a permanent negative income tax. Moreover, many opponents of the negative income tax did not expect widespread withdrawal of workers from the labor market. The withdrawal of only a relatively few able-bodied workers was sufficient reason for much of the opposition—and the experiment did little to remove these fears. Finally, the experiment's failure to improve the accuracy of cost estimates for alternative negative income tax plans also is unfortunate.

The conferees developed little consensus on these issues. The considerations leading to moderate tax rates were vigorously defended, as was the view that work effort is discouraged by high tax rates. It was argued that equity and politics, as well as the growth in cumulative tax rates among government cash and in-kind transfer programs, suggested that a negative income tax was still the leading practical alternative. On the other hand, it was pointed out that the recent expansion of these same income support and in-kind transfer programs has greatly reduced the urgency of a comprehensive negative income tax and thus the significance of the experiment's findings.

Significance of the Experiment

What, then, is the significance of the New Jersey income maintenance experiment for policy and for the idea of social experimentation? Eight million dollars were spent, about two-thirds of it in research costs. Aside from the direct financial costs, an enormous amount of time was spent by social scientists inside and outside the government in helping to design the experiment and in analyzing the results. Are the benefits worth the costs?

Most of the participants at the Brookings conference felt that the answer to this question is affirmative. It was generally agreed that the New Jersey experiment was conducted with diligence and intelligence, that the insights gained in program design have improved subsequent experiments, and that the administrative feasibility of a negative income tax has been demonstrated. In addition, the experiment corroborates and improves on other contemporary findings about the labor-supply response of workers to a negative income tax. As Barth, Orr, and Palmer acknowledge, however: "The experiment does not and should not decide for policymakers whether to extend cash assistance to the working poor or at what levels and with what benefit-reduction rates. Indeed, no empirical evidence could do so. Research, no matter how relevant and competent, cannot tell us what national policy ought to be. It can provide some hard data as one input to the process that balances competing demands for scarce public resources." Moreover, even with all the demonstrable advances it has made, the New Jersey experiment remains vulnerable to those who distrust its scientific underpinnings or prefer to disregard its policy implications.

Hindsight suggested to the conferees that subsequent social experiments could improve on the New Jersey experience in several respects. Treatments should be sufficiently different so that statistically significant results will be more likely to be obtained. For example, the failure to detect the relative effects of different guarantees and tax rates was one of the major disappointments of the experiment. For the same reason, sample sizes and selection should not be too parsimonious, given the uncontrolled turbulence of the environment and the likelihood of unpredictable attrition. Pre- and post-experimental data collection opportunities should be explored more fully. Finally, the design and analysis of results should have an interdisciplinary character—for, as one conferee put it, "in no other way can we hope to explain the richness of the real world." It seems clear that any major social policy experiment will face the same types of design trade-offs and constraints that were confronted in the New Jersey trial. Yet it is impossible to say whether the state of the art in social experimentation is advancing rapidly enough—and the tempo of social change is steady enough—for the larger, more complicated experiments now under way to improve on the performance of the New Jersey experiment.

Beyond its actual and potential contributions to research in the social sciences, the New Jersey experience doubtless will have a substantial impact on the ways in which proposals for social reform are considered. Without suggesting that social progress must await the results of research, the experiment demonstrates that a new social idea need not be adopted before its consequences are appraised on the basis of a carefully controlled field test.

ROBERT A. LEVINE

How and Why the
Experiment Came About

The idea of a negative income tax gained considerable support in economic and political circles during the years 1965–67, and the possibility of an experiment to test its feasibility attracted increasing interest. But the notion of an experiment was developed in a relatively casual manner, and little serious analysis of how to go about it had taken place by the time the grant was made. Consequently, many important decisions were made along the way on an ad hoc basis. This casual manner of planning focused attention on major problems rather than on details and thus may have been more effective in achieving its objective than a more careful approach.

The pathway leading to adoption of the experiment is obscure, but it had been clear from the beginning that an objective investigation—a controlled experiment—was needed to help estimate the effects of a negative income tax on work incentives of adult males. The focus on this objective was never lost, perhaps because attention was not diverted in the early days to experimental details. Recent experiments on proposed social programs have been planned more carefully, but probably they would never have been launched without the precedent of the New Jersey experience.

Origins of the Experiment

Conventional history holds that the notion of the negative income tax originated with Milton Friedman. This may well be the case, but Robert J. Lampman of the University of Wisconsin was thinking in similar terms at about the same time as Friedman. Clearly it was Lampman who, in February 1965, brought the negative income tax idea to the attention of Joseph

15

A. Kershaw, an economist and first director of the Office of Research, Plans, Programs, and Evaluation (RPPE) of the Office of Economic Opportunity (OEO), and through Kershaw to R. Sargent Shriver, then director of the OEO. Kershaw immediately appreciated the importance of the idea; Shriver also was taken with it as a long-run possibility, although it was not relevant to his immediate programmatic and legislative plans.

Refinement and Proposal: Winter to Fall 1965

In the summer of 1965, RPPE began work on a five-year antipoverty plan by commissioning a series of papers from both its own staff and outside consultants. A paper on income maintenance endorsed the negative income tax. At the same time, as chief of the research and planning division of RPPE, I put together an overall antipoverty planning strategy in which income maintenance was one of three major components and the preferred program for income maintenance was a negative income tax.[1]

The crucial role of income maintenance was accepted by the RPPE staff, but the negative income tax was more controversial. Alvin Schorr, deputy director of the office and an innovator in social work and welfare, argued strongly for a children's allowance that would be paid to all families with children, regardless of income. The economists on the staff contended that a program not related to income, such as the children's allowance, would provide a lot of money to the nonpoor in order to get a little to the poor. Kershaw accepted the argument of his fellow economists and pushed the negative income tax as part of the program he recommended to Shriver. Shriver also accepted it, and in September 1965 the antipoverty plan containing the negative income tax was sent to the White House. But, with the great increase in U.S. involvement in the Vietnam war in the fall of 1965, as well as the increasing political unpopularity of the OEO's community action programs, the plan never was taken seriously by the Johnson administration.[2]

Most proponents of the negative income tax believed, in the early days, that the greatest political problem that would arise in attempting to legislate an actual program would be the belief, among the public and in Con-

1. The other two components were job programs (particularly public employment) and social programs (including community action and education, as well as other activities).
2. See Robert A. Levine, *The Poor Ye Need Not Have with You: Lessons from the War on Poverty* (M.I.T. Press, 1970), pp. 59–72.

gress, that any form of income maintenance for adult males would bring about a large increase in idleness among those who otherwise would have worked. The whole thrust of the negative income tax, of course, was precisely to avoid this outcome—to provide such men with the financial incentives to work. But the advocates felt that, without evidence to the contrary, the conventional perception inevitably would prevail.[3]

That the necessary evidence to counter this belief—or perhaps to confirm it—could be gained experimentally was suggested by Heather Ross, then a graduate student in economics at the Massachusetts Institute of Technology, who in the summer of 1965 interned with the Council of Economic Advisers. There, as a member of a task force on income maintenance, she began to outline a method for experimentation on the negative income tax. She perfected her ideas during the following year—at the U.S. Department of Health, Education, and Welfare (HEW) and at the Brookings Institution—and formalized them in a proposal that she prepared for the United Planning Organization in Washington, D.C.; this proposal was reviewed widely and later became the basis for the New Jersey experiment.

Gathering Support: Fall 1965 through Winter 1967

Although the first five-year antipoverty plan was shelved, both the negative income tax and the experiment were discussed actively in governmental and nongovernmental quarters in the following year and a half. The tax idea itself was submitted to a good deal of current analysis; little attention was paid to the experiment.

INSTITUTIONAL INVOLVEMENT. Within the government, the OEO remained the strongest advocate of a negative income tax. In addition, a series of interagency study groups on income maintenance was convened under the leadership of the Council of Economic Advisers; representatives were included from the Budget Bureau, HEW through the office of the assistant secretary for planning and evaluation, and sometimes the Treasury Department, as well as from the OEO and the CEA. These discussions occasionally reached the office of President Lyndon B. Johnson's chief assistant for domestic policy, Joseph A. Califano, Jr., where discussion of real policy alternatives took place. At this level, neither the negative income tax nor any other form of income maintenance beyond increased social security was ever considered seriously.

3. Harold Watts had demonstrated, in an internal OEO memo, that existing cross-sectional data would not answer these questions.

Outside the government, continuing discussion and analysis took place at the Brookings Institution and at the University of Wisconsin. The formation at Wisconsin of the Institute for Research on Poverty, sponsored by the OEO with strong support from Kershaw, provided a locus for more substantial analyses of the negative income tax. From the beginning, the institute stressed research on income maintenance, but it played only a casual role in promoting the experiment at this time. The continued impetus came primarily from the OEO and to some extent from Brookings and HEW.

During this period a number of basic decisions concerning the experiment were made at the OEO, generally after some discussion with personnel from other agencies. One was to concentrate the experiment entirely on adult males, whose incentives and behavior were, in the economists' perception of political reality, the crucial political issue.[4] Therefore, the basic components of any experiment were to be concentrated on work incentives, but it was agreed that some, but not much, other information—carelessly labeled "sociological"—would be gathered as well, because the cost of obtaining it would be relatively small.

SITE SELECTION. Another crucial decision taken casually during this period concerned the location of the experiment. It was assumed from the outset that there should be a single experimental location rather than a nationwide sampling—that to do otherwise was believed to be administratively impractical. This assumption may have been correct, but it was questioned only once, by Guy Orcutt, then of the University of Wisconsin.

Washington, D.C., was dismissed as a possible location of the experiment: it was too visible and too atypical a social and political entity. New Jersey attracted interest for three reasons: first, the administration under Governor Richard J. Hughes was amenable to having the experiment; second, the highly regarded Mathematica, Inc., which was most interested in carrying out the experiment, was headquartered in Princeton; and, third, and most important, New Jersey was the only industrial state that both lacked an Aid to Families with Dependent Children–Unemployed Parents (AFDC-UP) program and was easy to reach from Washington. For the purposes of the analysis, it was important that neither the experimental nor the control group have any other income maintenance alterna-

4. It was assumed that the tax rate of the negative income tax—lower than 100 percent—would be superior to the absolute cutoffs implicit in existing welfare schemes for female-headed families. Changes in the law and more recent analyses, particularly in the Joint Economic Committee's series *Studies in Public Welfare* (1972–74), throw doubt on the assumption of major differences in this area between existing and proposed schemes.

tive available to them. Shortly after the experiment began, New Jersey adopted an AFDC-UP program, but the location decision was never seriously reconsidered on this account.[5]

DESIGN ALTERNATIVES. The final conceptual development during this period was laid out in a paper on social experimentation by Guy and Alice Orcutt.[6] The Orcutts suggested a range of experimental treatments much wider than is available through the traditional experimental concept of a control group and an experimental group or through a few separate cells of different experimental groups. To ensure a sample large enough to support inferences about each treatment, they suggested that statistically different treatments be combined and analyzed, particularly through the use of multiple regression techniques. This methodology was followed throughout the experiment.

As a relatively rigorous and controlled effort to obtain specific statistical information, the idea of an experiment did not develop much further. Instead, the proposed plan began to develop certain characteristics of a demonstration: to show on a small scale what might be proposed for later implementation on a large scale. Because of the size and cost, the experimental objectives were not fully recognized by persons who were used to thinking in terms of demonstration programs—in particular, the Community Action Program (CAP) of the OEO, which had organized tens of millions of dollars' worth of such projects.[7]

Because CAP funds were to be used, its stress on the demonstration aspect was important. The CAP carried the issue beyond the negative income tax, however, and asked for additional experimentation to examine other forms of income maintenance, particularly the nonincome-conditioned children's allowance, which had been proposed by Alvin Schorr. The request was not entirely unreasonable. That OEO policy as endorsed by Shriver was to promote the negative income tax was no reason to avoid examining other alternatives in the experimental-demonstration stage. The problem was the difficulty of visualizing a true experiment on the children's

5. For further discussion of the effect of the AFDC-UP program in New Jersey, see the following paper.

6. Guy H. Orcutt and Alice G. Orcutt, "Incentive and Disincentive Experimentation for Income Maintenance Policy Purposes," *American Economic Review*, vol. 58 (September 1968), pp. 754–72.

7. It is not clear that the CAP was incorrect. In retrospect, RPPE was naive in feeling that a pure experiment could be carried out on a multimillion-dollar scale. In fact, the political world has come to look upon the New Jersey experiment as a demonstration of how a negative income tax might work.

allowance: the CAP had no idea how to go about it, nor did Schorr, who had moved to HEW, nor Daniel P. Moynihan, another strong advocate of the allowance.

The CAP's motivation in advocating an experiment on the children's allowance again was primarily that of demonstration: to show how it would work and thus make it subject to political discussion, rather than, as in an experimental situation, to obtain information on how it would affect the recipient families. But for several reasons, neither the demonstration nor the experiment in children's allowances ever got off the ground. The essence of a children's allowance is that to avoid any stigma to the poor, it does not separate the poor from the near-poor; yet this very lack of income conditioning made an experiment difficult to conceive because, to give an experimental children's allowance to everybody in an area—the rich as well as the poor—was impractical. A nationwide children's allowance, by making changes in the regular positive federal income tax,[8] might be able to recapture some of the funds going to children of upper-income families, but it seemed difficult to do this on an experimental basis.

Discussions of the feasibility of the experiment also took place during this period between the OEO and the office of HEW's assistant secretary for planning and evaluation. HEW saw major political difficulties in such an experiment, and although it maintained an interest, it showed no inclination to help in the financing.

Getting the Program Started

By March 1967 the idea of a negative income tax was being actively considered, though it was not regarded as a serious proposal that could be enacted in less than a decade. And in regard to the experiment, the predominant mood was one of drift. Within the OEO, the political problem of mounting the experiment, together with the CAP's opposition to experimenting with the negative income tax and not a children's allowance, tended to neutralize RPPE's continuing support for the experiment.

In this atmosphere a meeting was held in March 1967 at the Ford Foundation in New York City. McGeorge Bundy, the foundation's president, was chairman of the meeting; other participants included the author, who

8. Such a plan for a universal allowance plus a tax recapture from the upper brackets was essentially what Senator George McGovern proposed in his abortive welfare reform proposals during the presidential campaign of 1972.

had succeeded Kershaw as director of RPPE, and representatives of Brookings, the University of Wisconsin, and several other organizations. The implicit objective was to determine whether the Ford Foundation would provide the financial support for a negative income tax experiment. The apparent answer was negative. In a review session after the meeting, James Tobin of Yale University and Joseph Pechman of Brookings suggested to me that if there was to be a negative income tax experiment, the OEO clearly would have to fund it.

RPPE therefore pushed ahead with development of the experiment. By June 1967 the OEO was ready with the initial grant. The guidelines had been laid down and arrangements had been made with the state of New Jersey and with Mathematica. The CAP was still holding out, but Shriver wanted the experiment and was willing to put the necessary pressure on his CAP director.

At this point, the OEO's assistant director for congressional relations sent Shriver a note to the effect that "this would not be an experiment in income maintenance; it would be an experiment in how to kill the OEO program on the Hill." The elections of 1966 had produced a Congress that was relatively hostile to the OEO and President Johnson's Great Society programs, and for the OEO, 1967 was a year of major battling for its survival and continued funding—an effort led by Shriver, who devoted almost his entire time to it. Under these circumstances, Shriver could not dismiss his aide's warning completely. He therefore suggested, first, that the grant be made in June out of funds for fiscal 1967, but that its announcement be withheld until Congress had left for its Labor Day recess; second, that the program be called "work incentives" rather than "negative income tax"; and, third, and most important, that the purely scientific aspect of the experiment—as compared with the demonstration aspect, which might have suggested to Congress that the OEO was pursuing a wild-eyed scheme or trying to usurp congressional authority to legislate—be emphasized by putting the grant through "that damned institute of yours at Wisconsin that doesn't seem to be doing much about much."[9]

Given the Shriver decision, the initial grant was negotiated quickly with

9. Establishment of the institute had been the subject of earlier conflict between RPPE and the CAP. Shriver had supported the institute but had received less assistance from it than perhaps he had expected. But in retrospect, Shriver's suggestion—that although the experiment would be carried out in New Jersey with Mathematica as the operating agent, it would be run through the institute—was a critical decision in the experiment. The institute, though it was brought in for no other reason than Shriver's political perception, made a major contribution to the experiment.

the institute and was approved by the director of the CAP on June 30, 1967. As scheduled, the announcement was made in August and the Institute for Research on Poverty, Mathematica, and the OEO staff went to work on the procedures that ultimately produced the first payments in the summer of 1968.[10]

Conclusions about Experimental Design and Outcome

The following pronouncements, ex cathedra, have grown out of reflections on the background of the negative income tax experiment, as described above. Their implications for future experimental efforts are of some importance.

First, the necessary beginning for any significant experimental effort is the definition of objectives, together with consideration of the relevance of an experimental format to these objectives. This procedure is in contrast to the point of view of a demonstration—exemplified by the CAP attitude—as well as to the more recent tendency to experiment on social programs only because experimentation seems to have become a popular technique. Unfortunately, experimentation is not always appropriate for major social efforts, nor is it always feasible. The early indication that other forms of analysis will not answer critical questions is an important precondition for acceptance of the need for experimentation.

Second, a precondition of success in an experiment is clarity of objectives and relevance, rather than a set of advance specifications about experimental details. Experiments are such complicated enterprises that detailed specifications should be prepared as a first step in the experiment itself, only after it has been decided that an experiment is in fact appropriate for obtaining the desired information.

Third, in the light of the subsequent development of the New Jersey experiment, economists should be careful when making political judgments. The primary purpose of the New Jersey experiment—to discover whether a negative income tax would decrease the work incentives of adult males— was based upon the economists' belief that work incentives were the crucial factor in determining the ultimate political acceptability of a negative income tax. In early 1970, Daniel Moynihan—by then in the Nixon adminis-

10. For details, see the following paper.

tration and a convert from children's allowances to this form of income maintenance—forced disclosure of the early results of the experiment in order to show that President Nixon's proposed family assistance plan would not decrease work incentives significantly.[11] This use of the early experimental results, however, really accomplished little, either in 1970 or subsequently. And it remains unclear whether or not the final results of the experiment, showing that effects on the work incentives of adult males are small, will play an important political role.

Fourth, as unrealistic as the political expectations of these economists may have been, those of the politicians seemed little better. Belying the warning to Shriver, the New Jersey experiment never caused political trouble. During the 1968 session of Congress, when HEW Assistant Secretary Alice M. Rivlin and I were testifying before the Joint Economic Committee, a practical, conservative congressman, Melvin Laird, praised the OEO for mounting the experiment and criticized HEW for not participating. Laird, the senior minority member of the appropriations subcommittee passing on both HEW and the OEO, was an advocate of the negative income tax.

All this suggests that social experimentation is as much a political process as a detailed scientific one. The primary result of the New Jersey experiment perhaps was to make the negative income tax visible and therefore more feasible than it otherwise would have been. In addition, some of the demonstration aspects of the experiment—for example, the definition of income, the length of the accounting period, and other vital administrative matters—played important roles in the structure of subsequent income maintenance proposals.

In any case, the fact that the experiment indicated few negative work incentives for males may have importance in pushing the idea of a negative income tax along. To use a word coined by Walter Williams, the almost universally expected result of any social experiment is "macronegative": that is, differences between outcomes for experimental and control groups are almost impossible to detect.[12] In most cases, macronegative results usually dash the hopes for a new social program; a lack of measurable

11. Because the Wisconsin and Mathematica economists were advocates of the negative income tax, not too much prodding was needed to get their cooperation in making this early disclosure.

12. Walter Williams, *Social Policy Research and Analysis: The Experience in the Federal Social Agencies* (American Elsevier, 1971), pp. 7–8.

effects as a consequence of new treatments is the norm. For the New Jersey experiment, however, the macronegative results may mark the beginning of a new life for the negative income tax idea because the meager measurable differences between the experimental and control groups imply that adult male recipients of assistance will not reduce their work effort by much. Thus, the experiment confirmed the hypothesis held by those of us who initiated it.

FELICITY SKIDMORE

Operational Design of the Experiment

The grant to undertake a controlled experiment in negative income taxation, made to the Institute for Research on Poverty in conjunction with Mathematica, Inc., was approved by the Office of Economic Opportunity (OEO) on June 30, 1967. The four volumes of the final report of the experiment were released in late 1973 and early 1974 by the Department of Health, Education, and Welfare, the inheritor of the experiment. The first fourteen months of the grant period were spent in planning, the next four years in actual operation of the experiment, and the final sixteen months in analysis of the data collected and production of the final report. The total cost of the experiment, including payments and administration, was almost $8 million.

Description of the Experiment

The eligibility criteria for a family's participation were:
—That it contain an able-bodied male between eighteen and fifty-eight years of age who was not going to school full time, not institutionalized, and not in the armed forces
—That its normal or expected income not be more than 150 percent of the official poverty line
Originally enrolled in the experiment were 1,216 such families, 725 in the experimental groups and 491 in the control group. They were enrolled sequentially in four sites: August 1968, in Trenton, New Jersey; January 1969, in Paterson and Passaic, New Jersey; June 1969, in Jersey City, New Jersey; and September 1969, in Scranton, Pennsylvania. In October 1969,

141 families in Trenton and in Paterson and Passaic were added to the control group.

The operating phase of the experiment lasted three years in each site. Every four weeks, each family in the experimental groups filled out an Income Report Form, on the basis of which their payments were calculated; the family received the indicated amount in biweekly checks. The Internal Revenue Service ruled these transfer payments to be nontaxable.

A negative income tax plan is characterized by two factors:

—A guarantee level, expressed as a percent of the poverty line: the payment the family receives if its other income is zero

—A tax, or reduction, rate: the rate at which each dollar of other income is taxed and earnings thereby reduced

Eight such negative income tax plans, representing combinations of three tax rates and four guarantee levels, finally were chosen for the experiment, as follows:

Guarantee *(as percent of* *poverty line)*	*Tax rate (percent)*		
	30	*50*	*70*
125	. . .	X	. . .
100	. . .	X	X
75	X	X	X
50	X	X	. . .

In addition to the negative income tax payments, known as transfers, every family receiving payments was paid $10 (included in their regular check) biweekly for sending in the income report form. The control families were paid $8 a month for sending in a small card giving their current address, but of course received no transfers. Every three months, an hour-long interview was held with both control and experimental families, for which they were paid $5. This other payment was considered to be taxable income.

Every effort was made to use the mails to transmit these forms and payments because, in contrast to welfare, the experiment was designed explicitly to minimize discretionary personal contact with the families. A field office at every site was found essential, however, to deal with those filing problems which did arise.

The personnel administering the interviews were, from the beginning, completely separate from those dealing with the report and payments forms. In fact, different names were used for the two groups in an effort to underline their independence in the eyes of the families.

The twelve regular quarterly interviews provided the principal source of data for the experiment. They comprised two sections: a twenty-minute section repeated every time on the status and participation of all family members sixteen years of age and older in the labor force; and a forty-minute section that varied by quarter and covered at differing frequencies items on such other kinds of economic behavior as expenditure and debt accumulation, as well as information on health and family and social behavior. Eight special interviews supplemented the quarterly interviews: a short 44-question screening interview to assess eligibility for inclusion in the experiment; a 340-question preenrollment interview to collect extensive baseline data on all the families that had been selected through screening but before they actually were enrolled; a follow-up interview held three months after the last transfer payment to explore activity in the labor force after payments had ended and to determine the families' understanding of the experiment and their reactions to the interviews and, for experimental families only, the transfer payments; an in-depth interview administered in January and February 1970 to a 10 percent subsample of experimental families to explore the program knowledge of the families and to ascertain how they viewed certain administrative and methodological problems; an annual income supplement interview administered every calendar year at the same time as the first quarterly interview of the year; a termination interview with experimental families leaving the experiment (this interview was dropped in late 1970); an attrition interview, after the experiment ended in each city, with families that had dropped out, covering income, work history patterns, and family composition to determine if their characteristics differed significantly from those who stayed in the active group; and a family composition questionnaire administered near the end of the experiment to determine whether any within-quarter changes in family composition had been missed.

All these features of the final experiment were not, however, the result of a carefully devised plan that could be put into instant operation at the site. They were, rather, the product of certain preliminary insights and decisions that had to be modified considerably in light of numerous realities and events that were not, or could not be, foreseen during preexperimental planning.

The following discussion of how this final design came into being and how it worked might be more neatly presented if each issue—site selection, for example, or ethnic balance—were covered just once, from beginning to end. Each of these considerations, however, arose and had to be dealt with in a dynamic context, continually interacting with related problems over time. Therefore, from the point of view of the manner in which the experiment's staff had to work and make those decisions about constantly recurring issues, all of which contributed to the final design, it has been felt preferable to present the discussion in time sequence rather than topically.

Decisions Made before the Contract Was Signed

The decisions that shaped the final experiment can be divided into those which were made beforehand and those which were made or, in many cases, remade more or less in the field. The first group comprised the primary objectives of the experiment, the location, the contracting, and the desirable duration of the project.

Concentrating on the Response of Male-Headed Families

Although most of the welfare population consisted of female-headed families, the OEO had decided before it made the grant that the population of interest would be able-bodied working-age males with dependents. The argument that led to the decision was as follows.

Public debate on the issue of a universal guaranteed income program of some kind generally had narrowed down to the question of the possible idleness of the working poor. Able-bodied males were the only people in American society who as a group had never qualified for public assistance. The only benefits for which they had been eligible in the past, such as unemployment compensation and social security, were dependent on their having had a history of regular employment. They were entitled to nothing simply because they were poor except whatever low-level grants might be made from local general assistance.[1]

For this reason, little was known about what their work effort would be if they were to become eligible for an income maintenance program. Over the past thirty years economists had done much empirical work on labor supply. But the data gathered and used had not been restricted to low-income workers and did not contain the kinds of variation in income or

1. Although by 1966–67 some twenty states had Aid to Families with Dependent Children–Unemployed Parents (AFDC-UP) programs extending aid to intact families, no data on them were available.

wage rates—particularly in the case of the poor—that were envisioned in the negative income tax plans under consideration.[2]

The need to learn more about the work behavior of female heads of household also was discussed during that period, but three arguments prevailed against the idea of including them in the experiment. First, female heads of households already were eligible for public assistance; therefore, conversion of the program from a state to a national basis could be expected to have a relatively small effect on them. Second, their participation in the labor force was comparatively low, and could be expected to remain so because they typically headed families with children and no other caretaking adult. Any new transfer program would be unlikely to reduce their work effort further and thus *add* significantly to transfer costs. The major policy interest, it should be remembered, was in whether transfer payments (and therefore program cost) would increase massively if a negative income tax program were adopted on a national scale. In fact, because the tax rates on earned income for AFDC beneficiaries had been running as high as, or higher than, 100 percent, a negative income tax with lower tax rates could be expected, if anything, to stimulate them to work more and therefore reduce their need for transfer payments. Third, the Social Security Act as amended in 1967 placed a maximum tax rate of 67 percent on AFDC. The research community expected a research component to be built into the New York City AFDC program to provide information on the labor force participation of female heads of families under the new (lower) tax rates.

Location of the Experiment in New Jersey

The decision to run the experiment in New Jersey had two unintended effects that, combined with other historical accidents, reduced the usefulness of the experimental evidence obtained: the contamination with welfare, and the fact that the white families in the sample had to be drawn largely from a site that differed in significant ways from the other sites, thus reducing the value of the results in generalizing to the country as a whole. But the reasons for choosing New Jersey seemed strong, were generally agreed upon, and proved decisive.

2. The recent group of studies using the Survey of Economic Opportunity—a two-year panel survey, principally of low-income households, commissioned by the OEO and carried out by the Census Bureau for 1966 and 1967—were subsequent not only to the planning but also to the early operation of the experiment. Glen G. Cain and Harold W. Watts (eds.), *Income Maintenance and Labor Supply: Econometric Studies* (Markham, 1973), pp. 5ff.

Although some of the most distinguished participants in the academic debate strongly favored a nationally dispersed sample, most people concerned with the feasibility of the operation felt that, in terms of cost, sample size, and administration, a national effort was impossible. In 1967 no administrative expertise, such as has been developed since by Mathematica and others, yet existed. Nor was it clear that plans offering differing payments (including zero) could be administered simultaneously without recipients' making their own comparisons and refusing to cooperate. If trouble arose, it was thought that geographical proximity of the administrators to the sites would help the experiment to continue functioning effectively.

Concern about community disruption also led the planners to put great weight on the cooperation and even participation of the state administration. Here, New Jersey seemed to score high marks. The head of the New Jersey Department of Community Affairs promised his full support, as did the New Jersey Economic Policy Council.[3] The New Jersey government also was prepared at that time to assume the administrative costs of disbursement of, and accounting for, the payments to experimental subjects.[4]

Another argument in favor of New Jersey concerned the potential problem of overlapping welfare payments. The planners of the experiment presumed that to select an unbiased sample and to produce usable data, it was important to avoid sites in which competing payment options existed. The AFDC-UP program, which in certain states extended aid to unemployed fathers and included generous state supplementation, could overlap seriously with the planned experiment. That New Jersey had no AFDC-UP program and was not projecting one was seen as an added advantage.

The planners also wished to have a relatively homogeneous sample. Previous work on the subject had suggested a reasonable sample size of about 1,000 families,[5] which assumed that the sample observations could be analyzed as one group. The existing literature on labor supply indicated differential responses according both to demographic characteristics and

3. Mathematica, Inc., "Proposal for an Experimental Study of the Negative Income Tax" (prepared for the Office of Economic Opportunity, May 31, 1967; processed), p. 30.

4. Institute for Research on Poverty, "Experimental Study of the Negative Income Tax" (research grant application to the Office of Economic Opportunity, June 27, 1967; processed), Budget Table.

5. Heather Ross, "A Proposal for a Demonstration of New Techniques in Income Maintenance" (United Planning Organization, December 1966); Guy H. Orcutt, "Experimental Study of Negative Income Taxation" (memorandum, March 1967); Glen G. Cain, "A Discussion of Sample Size for the Experimental Study of the Negative Income Tax" (memorandum, June 1967).

to the kind of labor market facing the potential worker. These considerations further supported the decision to restrict the experiment to males with dependents and suggested that the limited sample size and budget required a focus on one geographical area. These criteria pointed to the urban industrial Northeast, where the poor were predominantly wage earners living in large metropolitan areas.

As these decisions were being made, the proposed experiment came to be seen as a first step in a "test-bore" approach to income maintenance experimentation, one in which different sections of the labor force and the labor market would be explored in different experiments to reduce the risk of failure, in administration and in adequate depth of the data for analysis. Shortly after the New Jersey experiment was funded, the Ford Foundation awarded a grant to the Poverty Institute to plan an income maintenance experiment for rural areas, and the OEO awarded a grant to the institute for the execution of such an experiment in 1968. Since then HEW has funded an experiment in Gary, Indiana, the central focus of which is the female-headed family (plus day care), and one in Seattle and Denver that focuses on households with and without the benefit of labor market services and job training.

Awarding the Grant and Subcontract

The proposal by Heather Ross on which the finally funded experiment was built actually was a design for a demonstration on the work effort of able-bodied males. The concept of a control group and of a systematic statistical design, however, already appears clearly in the Ross proposal. The discussion it stimulated, along with later events, led to the funding of a somewhat different experiment, but the features of controlled experimentation and the concentration on the work effort of able-bodied males with dependents remained. The Council of Economic Advisers became interested in the Ross idea, and the OEO was enthusiastic enough to solicit similar proposals from various other groups experienced in statistical methodology and the economics of labor force behavior.

The OEO leaders decided to concentrate on the urban Northeast almost as soon as they became interested in the general idea of a negative income tax experiment. An analysis was made of the labor market in five northeastern states to determine which of them most nearly approximated the overall U.S. unemployment rate. When, on the basis of this analysis, New Jersey began to look like a good site, administrative feasibility suggested that likely research groups near potential urban sites in New Jersey be considered to conduct the experiment. Several such groups were contacted by the OEO. On May 31, 1967, Mathematica, Inc., of Princeton submitted a proposal for an experimental study of the negative income tax, listing Heather Ross as one of the people to be involved in the study.

The OEO decided to fund the experiment, but to make the actual grant to the Institute for Research on Poverty, which could then subcontract with Mathematica. Because the OEO planners wanted the true character of the project to be made clear and to protect it as much as possible from that publicity and political vested interest which demonstration projects had learned to expect, they looked to the institute, located at a respected university, to provide the necessary shield.

After negotiations between the institute and Mathematica over rights and responsibilities in the research, the contract was signed just before the end of fiscal 1967. Under it, the institute agreed to implement what was basically a Mathematica proposal, subject to its continuing approval of all basic design, management, and data-collecting activities. Mathematica retained responsibility for studies of the probable effect of a negative income tax on a recipient's work effort and for the conduct of experimental operations.[6]

As it turned out, these negotiated provisions were not strictly adhered to. Instead, the grantee and the subcontractor shared responsibility for most of the major decisions discussed in the next section, and for the final analysis. The thirty research chapters of the final report (including those on the labor supply response) were written by researchers from both Mathematica and the institute and were edited by Harold W. Watts of the institute and Albert Rees of Mathematica. The volume of the final report devoted to the operational aspects of the experiment was entirely the work of Mathematica, edited by David N. Kershaw and Jerilyn Fair.

Duration of the Experiment

The proposal finally funded by the OEO was internally inconsistent as to how long the experiment was to last. The timetable and the budget clearly stated the duration of the payment phase as three years, but in the body of the proposal the duration of the experiment is considered a potential variable.[7]

6. Poverty Institute, "Experimental Study," pp. 2–3.
7. Ibid., p. 9.

There is no record of substantive discussion about duration in the months following the grant. All sides appear to have assumed that three years was reasonable. Two years later, however, the possibility of securing additional funds to continue a long-term subsample became a live issue. The OEO refused to consider the request, partly because the sample families already had been told that the experiment would take three years and they could not now constitute a group with an uncontaminated time horizon.[8]

In retrospect, failure to vary the time duration appears to have been a mistake, not only because data on time horizons stand to be valuable for judging how permanent an income source the families consider the experimental payments to be,[9] but also because evidence has emerged consistent with the existence of a learning effect on the part of families. The income report forms and quarterly interviews asked for gross income. Both experimental and control families had trouble distinguishing net from gross. The hypothesis holds that the experimental group learned the distinction more quickly because they were asked for their income every month and the control group only every three months—a factor that led to a spurious income differential between the two groups.[10] Light could have been shed on the hypothesis of a learning experience if families had been on the experiment for differing lengths of time.

In the context of this possible learning effect, an even more unfortunate decision was taken: the control families would not be required to file income report forms every four weeks. The reason for the decision was the fear that the families would become sensitized with too much contact and would act progressively less like proper controls. The argument was brought forward, although it did not carry the day, that to constitute a true comparison group, the control group should have the same requirements as the experimental, including filing responsibilities. It was very generally phrased, however, and nobody realized that learning to report correctly would itself be a long-term process that could confuse the results.

8. The Seattle-Denver income maintenance experiment has duration as a variable: some families receive payments for three years, some for five.

9. Charles E. Metcalf, "Predicting the Effects of Permanent Programs from a Limited Duration Experiment," in Harold W. Watts and Albert Rees (eds.), *Final Report of the New Jersey Graduated Work Incentives Experiment* (University of Wisconsin—Madison, Institute for Research on Poverty, and Mathematica, 1974), vol. 2, pt. C, chap. 3 (cited hereafter as *Final Report of the New Jersey Experiment*).

10. Harold W. Watts and John Mamer, "Wage-Rate Response," in ibid., vol. 1, sec. 2, pt. B, chap. 6.

Data on the 141 families added to the control group a year after the beginning of the experiment have not yet been analyzed, but they can be used to shed some light on the learning curve of the control families.

Decisions Made or Revised during the Planning and Implementation Phases[11]

Establishment of preliminary administrative regulations and of basic facets of the experimental design took place before the experiment was set in motion. In many instances, certain discoveries about the real world, as well as various events that occurred once the experiment was under way, required that changes be made or were otherwise significant for our work.

Administrative Regulations

The first major task after the grant was awarded was to draw up a set of rules of operation as detailed as those that would have to accompany any legislation drawn up in the area. Rules affect behavior, and a non-exhaustive set could introduce unknown and uncontrolled variation. Work on the rules proceeded independently at Wisconsin and at Mathematica, and several meetings were held to reconcile differences. By the end of 1967 most of the rules of operation had been set. The main definitions concerned the nature of the filing unit (that is, the collection of people eligible to fill out a joint family income report form and receive the payment as a group); the definition of income; the accounting period; and the problem of the overlapping of experimental tax rates with those of existing programs.

FILING UNIT. The family was chosen as the filing unit for purposes of calculating and receiving payment. The family unit was defined as the head of the family plus his or her dependents. There had to be at least one dependent, not necessarily a child. There also had to be at least one able-bodied male between eighteen and fifty-eight years of age who was not institutionalized, in school full time or in the armed forces; he did not have

11. Certain descriptive parts of this section are summarized from David N. Kershaw and Jerilyn Fair (eds.), from their volume of the final report of the experiment, *Operations, Surveys, and Administration*, vol. 4 of *Final Report of the New Jersey Experiment.* Except where otherwise noted, the narrative is based on the unpublished memoranda now deposited at the Data Center of the University of Wisconsin and a diary kept for part of the period by the Mathematica central office.

to be the family head.[12] A dependent was defined as any blood or adopted relative living with the head or a person not so related but living with the head and receiving no more than $30 a month from sources other than the family income.

The decision to include able-bodied males with dependents even if they were not heads of families was made for three reasons.[13] First, the focus of the experiment could be said to be on male primary wage earners with dependents. A man supporting his mother or sister (with or without her children) could be expected to react to labor market choices in a way similar to married men supporting dependents. Second, 1960 Census tabulations suggested that the eligibility rates could be increased by about 5 percent if unmarried able-bodied males were included in addition to married male heads. Third, there was the fear that "taking out [these] families . . . even though they do not bulk large in the population may have a disproportionate effect on the degree to which the results of the study are accepted."[14] In the final report the labor force analysis was restricted to married men because of the difficulty of incorporating different family types into one analysis. The decision to enroll the eighty or so single men with dependents simply restricted the size of the sample available for post-experimental analysis.

The general intent of the family unit regulations was to simulate insofar as possible the conditions of a nationwide program. On two specifics, however, such simulation was not possible: when a member leaves or when a new member joins a family unit. There was much concern that the experimental rules be neutral with respect to incentives for change in family composition.[15] Thus, a decision was made that children who became of age could continue to receive the payment attributable to them as a family member when they left the unit, but they were not eligible to start a new filing unit of their own. This was to prevent the creation of a "dowry effect,"

12. Age fifty-eight was chosen so that none of the able-bodied males would become eligible for retirement before the end of the experiment.

13. This decision on the status of the family head was not enforced consistently until mid-1969, after Trenton had been in operation for a year.

14. Robinson Hollister and Harold W. Watts, "Comments on Criteria for Inclusion of Families in the Sample" (memorandum, May 8, 1968).

15. The *Final Report of the New Jersey Experiment*, vol. 4, pp. 125–30, discusses in more detail the inherent ambiguity of such a concept, shows how the various income maintenance experiments differ in their regulations regarding family unit rules, and argues that how the rules treat family formation or dissolution may have "critical implications for the cost and impact of a national program" (p. 130).

whereby children in experimental families would be more than usually marriageable for the three-year experimental period. To prevent experimental families from becoming artificially attractive as lodging places for relatives or friends, an analogous decision prohibited families from admitting new members for payments purposes except their own newborn children or other children after a six-month continuous period of residence within the new family.

When a spouse left the original household, the regulations provided for that spouse to take the fraction of the family guarantee allotted to him or her. The guarantees for both spouses were always equal. The children's guarantees went to the spouse who took custody.

DEFINITION OF INCOME. The definition of income was to serve as a measure of overall economic well-being that would enable the calculation of payments to reflect adequately and uniformly the differences from family to family. The Internal Revenue Code definition therefore was amended with this in mind. The definition of income for the experiment included, in addition to earnings, annuities and pensions; prizes and awards; life insurance in excess of $1,000; gifts; support payments; inheritances; trust distributions of capital totaling more than $100 a year; interest on all government obligations; any damages, insurance payments, and workman's compensation; all dividends; scholarships and fellowships in excess of tuition, books, and fees; income from a trust or estate; alimony and court-ordered support; the rental value of public housing to the extent it exceeded rent paid and the rental value of owner-occupied housing; any indirect or direct cash payments and the value of in-kind lodging from job or public[16] or private agency, including unemployment compensation, strike or other unemployment benefits, social security benefits, veterans' disability benefits, and training stipends; and income received from non-family members, such as roomers, living with the family.

The deductions allowed for in the experiment included: direct costs incurred in earning income for the self-employed (of which there were few); mortgage interest, real property taxes, and a fixed property allowance in

16. In the original rules, welfare payments were treated the same way: that is, added to income. In 1967–68 the only major welfare program in New Jersey was AFDC (restricted to female heads of families). Because eligibility for the experiment required that a family contain an able-bodied non-aged male, we expected minimal overlap with welfare. When the generous AFDC-UP program (for two-parent families) went into effect in January 1969, the rules had to be changed so that in any one reporting period a family could be eligible only for the experiment or for welfare. The rules permitted them to switch as many times as they liked.

computing income from owner-occupied housing (see additions to income above); $12 a week for a roomer receiving meals; alimony and court-ordered support payments up to $30 a month per supported person; the cost of caring for any child or incapacitated person if a member of the unit thereby was released for immediate earnings up to $80 per month for one dependent and a maximum of $120 for two or more. An annual disregard of $1,200 was also allowable for aged ineligible members of the unit. Capital gains were treated as income and capital losses were counted deductible to the extent of capital gains realized during the experimental period.

ACCOUNTING PERIOD. The accounting period is defined as the period over which income is counted for the calculation of a transfer payment. (The accounting period for the current welfare system generally is one month. That for the positive tax system is one year.) The period for which income is included affects the degree of equity in the system, as well as the degree of responsiveness to financial need. It also can be expected to affect patterns of work behavior and therefore the transfer cost of any program because the shorter the accounting period the more can be made out of the system by bunching earnings and then taking periods of not working at all. The goal of maximizing responsiveness always conflicts with the goals of producing annual equity and minimizing work disincentive and cost.[17]

When the regulations were being drawn up, these factors were appreciated to some extent, but the conceptual and administrative problems involved in achieving annual equity without losing most of the system's responsiveness to need were underestimated. It was not until the experiment had been in operation for a year in the pilot city, Trenton, that a satisfactory system finally was achieved.

When the experiment began, two methods of maintaining annual equity were considered. The first was to make regular payments every four weeks based on the family's income simply for the previous month and then reconcile payments at the end of the year. The second involved use of a twelve-month moving average, by which the current month's income was averaged with the preceding eleven months' income to reach an average income figure for the past year. Because a family would perceive an immediate increase in payments for any decrease in earnings, the OEO did not want to test the most responsive, one-month, system, viewing it as likely to produce a greater disincentive than would be feasible from a policy point of view. A compromise was reached under which a three-month moving

17. For illustration of this conflict, see Kershaw and Fair, *Operations*, chap. 4.

average was used for the payments calculation, with an adjustment at the end of the year.

Too little thought, as it turned out, had been given to the problem of recapturing overpayments, possibly because the amount of income variation that would be experienced by the families must have been implicitly underestimated, even though it was discussed at length. By the end of the first calendar year of operations in the pilot site—which in fact included only five months of payments—substantial discrepancies between what the families had received and what they should have received on an annual basis already had appeared for 40 percent of the families. One overpayment was as high as $463. Obviously, recapturing such large sums in one installment was not possible, and recapturing them out of a series of future payments also seemed unsatisfactory on the grounds that the responsiveness of the payments to income changes would be obscured.

The problem finally was solved in mid-1969. The planners of the upcoming rural experiment were formulating their regulations and had the problem of self-employed farmers whose incomes and outflows are bunched throughout the year. A carryover method of accounting was devised under which payments were based not only on the average family income during the last three months but also on any income in excess of the breakeven amount earned in any of the preceding twelve months. As long as a carryover sum existed, the payment was zero; if the remaining carryover from any month was still greater than zero after allocations from it had been made in each of the twelve succeeding months to bring the accounted income up to the breakeven point, the excess was dropped from any subsequent payment calculations.[18]

The reconciliation problem, however, had renewed discussion among the research staff about accounting periods and particularly about an entirely retrospective twelve-month moving average. Wisconsin felt that the accounting period itself also should be a variable of interest, but Mathematica was unwilling to disturb the families already enrolled by changing the method of calculation in any more drastic a way than the new carryover provision.

The OEO agreed that the twelve-month system was important because of possible differences in work incentive. As enrollment was taking place in Jersey City and Scranton, therefore, sixty-five families were assigned to the retrospective twelve-month moving average accounting system. In retrospect, it was a bad decision: sixty-five was too small a number to pick

18. The method was devised by William Klein and D. Lee Bawden. For more details, see ibid., pp. 88–89.

up any but the grossest differences in work incentive. Furthermore, no real policy interest ever existed in such a system because of its lack of responsiveness to changes in need. For the final statistical analysis, the sixty-five families were lumped together with the rest who were on the three-month moving average system.

OVERLAPPING TAX RATES OF OTHER PROGRAMS. Because a situation in which the families had no contact with, or participation in, other tax and transfer mechanisms was considered impossible, the only feasible alternative was to decide which other tax rates were important to control for and then to formulate a means of counteracting their effects. The issue narrowed fairly readily to the question of the positive income tax.

First, a decision was made not to be concerned with those programs which could be expected to remain in operation even if a negative income tax were adopted nationally: for example, sales taxes. But any work-conditioned tax rates that might affect the work effort of the control and experimental groups differently were recognized as needing to be controlled to enable any experimental effects to be isolated.

The welfare system was an obvious candidate for caution on both counts. It could be expected to vanish with the implementation of a national program, and it was a work-conditioned program whose benefits depended on the amount the recipient earned. As noted above, the planners had picked New Jersey in part because—with the population of interest being families with an able-bodied male of working age—the absence of AFDC-UP meant that the problem of a welfare overlap did not arise. The designers realized that during the course of the experiment certain families probably would become female headed and thus potentially eligible for AFDC, which required that no male head be present; but they assumed that the number of such cases would be small and could be handled adequately simply by including welfare payments in the experimental definition of taxable income. Originally, medicaid and the food stamps program were considered equally minor: medicaid because it was tied to AFDC eligibility, and the food stamps because they were a small program in New Jersey at the beginning (and remained so throughout much of the experiment).

Social security was not regarded as a problem because it was not seen at that time as likely to disappear with welfare reform. Although it was a work-conditioned program, it was considered to be part of the status quo for both the control and experimental groups and unlikely, therefore, to affect work choices.

That left the positive income tax system, which was handled—not entirely satisfactorily—in the following way. Because the maximum income level at which no positive tax was paid was lower than the income level, or breakeven point, at which the experiment's payments were reduced to zero, superimposing one system on the other without making some adjustment would produce a range of incomes over which experimental families would face a very high tax rate (composed of the tax rate of their experimental plan plus the positive income tax rate applicable to their income). If positive taxes paid were reimbursed in full for people below their experimental breakeven point but not at all for people above it, a tax rate "notch" would be produced whereby an increase in income of one dollar could bring about an actual decrease in disposable income. A decision was made, therefore, that families would be reimbursed in full or in part for positive taxes paid so as to maintain a constant tax rate—dictated by the particular experimental plan to which they were assigned—up to the tax breakeven point, defined as the point at which the yield from the positive tax system is equal to the yield if the tax rate of the negative income tax plan were extended past the breakeven level into the income range covered by the positive tax system. Thus, families paying no positive tax were unaffected; families with incomes below the breakeven point of their particular experimental plan had all taxes reimbursed; and families with incomes over the breakeven point for their experimental plan but not as high as their tax breakeven point were partially reimbursed.

In theory, this was a straightforward solution. From an experimental point of view, however, it proved unsatisfactory because the administrative procedures adopted for the rebate produced a long time lag between the time the families paid their positive taxes and the date of their rebate check. Rebates were calculated on the basis of W-2 forms and 1040 tax forms that were requested from the families, most of whom were quite willing to hand them over. But using the 1040 forms meant, for example, that taxes which had been withheld in January 1969 could not be rebated until after the 1040 forms had been completed, any time between January 1 and April 15, 1970.[19]

Experimental Design

The main attributes of any design are composition of the sample, specification of experimental variables, and allocation of the sample to experi-

19. Kershaw and Fair, in ibid., pp. 99–100, note that in the Seattle-Denver income maintenance experiment, tax rebates are made concurrently with the payments on an estimation basis. A final year-end reconciliation then must be made, with lags as long as those in New Jersey but involving much smaller amounts.

mental cells. The following sections—which discuss the reasons behind, and the consequences of, the decisions in these areas—do not attempt to evaluate various design strategies from a methodological point of view.

INCOME FACTOR IN COMPOSITION OF THE SAMPLE. The decision to restrict the sample to families containing an able-bodied, working-age male and at least one dependent has been discussed, as has the decision to restrict the geographical area to urban industrial sites in New Jersey. Here I shall discuss the other decision affecting composition of the sample: the decision to restrict it to families with normal family income not more than 50 percent above the poverty line.

The original intention was to restrict eligibility to officially poor families: those with average incomes below the social security defined poverty line. As design work began in earnest, however, it became clear that some families had to be included whose incomes were over the breakeven point of their respective negative income tax plans—that is, currently were not receiving actual experimental payments, although they would be eligible should their income drop. One of the big questions in preparing any program cost estimate was the number of families that would be prepared to cut their work effort in order to bring themselves down to the level at which they could receive payments from the experiment. By December 1967 the decision had been made to raise income eligibility, and the remaining question was whether it should be 25 or 50 percent above the poverty line. The decision was to be made on the basis of one-in-one-thousand sample Census tabulations showing the increase in the eligibility rate to be expected. In mid-January 1968 the income cutoff level was set at 50 percent above poverty. Without this decision the eligibility rate would have been very low indeed.

The concept of income being discussed was not current income but rather some measure of normal,[20] expected, or permanent income, to minimize possible bias. At any given level of current income, the group of

20. For the final analysis two rather statistically sophisticated measures of normal income were formulated. The original hope was that the same could be done for the normal income measure on which the sample was selected and stratified. The exigencies of the field work schedule and data processing facilities were such, however, that the estimates for eligibility purposes were made by inspection of the screening and preenrollment questionnaire to see whether certain features of the family—education and training of the wife, for example, if she was not working—would lead to the presumption that their normal income probably was significantly higher or lower than the average given for the past year. The sample was differentiated on the basis of three normal income strata: 0–99 percent of poverty, 100–124 percent, and 125–150 percent.

people who fall below that level will comprise those whose regular income is low, but it also will include those whose usual income is high but who happen to be in an income slump. It will not, however, include those whose usual income is low but who are having a short-term increase in income. Any measured income change over time for the group as a whole will include income increases for those who are in fact simply returning to their usual (high) level, but will pick up no decreases of people returning to their usual (low) level, because they were by definition excluded from the group in the first place. Therefore, income increases will be overestimated. A longer-term measure will lessen this overestimate.

From a research point of view, the higher the income cutoff—within reason—the better the estimates of cost and work effort would be. But two considerations argued against raising it further: the concern, first, of those persons close to the field operations that the payment amounts not be insignificant for a large group of sample families, and, second, of the OEO that substantial amounts not be paid to the technically nonpoor.

As the field work began in the second half of 1968, it became clear almost immediately that the number of eligible families was much lower than the estimates made from the 1960 Census. The ratio of eligible families in our pilot site, Trenton, was only 4.3 percent of families contacted, and of the eligible poor, constituted less than 2 percent of all contacted households.[21] The question arose as to whether the eligibility requirements should be expanded—and, if so, how. A reassessment of the decision to exclude female-headed families was rejected. Raising income eligibility levels was looked on favorably by all researchers but regarded as politically inconceivable by the OEO.[22]

The decision to retain the income cutoff at 50 percent above the poverty line inevitably left working wives very underrepresented in the sample. Stratification by family income, given the wage rates prevailing in New Jersey, meant that families with two regular wage earners, unless the family was quite large, almost certainly would be excluded from the sample. The percentage of wives who remained in intact families and worked regularly throughout the experiment was only 15 percent (although 40 percent worked at one time or another), which left an uncomfortably small sample

21. Heather Ross, "Reassessing Our Eligibility Requirements" (memorandum, October 21, 1968); and "An Experimental Study of the Negative Income Tax" (Ph.D. dissertation, Massachusetts Institute of Technology, 1970), p. 46.

22. Minutes, Mathematica–OEO–Poverty Institute meeting, Washington, D.C., November 1, 1968.

for analysis—especially because of the fact, also unanticipated, that the three ethnic groups ultimately had to be analyzed separately.

SPECIFICATION OF EXPERIMENTAL VARIABLES. Before the experiment was funded, the possibility was discussed of using the size of payment as the experimental variable instead of varying tax rates and guarantee levels, adjusted for family size, explicitly. From the beginning of the design discussions, the experimenters themselves agreed on the latter strategy.

The guarantee levels were specified as percentages of the poverty line; in fact, the official poverty lines were altered for the experiment because it was felt that there was no analytical justification for using nutritional requirements alone as the basis of need, as the social security poverty levels did, especially regarding the variation in need by family size. The poverty lines used for the first year of the experiment are shown below, compared with the Social Security Administration index for 1967–68:[23]

Poverty line (dollars)

Number in family	New Jersey experiment	Social Security Administration
2	2,000	2,115
3	2,750	2,600
4	3,300	3,335
5	3,700	3,930
6	4,050	4,410
7	4,350	4,925
8 or more	4,600	5,440

These figures were increased in July of every year by the percentage change in the consumer price index. The question then became which guarantee levels and tax rates to test.

By the end of 1967 the researchers had come to general agreement that the values of the experimental parameters were primarily a matter of policy interest rather than of statistical design and had rejected "the thoroughgoing orthogonality of Orcutt."[24] In March 1968 three guarantee levels—50, 75, and 100 percent of the poverty line—and three tax rates—30, 50, and 70 percent—were decided on.

23. Albert Rees, "Variations in Support Levels with Family Size" (memorandum, February 12, 1968); and "An Overview of the Labor-Supply Results," *Final Report of the New Jersey Experiment*, vol. 1, sec. 1, pt. A.

24. This was a reference to the unpublished paper by Guy Orcutt, "Experimental Study," in Heather Ross, "Meeting at Institute for Research on Poverty" (memorandum, December 6, 1967), p. 3.

The general rationale for the choice of guarantee levels was that levels higher than the poverty line were regarded as politically impossible to achieve; the most likely level was considered to be 75 percent, and 50 percent was chosen as the lowest feasible level. On the tax rates, 50 percent had been used by many economists in their exposition of the negative income tax and therefore had come to be considered a central point; 70 percent, just slightly higher than the new rates on public assistance, was regarded by most social policy experts as the highest feasible rate but still rather punitive; and 30 percent was considered a reasonable lowest bound. The combination of a 50 percent guarantee and a 70 percent tax rate was rejected as too low in terms of political feasibility, and the 100 percent guarantee with a 30 percent tax rate was rejected as too high.

The field operations began in the summer of 1968, and these decisions were called into question immediately. Only about half the number of eligible families expected actually had been discovered and only about 30 percent of these had incomes below the poverty line. This meant that payments to the families would run about 40 percent below the target set earlier in 1968: an average per family of $1,500 a year.[25] People at Mathematica felt increasingly dissatisfied with how relatively high the incomes of the sample were turning out to be in comparison to the guarantee levels and how many family incomes were going to fall above the breakeven point of their assigned plan. The possibility was raised of either increasing the general level of all the guarantees or introducing a more generous plan or plans.

In the fall of 1968 the problem of how generous the experimental plans were was aggravated by New Jersey's decision to introduce, as of January 1, 1969, an AFDC-UP program with the following support standard:

Number in family	Support standard (dollars)
2	2,300
3	3,175
4	3,800
5	4,250
6	4,650
7	5,000
8 or more	5,300

These levels were generous enough to dominate the 50 percent guarantee–50 percent tax rate and the 75 percent guarantee–70 percent tax rate plans over almost the entire eligible income range, and most of the others over

25. Ross, "An Experimental Study," p. 101.

parts of that income range. The Poverty Institute had not been sympathetic to previous arguments about raising the generosity levels, but the certainty that an AFDC-UP program would be introduced, with one of the highest support standards in the country, persuaded them that something had to be done. On November 1, 1968, representatives from Mathematica and the institute went to Washington to persuade the OEO that changes had to be made. A new guarantee of 125 percent was added to the policy options. It was to be combined with both the 50 percent and 70 percent tax rates, but the latter subsequently was dropped from the final design. The set of experimental plans appeared to be completed to the satisfaction of all concerned.

ALLOCATION OF THE SAMPLE. As the allocation of families in the initial sites proceeded, however, increasing disagreement appeared between Mathematica and the institute as to how the sample should be allocated among the experimental plans. Divergence between the two groups of researchers appeared as early as the spring of 1968; disagreement continued through the process of assigning families in both Trenton and Paterson-Passaic. The dispute finally had to be referred to the OEO and an outside expert, James Tobin, for resolution, in June 1969, just as families in Jersey City were being enrolled.

The disagreement had a complex background, and a full picture of the relevant issues is necessary to understanding this aspect of the experimental design.

The objective of the experiment was agreed to be that of securing an estimate of the cost of a national program—or at least the cost of covering urban wage earners in the Northeast. It was agreed also that central to this objective was the proper distribution of eligible families among the various experimental cells so as to maximize the information obtained subject to the budget constraint imposed by the OEO.

As 1968 progressed and it became imperative to begin enrolling families in Trenton, Mathematica started to press for decisions on sample allocation. Researchers at the institute were working on a relatively sophisticated statistical model and would not allow final decisions to be made on the allocation because early calculations already were showing severalfold differences in cost per unit of information according to the way the sample was allocated. Therefore, the allocation of Trenton families to experimental cells represented a compromise. It rapidly became apparent that the various model allocations were leaving many more people without positive payments—that is, they were either in the control group or in plans in which they were above their breakeven—than anyone had foreseen or than was comfortable from the point of view of the field staff. The experiment was being somewhat less than enthusiastically received by certain community groups, and the field staff were only able to hold off militants in Paterson-Passaic by explaining that the experiment would bring money into the community. High and continuing attrition also was being encountered because of a lack of financial incentive to continue. An additional concern was expressed, especially by Mathematica sociologists: with a large proportion of the sample either above their breakeven points or receiving very small payments, certain research areas—for example, where the experimental interest lay in whether or not payments were received rather than the varying size of the payments—stood to suffer from a paucity of data on the payments group.

After the OEO approved two new experimental plans with the 125 percent guarantee, the institute produced new allocation calculations that were presented to Mathematica in December 1968. The allocations were extremely uneven, with many families assigned to low-payment plans and the control group.

The Wisconsin position was that the central behavioral response was with work effort. The model therefore should be designed to optimize information on that, with other responses estimated as well as possible from those data which emerged. Wisconsin argued further that the specifications of the model in principle had been accepted by Mathematica, and that any dissatisfaction with the model results should lead to changes in the assumptions made rather than to jettisoning of the model itself.

The specifications of the model were several. First, the budget constraint dictated that the cost of an observation be weighed in any assessment of the information that observation would be expected to contribute. For example, for the cost of every low-income–stratum family on the 125–50 plan, thirty-three high-income families could be assigned to the 50–50 or 75–70 plan. Second, policy considerations implied that certain plans were more important in terms of national options than others, so that each plan should be assigned a policy weight. The policy weights given to the various plans were as follows:

Guarantee (as percent of poverty line)	*Tax rate (percent)*		
	30	*50*	*70*
125	. . .	5	. . .
100	. . .	10	3
75	6	10	3
50	3	4	. . .

As can be seen, the 100–50 and the 75–50 plans were considered to be most realistic in terms of policy.

Third, there was an income level above which a negative income tax plan could be expected to have no effect on the work behavior of the family. This level would be above the breakeven point and could be expected to increase as the tax rate increased. Fourth, attrition would be a function of plan generosity: the lower the expected payment, the higher the expected attrition. Fifth, variance in earnings behavior would be greater for the control families than for the experimental because, for the same labor market conditions, the effective wage change would be smaller for those receiving benefits. Sixth, the response function would be continuous across cells: that is, information could be learned about some cells from the behavior of people in adjacent cells.

None of these specifications was objected to as such by Mathematica. Throughout early 1969, changes in the assumptions relating to the specifications were suggested by all parties, new allocation patterns were calculated, and their merits discussed. In January 1969 the number of experimental cells with the 125 percent guarantee was reduced from two to one, with the 125 percent guarantee and 70 percent tax rate plan eliminated—a decision that proved to be one of the more costly in terms of the interpretability of the final results.

It turned out that few of the New Jersey sample families actually faced a 70 percent tax rate because one of the two 70 percent tax plans (75–70) was so dominated by the new welfare program in New Jersey that almost all families on that plan were either welfare recipients or over their breakeven points. Thus, not only did few experimental families actually receive positive payments calculated on a 70 percent tax rate basis, but doubt must be cast on the economic rationality of those below their breakeven who chose to remain on the 75–70 plan rather than transfer to welfare. Consequently, the experiment provided little evidence that can be used to illuminate the behavior of people exposed to so high a rate. If the 125–70 plan had been retained it would have dominated welfare over the whole range and provided—because the effects turned out to be so small—a valuable comparison point that is now lacking.

In January 1968, William J. Baumol, one of the principal investigators, had suggested the need for a plan with a tax rate of 100 percent. Harold W. Watts responded by saying that only in the unlikely event that no appreciable differences emerged in earning behavior over the 30 to 70 percent range would there be a need for direct experimentation with the relatively expensive 100 percent rates. He suggested that if the early returns showed no appreciable differences, a deliberately sequential design could allocate a second group of experimental families to a new 100 percent rate scheme. Both the suggestion and response were forgotten by the time the early results appeared. It is interesting to speculate what the results would have been had Watts' suggestion been remembered and implemented. The experiment also considered implementing a zero tax-rate cell in March 1970, when funds were offered from a private source to finance a cell whose families would receive a flat payment regardless of income. This was not pursued beyond one memorandum to the OEO.[26]

As the spring of 1969 progressed, it became clear that whatever assumptions were changed in the model, the resulting allocation would not be very even, and substantial numbers both of control and experimental families would be above the breakeven point for their plan. Mathematica became increasingly disturbed and decided the matter had to be referred to outside arbitration, as mentioned above.

The disagreement perhaps can be captured by saying that the Wisconsin model took as the objective of the experiment the measurement of the cost of a national program in the strictest sense. Other objectives were not considered to be of sufficient importance to modify the model. Mathematica, on the other hand, particularly by the spring of 1969, after nine months of partial operation of the experiment, saw other objectives as independently important. First, studying the feasibility of running a self-administrable transfer program was important; excessive attrition and few large-payment families would make this less possible. Second, the sociological analysis would suffer if only a small number got payments large enough to make a substantial financial impact on the families. Third, the model would have to be simple enough to be able to explain to the public at the end of the experiment; not to win public acceptance of the outcome would be to fail. Fourth, the feasibility of field operations depended on community acceptance of the experiment, which in turn depended on sufficiently high levels of payment.[27]

Both sides agreed to accept James Tobin's judgment as final and took him their arguments. Mathematica, in fact, formulated a compromise plan

26. William J. Baumol, "Second Control Group" (memorandum, January 11, 1968); Harold W. Watts, "Second Control Group" (memorandum, undated); and Watts, "Possibilities for Experimentation with Leonard Greene's Plan" (March 6, 1970).

27. Kershaw and Fair, *Operations*, pp. 148–49.

by which the cells would be divided into five regions in terms of size of payment. They argued that at the end of the experiment there should be a minimum number of families in each income stratum in each payment region (high, medium, or low dollar amounts).

Tobin decided to solve the problem by working his own best assumptions through the Wisconsin model and making certain judgmental deviations. His solution contained several main points. First, to tackle the attrition problem, the flat payments to the experimental families for filling in their income report forms were raised from $2.50 every two weeks to $10.00 every two weeks; and a payment of $8.00 a month for the control families was substituted for the previous $5.00 for every quarterly interview. Second, the cost of these payments was added to the transfer cost of each observation for the purposes of the model computations, and the expected remaining attrition rate was set at 20 percent. Third, the conditional variance of response was set twice as high in cells in which the guarantee level exceeded initial income or initial income exceeded the breakeven level as in the other cells, on the grounds that they had the maximum likelihood of a work disincentive response. Fourth, the total transfer budget constraint specified by the OEO and the 33 percent constraint on how much of that budget could go to the high 125–50 plan were accepted. Fifth, the agreed-on weights given to the various tax plans on the basis of realistic policy interest were accepted.

The allocation resulting from these calculations was altered in Tobin's final judgment in three respects. First, Tobin gave some weight to an analysis-of-variance approach in order to assure enough direct observations in plans having high policy interest. This had the effect of shifting observations into the 100–50 plan. Second, to provide a sufficient spread of observations to meet the informational requirement of studies other than the central work response, he allocated nine more poor—that is, lowest-stratum—families to the 125–50 plan than the calculation indicated. This violated the OEO constraint of 33 percent of the transfer budget by using up 36 percent, but the OEO acquiesced. Third, he arbitrarily decided that no cell in any city should contain between zero and five families. The Tobin allocation is given in Table 1.[28]

The only administratively difficult consequence of the Tobin judgment was that about 150 new controls were to be added to the sites already in

28. James Tobin, "Sample Design for NIT Experiment" (memorandum, June 1969).

Felicity Skidmore

Table 1. Number of Families Assigned to Each Experimental Cell and to Control Group, Tobin Allocation Model

	Income stratum[a]			
Cell and group	Low	Medium	High	Total
Experimental (percent guarantee and tax rate)				
50–30	5	31	12	48
50–50	29	37	5	71
75–30	30(5)	14	50(5)	94(10)
75–50	5	57(10)	36(10)	98(20)
75–70	13(5)	51(15)	0	64(20)
100–50	22	34(5)	20	76(5)
100–70	11	26	33(10)	70(10)
125–50	50	8	80	138
Experimental, total	165(10)	258(30)	236(25)	659(65)
Control, total	238	165	247	650
Both groups	403(10)	423(30)	483(25)	1,309(65)[b]

Source: David N. Kershaw and Jerilyn Fair (eds.), *Operations, Surveys, and Administration*, vol. 4 of *Final Report of the New Jersey Graduated Work Incentive Experiment* (University of Wisconsin—Madison, Institute for Research on Poverty, and Mathematica, 1974), p. 157.

a. The numbers in parentheses refer to those additional sixty-five families on the twelve-month retrospective accounting period system, as described in the text.

b. This differs from the 1,357 total because of a sampling shortfall. It was possible, for example, to find only 141 new control families in the cities that were already in operation.

operation—Trenton, Paterson, and Passaic. Those sites had to be re-screened, and those eligible families found were given a special makeup preenrollment interview.

Decisions in the Field

The actual fielding of the New Jersey experiment took more time and budget resources than anyone had dreamed in 1967. Brief summaries of specific parts of the field operations and some of the problems encountered are covered below.

COMMUNITY AND STATE COOPERATION. The main difficulty anticipated was possible community disruption as a consequence of assigning families to plans of differing generosity and some to no plan at all. This turned out not to be a problem, although community militants tried for a time to get the experiment out of Paterson and Passaic altogether. The cooperation of New Jersey state and local authorities, on the other hand, was expected to be an important ingredient, but this cooperation failed to materialize. Actually, it was not needed except in the area of overlapping welfare payments, where its absence did aggravate the problem.

COST ESTIMATES. The problems of regular screening and interviewing of large numbers of families were underestimated, at least partly because of the unexpectedly low number of eligible families, which required virtual saturation sampling. The original plan, to subcontract the screening and interviewing to a professional survey organization, had in fact to be abandoned because of major slippages in timetable on the part of that organization. The difficulty of effective processing of enormous amounts of person-specific microdata produced by an hour-long interview every three months, in which two-thirds of the questions were not repeated regularly, was drastically underestimated. This underestimate can be measured by the fact that the original data processing plan called for the state of New Jersey to donate adequate time on the state's Trenton computer.[29] Finally, reaching agreement from all research groups to a design for allocating the sample, as described above, was not originally foreseen as being more time consuming or delicate than could be encompassed, along with all other preparations, in the first seven months.

The extent of the schedule slippage can be measured by the fact that the original proposal presumed a completion date for the final report of June 30, 1971, whereas it was completed only late in 1973. Part of this lag was because the report took a year to prepare rather than six months after the last transfer payment was made. In addition, the sites had to be enrolled sequentially over a year, so that the total period during which payments were made became four years rather than three. Finally, the initial planning phase, before even the first site was enrolled, covered fourteen months instead of the planned seven.

Another measure of the underestimation is the budget underestimate. The original estimate for the experiment—for a four-year period—was just over $4 million. The final cost, including transfers, was almost $8 million. The originally estimated transfer budget, $2.9 million, was almost on target, with final payments amounting to $2.4 million.

There was no indication that anyone thought the estimates to be optimistic while the proposal was being drawn up and funded. The survey organization contracted for the original screening underestimated its own budget and timetable substantially—and it had had extensive interviewing experience. Moreover, no one seems to have learned from the experience.

---

29. Poverty Institute, "Experimental Study," Budget Table.

Subsequent experiments by other organizations, even with the benefit of the New Jersey experience, have drawn up optimistic schedules that they were warned could not be met—and all have fallen behind.

SITE SELECTION. Early in the experiment it was decided to enroll sites sequentially—because of the difficulty of getting field operations under way and also because, quite reasonably, the first site was regarded as a pilot site from which lessons could be learned for the others. The proposal acknowledges that "we cannot be certain that in a city the size of Trenton we will be able to find a sufficient number of male-headed poor families with children to complete our sample,"[30] but the main reason given for wanting more than one city was to test the effects of differences in industrial composition and tightness of the labor market. As it turned out, enough eligible families could not be found in four New Jersey cities, and it was necessary to go outside New Jersey to complete the sample.

Trenton was chosen as the first site because of its proximity to Princeton and Mathematica, because it was the seat of the New Jersey state government, and because of the cooperative attitude of United Progress Incorporated of Trenton. Of other possible cities, Newark was eliminated because of the 1967 riot and because of its militant local CAP group; and Camden because there were reports of impending riots and because it was dependent on the Philadelphia labor market. Elizabeth was eliminated after the small yield in Trenton because it was no larger than Trenton.

When the Trenton sample was complete, ethnic balance became an obvious problem: despite the figures from the 1960 Census, 66 percent of the sample was black, 16 percent was white, and 18 percent was Puerto Rican. The Paterson-Passaic sample was as bad: 39 percent black, 51 percent Puerto Rican, and 10 percent white. We hoped that Jersey City would be white enough to redress the balance, but again we found a high proportion of Puerto Ricans. Even when we took only every second Puerto Rican family, the sample in Jersey City was 51 percent black, 13 percent white, and 36 percent Puerto Rican.[31]

Thus, a site had to be found in which the low-income population was predominantly white. In no other low-income areas in New Jersey could we even presume that efficient sampling would produce the requisite number of whites. Pennsylvania had been excluded because the state had an AFDC-

30. Ibid., p. 19.
31. The 1960 Census had shown Paterson as being 15 percent black and Jersey City as 13 percent black; and the percentage of Puerto Ricans was small enough not to be considered worth mentioning in Poverty Institute, "Proposal," p. 20.

UP program, but now so did New Jersey. The large industrial areas close to existing experimental sites were Scranton–Wilkes-Barre–Hazelton and Allentown–Easton–Bethlehem. Preliminary information on income level eliminated the latter three. Of the first group, Scranton was presumed to have the largest low-income population and, after preliminary sampling, it was selected. The overwhelming majority of those sampled were white. The experiment now had an ethnically balanced sample—roughly one-third fell into each of the three major ethnic groups—but the ethnic groups were not balanced within the sites.

SELECTING THE SAMPLE. Encouraged by the OEO, the decision was made that sampling was not to be restricted to urban areas identified by the 1960 Census as poverty areas: an important group of low-income families, it was felt, those who chose not to live in patently poor districts, might otherwise be missed. Trenton showed us that sampling outside Census poverty tracts was yielding practically nothing. Even within the poverty tracts, sample areas had to be redrawn by staff members on the basis of close observation.

The short screening interview was designed simply to ascertain family eligibility. When noneligible answers were given, the interview was terminated, a step that was seen to have been an error when the research staff later had to assess what additional sample yields could be expected from expanding the eligibility criteria.[32]

Those families selected as eligible on the basis of the screening were then given an hour-long preenrollment interview to collect baseline data. From these two interviews, a final decision was made on each family's eligibility and the experimental cell to which it would be assigned. It was assumed at first that the more thorough the enrollers' understanding of the theory of the program, the more effective they would be, so graduate students from neighboring campuses were chosen to enroll the families. The Trenton and Paterson-Passaic experience indicated, however, that the most important attribute for an enroller was a thorough understanding of the attitudes of those to be enrolled. Therefore, the enrollment personnel for the last two sites were chosen from the community itself.

---

32. Ross, "An Experimental Study," p. 127. Ross notes that in fact a decision was made after Trenton not to terminate interviews with families who obviously were ineligible, but that the "additional task of non-termination interviews proved too much for our new interviewing staff with both them and us performing unfamiliar duties for the first time. . . . Although the [interviews were] carried on to completion, the results were of little use."

In all, 1,513 sampled families were found to be eligible for enrollment. The search for additional control families in Trenton and Paterson-Passaic turned up another 141, a total of 1,654, of which 1,357 were enrolled. The selected-out Spanish-speaking families in Jersey City amounted to 135, and 62 families in Scranton were randomly eliminated because their assigned cells were full. Out of the total eligible sample, 30 families could not be located for enrollment and 8 were no longer eligible because they had lost their critical male earner. Finally, 62 families chose not to participate. There were no sizable inherent differences in demographic characteristics among experimentals, controls, and refusals.

INTERVIEWS. Bids to carry out the interviewing were solicited from professional survey organizations, all of which were "influenced too much by the customary presentation of competitive bids and not enough by the unique requirements of this experiment."[33] The best bid was accepted, but soon it became clear that unusual procedures were necessary and that they were not forthcoming. Mathematica, therefore, decided to conduct its own interviewing, employing "tighter controls . . . longer and more in-depth training, and a much greater stress on minority staff and interviewing personnel."[34]

Each wave of interviews required from four to six weeks in each site and from fifteen to twenty interviewers. Interviewing in urban areas was found to require a substantial commitment on the part of the interviewer, and the high turnover of interviewers necessitated continuous hiring and training. Some assaults and robberies occurred, the incidence of which no doubt was increased because the need to collect earnings data required interviews to be undertaken when the wage carner was most likely to be at home—after dark.

It was learned on the job that questions had to be constructed with special attention to the particular socioeconomic characteristics of the sample. Many of the questions had been developed elsewhere, but pretesting and field experience made it clear that the wording had to be simplified.[35] Some 25 percent of the Puerto Ricans had to be interviewed in Spanish, a problem exacerbated because sociological and attitudinal questions seemed to translate poorly.

A major unexpected lesson from the interviewing portion of the study

33. Memorandum from F. Stephan to Mathematica, quoted in Kershaw and Fair, *Operations*, p. 68.

34. Kershaw and Fair, *Operations*, p. 68.

35. Ibid., p. 210.

related to the critical data on labor force and income. What seemed an eminently sensible decision, to use questions from the Current Population Survey, was made in the planning stage. A set of well-known standard questions, it was assumed, would minimize the risk of unusable data and maximize the likelihood of being able to make nationwide comparisons using other data sources. By mid-1969, however, these questions were seen to be seriously inadequate because they provided only a one-week snapshot out of every quarter. Consequently, no complete and continuous work and income history was developed for comparison with the family income report forms. For large parts of the sample these forms also occasionally picked up atypical weeks such as those containing holidays.

In July 1969, therefore, the labor-force core of the questionnaires was amplified by "expanding the 'last week' set to 'last month by weeks.' The definition of 'last month' was associated with pay periods, which simplified the interview, increased accuracy, and aided the matching of interview income data with IRF data."[36]

WELFARE. As described above, on January 1, 1969, New Jersey introduced a generous AFDC-UP program for which most of the experimental sample were eligible and that dominated most of the experimental plans over at least some of the relevant income range. Throughout the fall of 1968, alternatives were discussed as to how to treat this problem, and a new experimental guarantee of 125 percent of poverty was added to forestall defections to welfare. In addition, for all the sites except Trenton the rules of operation were changed so that experimental families would have to decide at each payment period whether to accept welfare or experimental payments. Even if they chose welfare, they were to remain in the sample for the purposes of sending in income report forms and answering the quarterly interviews, and they could change back and forth as many times as they liked between welfare and experimental payments.

The Trenton sample was to be allowed to continue as it had started, reporting any welfare payments to the experiment as income. In November 1969, however, the Mercer County prosecutor's office began investigating overlapping payments and subpoenaed the records of fourteen families. Mathematica moved to quash the subpoenas, and after weeks of negotiating with the prosecutor and monetary haggling with Mercer County, the experiment agreed to pay back approximately $20,000 of welfare overpayments that the families had received. Later, Passaic County also attempted

36. Ibid., p. 207.

to collect money from the experiment, but because the rules for the Passaic sample were unambiguous, Mathematica was able to threaten a counter suit, and the case was dropped. The Trenton rules had to be changed to conform to the rest of the cities, and a system of quarterly checks with the welfare departments for overlap was instituted.

THE FAMILY ASSISTANCE PLAN. In 1967 it was inconceivable to anyone that political reality would overtake the experiment. In August 1969, however, the family assistance plan, with a negative income tax component built into it, was announced by the Nixon administration as a welfare reform measure. The experiment was the only potential source of empirical data relevant to the proposed legislation. In January 1970 representatives from the experiment were called to testify before the House Ways and Means Committee. They replied to questions in general terms, but they had no hard data for the committee and, in fact, had not decided whether to provide preliminary data even if available.

After their testimony, the Poverty Institute, Mathematica, and the OEO all felt that preliminary results, even if it meant hand tabulating, should be released. Therefore, *Preliminary Results of the New Jersey Graduated Work Incentives Experiment* was issued on February 18 by the OEO. This decision opened the experiment to extensive and critical examination by the General Accounting Office (GAO) and set in motion an attempt by the Senate Finance Committee to obtain confidential files on individual families. In addition, the research staff of the experiment came in for professional criticism for allowing themselves to be used for administration advocacy.

The end to the story was relatively happy. In testimony before the Senate Finance Committee on August 18, 1970, the experiment staff, the OEO, and the GAO all were called to testify. The GAO, although critical of the preliminary report itself, supported the experiment, and the threat of a congressional subpoena dissolved. The Poverty Institute—which realized that it had made a major mistake by letting its government sponsor use its name for a release that in fact it had not approved—issued its own appropriately tentative version of the preliminary results for the research community.

The general lessons to be learned are summarized in volume 4 of the *Final Report* as follows:

Congressional interest and concern pose a more sensitive issue. It is helpful to establish a relationship with the GAO when the experiment is launched. . . . When results are obtained they should be published with suitable qualifications, and the GAO should see them before they are released. . . .

When an experiment becomes as relevant to the policy-making process as

New Jersey did, it requires a difficult but essential balance between the interests of research and policy. . . .

The approach subsequently taken with H.R.1 ("Social Security Amendments of 1971") is probably the best course. The research staff disclaimed for the experiment any central relevance to the legislation but indicated to both the House Ways and Means Committee and the Senate Finance Committee that they were very willing to act as a resource for questions which fell within the scope of the experimental experience. The Ways and Means Committee took advantage of this offer. . . . Neither OEO nor the experiment staff supported or criticized the legislation, only supplying answers to specific questions raised.[37]

TERMINATION. The final major decision to be made about operation of the experiment concerned how to terminate payments to the families. At the start of the experiment the families were told the duration of the payment phase and given a wallet-sized card with the termination date printed on it. After the enrollment, however, the final payment date was never mentioned again. Ethical concern had been expressed from the beginning about creating possible hardship by accustoming families to income augmentation and then withdrawing it.[38] Discussion intensified as the time for the last payment in Trenton approached: about whether to let the families down gently, with payments that tapered off, and about our responsibility to warn them of the approaching end to the payments. Finally, it was decided to remind the families of the last payment date once, just after the final quarterly interview. The field offices remained open as referral agencies for any hardship cases, but not a single family came to them for assistance.

The only data that give information on the experience and attitudes of the families after the experiment are from a questionnaire, administered three months after the last payment and designed to measure responses to termination. The families reacted rationally in the sense that the relative importance of the payments to their total income affected how much thought they had given beforehand to the termination of those payments and what preparations they made for it. But no major differences emerged in the special budgeting, emergency, or medical needs they said they actually had encountered during the payments period.

As far as needing financial help after the payments had stopped, of the 179 families who answered that they had needed help, 94 did not apply for help, and only 8 applied for help and were denied. Finally, families were asked to make a before-and-after comparison. About 88 percent estimated

37. Ibid., pp. 288–90.
38. Minutes, meeting in Madison between Mathematica and the Poverty Institute, December 13, 1967.

that they were as well or better off after the experiment. As Kershaw and Fair express it: "Although it may be that the simple passage of time improved the experimental families' *absolute* level of well being, these figures provide one more general indication that short-term experiments can be conducted without serious adverse effects on participants."[39]

Conclusion

Looking back over the New Jersey experiment and the decisions made by—or forced on—the experimenters, the obvious concluding question is: what did those decisions do to the data base that was collected?

First, it must be noted that many decisions were made or changed during the first year of operation in the pilot site of Trenton. (a) The questions in the labor force core of the interview questionnaire were changed to elicit more detail and to provide data more easily comparable with the payments data. (b) The treatment of welfare changed, from a system allowing families to receive welfare income as long as they added it to their experimental payments, to a system whereby families had the choice of receiving either welfare or experimental payments in any one month. (c) The accounting treatment of income over the breakeven point was not clarified until mid-1969, so for the five months of operation in 1968 many Trenton families piled up overpayments from the experiment not all of which were reclaimed. (d) The regular taxable payments to keep families in the sample were set at $10 every two weeks for experimentals and $8 a month for controls in mid-1969. Before then, the experimental families had received a minimum payment of only $2.50 every two weeks and the control families only $5 every three months for the interview.

For all these reasons, the data for Trenton must be regarded as less reliable than the data for the other sites. In the analysis undertaken for the final report, Trenton data were included. At some future time it might be wise to reanalyze at least the crucial labor supply response without the Trenton data to see whether the results actually are sensitive to their inclusion or exclusion.

Second, with regard to the data in general, the extremely low number of eligible whites in the New Jersey cities would have been hard to predict. The experiment was fated to be in operation during the years farthest from

39. Kershaw and Fair, *Operations*, p. 304.

the most recent census year. The 1970 Census permits comparison with the experiment to examine how representative the experimental sample actually was of the total low-income population in the sampled tracts. This is being done. Such data, of course, were unavailable in 1967 and 1968.

However unavoidable, the experiment has left a data base for which direct ethnic comparisons must be interpreted with caution. The results show significant ethnic differences in all the analyses of labor supply—for which no satisfactory explanations have as yet been made. Further work will be done on the question, in which one important task probably should be to analyze the Scranton whites and the New Jersey whites separately. Evidence already exists that they differ. Scranton whites were more likely to own their own home, for instance, and their attrition rate was significantly lower than that of any other group in the sample.

Third, the introduction of an AFDC-UP program in New Jersey had the effect of dominating almost completely one of the two experimental plans with a 70 percent tax rate (the 75–70 plan). Therefore, observations on families that were facing this tax rate, were below their breakeven point, and were not on welfare are underrepresented in the data. Because differences among tax plans were difficult to detect, these missing observations were costly.

Finally, looking back on the data collected and the analysis they produced, one must agree with Albert Rees that perhaps the main conclusion is that we underestimated the robustness of the null hypothesis. Although all the planners were confident that the withdrawal rate of non-aged male family members from the labor force would not be drastic, a review of the memoranda written during the planning phase makes clear that everyone assumed that there would be a well-behaved, detectable response on the part of able-bodied males and that it would be a disincentive response. If this had not been the uniform presumption, the experiment might have been planned to produce larger average payments and include a wider range of tax rate variation.

But this is all with the benefit of hindsight. The historical record recounted above shows that the experiment was designed, fielded, and brought to a conclusion responsibly and with carefully considered—if not always infallible—judgment. The information produced remains, with all the qualifications, as a unique resource for exploring economic behavior under conditions of experimental control.

ALBERT REES

HAROLD W. WATTS

An Overview of
the Labor Supply Results

This chapter provides a summary of the findings of the
negative income tax experiment for readers who are not concerned with
the finer points of methodology and technique.[1]

Expectations

From the outset, the sponsors of the experiment and the researchers expected that the payment of substantial amounts of unearned income to
poor families would reduce the amount of labor they supplied, though not
by large amounts. These expectations were based in part on theory and in
part on the results of nonexperimental empirical research. We begin by
reviewing what will be called here the static theory of the labor-leisure
choice.

Static Theory

Figure 1 represents the labor-leisure choices of a hypothetical worker
who is capable of earning $2 an hour. Each indifference curve represents all

This paper is adapted from *Final Report of the New Jersey Graduated Work Incentive
Experiment*, vol. 1 (cited in note 1). The first two sections and part of the third appeared
in slightly different form in the *Journal of Human Resources*, vol. 9 (Spring 1974), pp.
158–200.
1. A full account of the methods of analysis and the design of the experiment appears in Harold W. Watts and Albert Rees (eds.), *Final Report of the New Jersey Graduated Work Incentive Experiment*, vols. 1, 2, and 3, and David N. Kershaw and Jerilyn
Fair (eds.), vol. 4 (University of Wisconsin—Madison, Institute for Research on Poverty,
and Mathematica (1973, 1974) (referred to later as *Final Report of the New Jersey
Experiment*).

Figure 1. A Hypothetical Worker's Response in Hours of Work to a Negative Income Tax

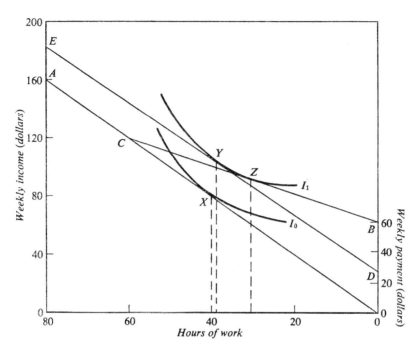

combinations of money income and leisure that give the worker equal satisfaction. Higher indifference curves represent higher levels of satisfaction.
We assume that the worker is able to vary his weekly hours by such devices
as voluntary overtime, part-time work, and holding multiple jobs; we also
assume, for simplicity, that all hours worked are paid at the straight-time
rate.

In the first situation, the worker is in equilibrium at point X on indifference curve I_0, where he works forty hours a week and receives a weekly income of $80. He is then offered a negative income tax plan that guarantees
him $60 a week if he has no earned income and taxes earned income at 50
percent by reducing the benefit payment as earned income rises. This plan
has a breakeven at point C at an earned income of $120; to the left of this
point he receives no payments. The opportunity set facing the worker is
now BCA rather than $0A$, and he chooses point Z on indifference curve I_1.
His hours and earned income have decreased, to thirty and $60, and his
total income has increased, to $90.

INCOME AND SUBSTITUTION EFFECT. The reduction in hours from X to Z can be divided into an income effect and a substitution effect by drawing, parallel to $0A$, line DE, which is tangent to I_1 at Y. The distance $D0$ shows the amount of payments that would yield as much satisfaction as the original negative tax plan if the tax rate were zero. The horizontal distance from X to Y is the pure income effect on hours, since the wage rate—or the price of leisure—is the same at both points. The horizontal distance from Y to Z is the pure substitution effect of the tax rate, since the level of satisfaction is the same at both points. The income effect refers to the combined effect on welfare or satisfaction of the guarantee and the tax, and not that of the guarantee alone. A guarantee of \$60 a week with no tax would enable the worker to reach an indifference curve lying above I_1.

As Figure 1 is drawn, the income effect and the substitution effect of the negative income tax each reduces the hours of work. The negative substitution effect follows from the usual constraints of neoclassical utility theory on the shapes of indifference curves. If the curves are convex from the southwest and BC is flatter than $0A$, then Z must lie to the right of Y. No such necessary relation exists between X and Y. The expectation that Y will lie to the right of X rests on the empirical evidence that as real income has risen through time, hours of work have tended to fall and that, in cross section, hours of work tend to be shorter in high-paid than in low-paid jobs. In other words, empirical evidence indicates that leisure (the term used for convenience to include all nonwork activity) is a normal good. That leisure is not an inferior good might be expected from the fact that most inferior goods have preferred close substitutes, and there is no close substitute for leisure.[2]

In the case of wage increases the income effect is negative also, and it may be sufficiently large to outweigh the positive substitution effect of a wage increase, which of course makes leisure more expensive. In the case of a negative income tax, both the income effect and the substitution effect will tend to reduce the amount of work supplied. The experiment enables us to observe points X and Z as the behavior of the control and experimental subjects, respectively. (It should be noted that point Y is not observable.)

GENERALIZATION TO THE FAMILY. The preceding discussion is cast in terms of the choice of hours of work by a single worker. If we think of the family as a single decisionmaking unit having a collective indifference map,

2. An inferior good is a good the consumption of which falls as income rises.

the same analysis would apply to a family. Moreover, it would apply to decisions about labor force participation as well as about hours. Thus, a negative income tax might be expected to induce some members of the household to withdraw from the work force, particularly those whose wage rate is low and who have good nonmarket uses for their time. Teenagers might withdraw to devote full time to schooling or wives to devote full time to keeping house.

Our expectations about labor force participation rest more heavily on substitution effects than do those about hours of work. As real wages have risen through time, male labor force participation rates have fallen, suggesting as in the case of hours that negative income effects outweigh the positive substitution effects of real wage increases. For married women, however, the evidence is mixed. In cross section, holding education constant, the participation rate of wives falls as husbands' incomes rise. The participation rate of wives has risen through time, however, as real wages have risen. Either the income effects are smaller than substitution effects in this context or they are offset by other changes in the opportunity set confronting wives—such as the availability of work-saving home appliances and prepared foods.

MULTIPLE TAX RATES AND GUARANTEES. In the presentation above, we have assumed only one guarantee-tax specification of the negative income tax plan. In the actual experiment, there were eight, combining four different guarantee levels and three different tax rates. The general expectation from the theory is that the plans with higher tax rates will have larger substitution effects and hence will produce greater reductions in labor supply—though this is true only among plans that permit the family to achieve the same level of satisfaction. Similarly, one would expect from the empirical evidence on hours of work that, at the same tax rate, the plans with the most generous payments would cause the largest reduction in labor supply, whether generosity is measured in guarantee levels or in the average payments that would be made at the family's normal (that is, pre-enrollment) income.

Dynamic Considerations

The theory sketched above is too simple in at least three respects. First, it assumes that the wage rate confronting each worker is exogenously given and that he can do nothing to affect it. Second, it assumes that the negative income tax is a permanent change in the opportunity set facing the worker.

Third, it assumes that the negative income tax plan is introduced into a world without existing welfare plans. Relaxation of these assumptions gives rise to what can loosely be called dynamic modifications of the standard theory.

ENDOGENOUS WAGE CHANGE. When a worker can influence his wage through his own choices, it is appropriate to regard the wage rate, as well as the number of hours he is willing to work, as a component of labor supply. In this context the wage rate can be viewed as an index of the quality of the hours supplied.

The worker could change his market wage in at least three different ways. In the first instance, he might withdraw from the labor force or reduce his hours in order to undertake training that would raise his wage at some future time. A permanent negative income tax would make it easier to do this by providing some income during the period of training. A temporary experiment provides an even stronger incentive in the short run, since the training would have to be completed before the end of the experiment. These considerations suggest that there might be a greater reduction in labor supply early in the experiment than the static theory suggests, but that toward the end of the experiment this might no longer be true. If labor supply is measured in earnings rather than man-hours, the effect toward the end of the experiment could even be to have a larger labor supply from the experimental group than from the control group. At the beginning of the experiment, however, few of us gave sufficient weight to this line of argument to expect this result.

A second set of arguments suggests that earnings might fall more than hours throughout the experiment. The jobs open to a person of given skill and experience usually differ in the extent to which they are pleasant or unpleasant. Some involve heavy physical labor, disagreeable working conditions, inconvenient working hours, or inaccessible places of work; others are lighter, more pleasant, and more convenient. Under conditions of sustained full employment, the less desirable jobs can be filled only at higher wages; the wage differentials thus called forth are known as compensating differentials.

The payment of a negative income tax could lead workers to shift toward more pleasant but lower-paying jobs, sacrificing compensating differentials previously earned. Instead of substituting leisure for labor, they would substitute more agreeable work for less agreeable work. Such behavior would cause earnings to fall more than hours.

To the extent that average hours are reduced, there is another source of reduction in hourly earnings. By choosing not to work voluntary overtime, workers would reduce the hours paid at premium rates. In shifting from full-time to part-time jobs, workers might have to accept lower straight-time rates. It is not uncommon for part-time workers to receive less for similar work than full-time workers; for example, such differentials often are specified in collective bargaining agreements covering clerks in retail food stores.

Another possible influence of experimental payments on wages is through their effects on job search. One of the standard arguments in favor of unemployment insurance is that it permits the unemployed worker to search for a suitable job, rather than being forced by lack of income to accept one of the first job offers he receives even if the wage offered is very low. More generally, any payments that are increased when a worker is not working will lower the cost of search, increase the optimum length of search, and increase the expected wage of the job offer finally accepted. Negative income tax payments fall into this category, as supplements to unemployment insurance and as perhaps the only important income replacement for workers ineligible for unemployment insurance payments. Low-income workers are more than usually likely not to receive unemployment insurance: some are in uncovered industries such as local government, domestic service, and agriculture, others are new entrants into the labor force or new residents in the state, and some will have quit their last jobs or have been discharged for cause. Because experimental and control families were selected from the same population and faced the same demand conditions, any difference between the two groups in the incidence and duration of unemployment should be considered as a change in labor supply rather than a result of deficient demand.

DURATION OF THE EXPERIMENT. The effects on labor supply of the limited duration of the experiment also do not all work in the same direction. Consider the male head of household with a steady job involving hard work and long hours. If he knew that the negative tax payments were permanent, he might instead take a job with lighter work and more normal hours. For a period of only three years, however, such a shift might seem too risky. At the end of the experiment he would need the higher earned income but might be unable to get his old job back. For the steadily employed male head therefore, an experiment of limited duration probably will have smaller effects on labor supply than a permanent program.

For other members of the household whose attachment to the labor force is less secure, the effects of limited duration may be quite the opposite.

Wives, teenagers, and other adults in the household are likely to be in and out of the labor force as family circumstances change. To the extent that periods of withdrawal from the labor force are planned in advance, a temporary experiment encourages the concentration of such periods during the experimental years, when the costs of not working are lower than normal. Similar behavior may be expected from male heads who have a history of frequent job change. This may be particularly true toward the end of the experiment.

PRESENCE OF WELFARE. As has been noted, New Jersey did not give welfare payments to households with a male head at the beginning of the experiment, which was a major reason for choosing New Jersey as the experimental site. The introduction of an Aid to Families with Dependent Children–Unemployed Parents (AFDC-UP) program three months after the Trenton enrollment, but before enrollment in the other sites, complicated the comparison between control and experimental families. In the ninth experimental quarter, 25 percent of control families and 13 percent of experimental families were on welfare—the highest percentages for any quarter. Among experimental families, the percentage varied by plan, decreasing with plan generosity: ninth-quarter figures show that 23 percent of families on the 50–50 and 75–70 plans chose welfare, compared with only 7 percent on the 125–50 plan. It also varied by site, from 6 percent of all experimental families in Jersey City to 21 percent in Paterson and Passaic in the ninth quarter.

The general effect of welfare is to make the observed differences between experimental and control groups smaller than they would be in the absence of welfare. This underestimate occurs essentially because welfare may induce some withdrawal of work effort in the control group. On the other hand, the estimates derived from an experiment in the presence of welfare may represent more accurate estimates of the effect of a new national income maintenance program that is superimposed on existing programs. A careful analysis of the effects of welfare on the experiment suggests that the presence of welfare did not have a major effect on the estimated labor supply differentials.[3]

These three arguments lead us to expect certain patterns in the experimental results. But they do not substantially modify the overall expectations generated by the static theory because, for the household as a whole, they tend to be offsetting.

3. Irwin Garfinkel, "The Effects of Welfare on Experimental Response," in *Final Report of the New Jersey Experiment*, vol. 2, pt. C, chap. 2.

The Nonexperimental Literature

A substantial empirical literature on labor supply has been developed in recent decades. This literature was important in forming our initial expectations. The studies fall into three general groups—studies of hours of work, studies of labor force participation, and studies concentrating on the effects of nonlabor income.

HOURS OF WORK. The studies of hours of work—which suggest that the income effect as well as the substitution effect of a negative income tax will be to diminish the amount of work supplied—lead us to expect some reduction in labor supply for the experimental group.

These studies have not been confined, however, to low-income workers. They suggest that at or near the mean wage, increases in wage rates are associated with decreases in hours worked, but this need not be true at wages well below the mean, when the desire for added consumer goods may be stronger and the desire for additional leisure weaker. Low-income workers may have a desire to reach the average level of living of their communities that is stronger than that of middle-income workers to rise above it. Indeed, this is exactly what is shown by the usual textbook diagrams of the backward-bending supply curve of labor, which show at very low wages a forward-rising curve that becomes vertical and then bends back as some higher level of wages is reached. Unfortunately, the forward-sloping portion of the curve has no empirical basis. Moreover, even if substitution effects are stronger than income effects at low wages, the total effect of a negative income tax still will be to reduce hours, since the tax-induced reduction in net wage rates will not produce an income loss—as would a wage cut with no income transfer. The unique feature of a negative income tax plan is that income is increased at the same time the net wage rate is reduced.

LABOR FORCE PARTICIPATION. The relevant portion of the literature on labor force participation deals with the differences in strength of attachment to the labor force by age, sex, and marital status. The studies of such attachment show very high rates of participation by married men with wife present, rates that are affected only weakly by differences in education or the strength of demand. Average rates of participation are much lower for teenagers, the elderly, and married women, and such forces as differences in education or in strength of demand induce much larger differences in participation rates.

Because of these studies of participation rates, we never expected any substantial fraction of the male heads of household to withdraw from the labor force when they received payments. It seemed much more likely that their response would be shorter hours or longer periods of search between jobs. For wives, teenagers, and the elderly, however, reductions in rates of labor force participation seemed a more probable outcome.

We were aware, of course, of the popular belief that large transfer payments will cause widespread idleness. Certain events have tended to support this idea: for example, the experience with unemployment benefits for returning veterans after World War II, payments that sometimes were referred to as "rocking-chair money." Many of the veterans involved, however, were single rather than heads of household, and they lacked recent—or any—civilian work experience. Popular beliefs about the effect of welfare on work behavior also are based largely on experience other than that of male household heads—mothers without husbands, for example. And even now, the point of view tends to be based on anecdotal information rather than on systematic evidence. If there were people who expected our experimental treatment to cause large declines in the participation rates of male heads of households, they were not in our research group.

NONLABOR INCOME. Several studies of the effects of nonlabor income on labor supply were designed explicitly to simulate the effects of a negative income tax program from nonexperimental data. Nevertheless, they were not influential in forming our expectations—in part, of course, because most of them have appeared since we began the experiment. The most striking thing about them is the wide range of values of their results, a lack of agreement that weakens confidence in any of the findings.[4]

These studies face a problem that may be insurmountable. Much of the nonlabor income reported in income surveys consists of transfer payments such as unemployment compensation, workmen's compensation, old-age, survivors', and disability insurance, and temporary disability insurance. All these payments except survivors' insurance are totally or partially work conditioned—that is, they cannot legally be received by those who work or by those who work and earn more than a stated amount. Work behavior—past and present—determines whether nonlabor income is received and in what amount. If any of these types of work-conditioned transfers are included in the measure of nonlabor income used to simulate a negative

4. See Glen G. Cain and Harold W. Watts (eds.), *Income Maintenance and Labor Supply: Econometric Studies* (Markham, 1973), especially chap. 9.

income tax, the size of the negative effects on work effect will be overestimated, perhaps greatly. Of course, certain types of nonlabor incomes are not work conditioned, notably dividends, interest, and certain types of pensions. But the amount of dividend and interest income of the non-aged poor is negligible, and pensions tend to be received by those past prime working age. The nonlabor income of the working poor that is not work conditioned is hard to find in such existing data bases as the U.S. Bureau of the Census or the Survey of Economic Opportunity of the OEO. Some investigators, searching for this needle in the haystack, seem to have seized in desperation at the handiest pitchfork instead. Even those who are clearly aware of the problem of work-conditioned transfers sometimes report amounts of nonlabor income—supposedly not work conditioned—that are so large as to call their definitions or procedures into question.

A second general difficulty with the simulation studies of negative income taxes is that they sometimes truncate their samples by eliminating households with current income above arbitrary levels. This will tend to include a disproportionate number of households that supply, perhaps temporarily, less than average amounts of labor—a selection that could bias the estimated coefficients toward large supply effects. Truncation on a measure such as hourly wages, which is uncorrelated or less highly correlated with the amount of labor currently supplied, would be far preferable. Granted, the New Jersey–Pennsylvania experiment sample also is truncated on family income, which may not have been the best variable to choose for this purpose. But the problem is far less serious in a study that estimates labor supply effects in a period subsequent to that used to select the sample and derives these estimates from a comparison of experimental and control groups in which the experimental group receives an exogenous treatment.

Finally, the nonexperimental studies estimate substitution effects from cross-sectional differences in average hourly earnings that may not be entirely independent of the effects of the amount of labor supplied. Those persons who work more than forty hours a week will receive premium pay for overtime; those who want to work only part time may have to accept lower hourly earnings. In an experiment, differential tax rates create a truly exogenous source of differences in net wages.

Despite these deficiencies, the studies that focus on the effects of nonlabor income reinforce the more general labor supply studies in one important respect: they consistently find larger supply effects for women than for men—and, indeed, the estimated effects for men are sometimes close to zero.

Summary of Expectations

The researchers involved in the experiment never agreed on and set down in advance a summary of what they felt was the most likely outcome for labor supply. In retrospect, this is unfortunate. Any attempt to do so now is bound to reflect to some extent our present knowledge of the results and thus to understate the degree to which we have been surprised. Despite this caveat, it seems useful to attempt a summary in retrospect.

We never expected able-bodied male heads of households to withdraw from the labor force in response to temporary payments too small to support large families. We did expect some of them to reduce their hours of work or to spend more time searching for new jobs when they lost or quit a job. We expected some teenagers to return to school or stay in school longer as a result of the payments. We expected some working wives to leave the labor force to spend all their time in household work.

On the whole, the reduction in labor supply we expected to find in the experimental group was on the order of 10 to 15 percent. We did not expect to find any differential effects by ethnic group. We did expect to find, however, that higher tax rates, as well as higher guarantees, would produce greater reductions in labor supply.

The Data Analysis

The results presented in the final report are more complex and somewhat more ambiguous than we anticipated, and they are not easy to summarize. In attempting to do so, we must explain why we regard some of the results as more salient than others. This in turn requires some brief discussion of our methods of analysis, which will deal with dependent variables, the control variables, the treatment variables, and the time period.

Dependent Variables

There are at least four possible measures of the amount of labor supplied by the household: labor force participation rates, employment rates, total hours of work, and total earnings. Total hours of work accounts for those persons not at work as supplying zero hours, and therefore the average level of this variable will be below the average weekly hours of persons who are at work. With hours defined this way, the measures listed above are in order of increasing comprehensiveness. Employment includes changes in labor force participation and in unemployment, which (as pointed out earlier) must be considered as a supply phenomenon in the context of differences between experimentals and controls. The hours measure includes variations in the two preceding variables and, in addition, variations in hours per week of persons at work. The earnings measure reflects variations in all three preceding variables, as well as in earnings per hour worked. Hourly earnings, as we have noted above, may be influenced by choices made by the worker and are to that extent a component of labor supply.

Therefore, it would seem that earnings furnishes the best summary measure of the effects on labor supply. Unfortunately, however, in the use of the earnings variable there is a possible bias that is not present in the other measures. Experimental families filled out a family income reporting form every four weeks, which control families did not. The experimental families therefore may have learned more quickly than control families that what was to be furnished was gross rather than net earnings—that is, earnings before taxes and other deductions, not take-home pay. This differential learning process could have caused a spurious differential in earnings in favor of the experimental group, especially during the early part of the experiment.

The analysis of differences in hourly earnings between experimentals and controls supports the idea of this learning effect.[5] For all three ethnic groups, reported average hourly earnings of male experimentals rise relative to those of controls early in the experimental period. For white and Spanish-speaking males, this differential later is reversed or disappears. For black males, it grows even larger toward the end of the experiment, a phenomenon that seems to result from an unusually small rise in hourly earnings in the black control group.

Because of the possible bias in the earnings measure, we emphasize the hours measure in summarizing the results. An exception is made in discussing the labor supply of the household as a whole, where despite its defects the earnings measure serves as an appropriate way of weighting the hours of different members of the household by the value of the labor they supply. (Family earnings, it should be recalled, are the basis on which payments were determined.)

5. See *Final Report of the New Jersey Experiment*, vol. 1, sec. 1, pt. B, chap. 1, and vol. 1, sec. 2, chap. 6.

Control Variables

In measuring supply effects, a large set of control variables typically was
entered on the righthand side of the regression equations—variables such
as age, education, family size, and prior earning and work experience. The
random-within-strata design that was used to allocate families to different
treatments makes it necessary to measure response behavior by comparisons that are adjusted to achieve equivalence in terms of variables that
define the stratification. If the response is different among the strata, it is
necessary to make separate or conditional estimates reflecting such differences. Inclusion of these variables also was warranted by the fact that even
in a simple random design it is important to control for systematic differences that may survive the randomization process.

The control variables are used in two different ways. First, they are
entered into the labor supply equations as variables in their own right.
Second, they often are combined multiplicatively with the variables representing experimental treatments to determine whether the treatment has
differential effects in different subgroups of the treated population. A
control variable that is highly significant in the first of these contexts may
not be significant in the second.

One of the most important control variables is the preenrollment value
of the dependent variable. Thus, if the dependent variable is hours, hours at
preenrollment usually are entered on the righthand side. This procedure
captures the effect of many taste variables that cannot be specified individually, but it also will reduce the significance of the control variables that are
specified separately. This kind of control variable cannot be used in a nonexperimental study based on a single body of cross-sectional data.

Some of these control variables, although they could have been expected
to be very significant, in fact were not. Thus, after control for ethnicity,
there was little systematic difference among experimental sites. In most
cases, therefore, separate results by site will not be summarized here. On
the other hand, health status was found to be an important variable. All
the results summarized below control for it and thus can be interpreted as
results for individuals in good health. Ethnicity turned out to be tremen-
dously important, even in the presence of several other control variables.
For this reason, most of the regressions were run separately for the three
ethnic groups (white, black, and Spanish speaking), and the results will be
summarized separately.

It is also important to control for potential earned income, since average income levels are not the same in experimental and control groups (because of the complexities of the design model), and since differential responses may occur at different income levels. The income variable used for this purpose should be free of any influence from the experimental treatment. For this purpose we have used estimates of normal hourly earnings, either based entirely on observations from the control group or derived by methods that isolate and abstract from treatment effects.[6]

The foregoing brief account is by no means a complete listing of control variables. To discuss each of them in this summary is unnecessary and would be tedious. Two other important ones should be mentioned, however. First, in studying the labor supply of wives, rather elaborate control variables are used for the number and ages of children. Second, education often appears as a control variable, though it is less powerful than in most labor supply studies because of the limited range of income in the sample.

Treatment Variables

In one sense the treatment in this experiment is very simple: it consists of giving families cash payments. These can be specified much more precisely than the more amorphous treatments involved in experimental evaluation of counseling, training, or psychotherapy programs. In another sense, however, the treatment is complex. There were eight different payment plans, and within each of these the payments varied by family size. The number of experimental families by payment plan has been shown in the preceding paper, by Felicity Skidmore.

In the design stages of the experiment, we all confidently expected the treatment to produce significant overall effects on labor supply, and attention was focused on measuring differential effects of the treatment plans. In retrospect, this emphasis may have been somewhat misplaced, since the overall effect of the treatment is not always unambiguous in direction.

In general, two different methods of introducing treatment effects are used. The first is to introduce a "dummy," or binary, variable, which permits estimation of a basic or central response, and additional variables to catch additional differences among the tax rate and guarantee level combinations. The second method again allows for a basic response level for all

6. For full descriptions of these normal wage variables, see *Final Report of the New Jersey Experiment*, vol. 1, sec. 1, pt. B, pp. BI-24 to BI-61.

families eligible to receive benefits, but also introduces the benefit payment level as the basis for measuring different responses among differently treated families or earners. The payments reflect the guarantee level, the tax rate, family size, and earned income. To avoid introducing experimental response into the treatment variable, the preenrollment level of income is used in calculating payments. The payments calculation is useful in identifying families who are initially above the breakeven point of their plans, because although they will be in the experimental group, they will appear with zero payments.

In practice, two of our plans were dominated by New Jersey welfare throughout most of the experiment, and attrition from these plans was high. These were, of course, the two least generous plans: the 50 percent of poverty guarantee with a 50 percent tax rate (50–50 plan) and the 75 percent guarantee with a 70 percent tax rate (75–70 plan). In much of the analysis, these plans are omitted from the treatment group.

The average size of payments to continuous husband-wife families—those who received payments in a given four-week period for each of the three years of the experiment—is shown below, by experimental site:

Site	Average payment (dollars)			Percent change, first to third year
	First year	Second year	Third year	
All sites	91.03	93.25	96.84	6.4
Trenton	69.93	71.91	58.67	−16.1
Paterson-Passaic	79.43	80.67	84.92	6.9
Jersey City	107.80	109.86	120.35	11.6
Scranton	91.46	94.72	98.26	7.4

The average payment per period of course can be converted to annual averages by multiplying by 13. Thus, the first-year annual average for all such families is $1,183. The average payments for all families are slightly lower than for continuous husband-wife families. We show the data for the latter here, since most of the labor supply analysis is based on these families.

The above data show a mildly rising trend through time, except in Trenton.[7] This trend arises from two sources. First, guarantee levels were escalated annually during the course of the experiment to reflect rises in the

7. There is no way of arriving at a scientific explanation of why Trenton shows a fall in payments because so many things vary among the sites. But the explanation is not particularly crucial to our measurement of response based on control-experimental contrasts within sites.

consumer price index. The increase, based on July to July changes in the CPI, was implemented in all sites in which payments were being made in September 1969 (5.5 percent), October 1970 (5.9 percent), and September or October 1971 (4.4 percent). Because of differences in the timing of the experimental period in different sites, Trenton received the first two cost-of-living adjustments, totaling 11.7 percent; Paterson-Passaic and Jersey City received all three, totaling 16.6 percent; and Scranton received the last two, totaling 10.5 percent. In Paterson-Passaic the third increase in guarantees was in effect for less than a full year before the end of payments; in Scranton it was in effect less than two months and in Jersey City about seven months. Comparing these increases with the increases in average payments shown above, it can be seen that in every case the increase in payments is less than the increase in guarantees—and by substantial amounts in all sites but Jersey City.

Second, rising unemployment rates tended to produce increasing average payments over time. A weighted average unemployment rate for the four sites rose from 4.4 percent in 1969 to 7.1 percent in 1971, a factor that also would tend to produce rising payments as members of the experimental families who lost jobs experienced greater difficulty in finding new ones.

In light of the increases in guarantees and the rise in unemployment, the smallness of the rise in average payments over the life of the experiment suggests that there was neither an increasing withdrawal of labor supply nor any growing falsification of income reports as experimental subjects learned to "beat the system." Either kind of behavior would have produced more rapidly rising payments.

The same kind of data are shown below, by ethnic group:

	Average payment (dollars)			Percent change, first to third year
Ethnic group	First year	Second year	Third year	
All groups	91.03	93.25	96.84	6.4
White	87.65	91.03	90.11	2.8
Black	97.65	96.59	102.83	5.3
Spanish speaking	86.96	92.23	100.32	15.4

The average payments rise most rapidly for Spanish-speaking families. Because these payments rise more than those for all ethnic groups in any one site, something more than the distribution of ethnic groups by site must have been at work.

The average four-week payments for the second year to continuous husband-wife families are shown below, by experimental plan:

Guarantee level (percent)	Tax rate (percent)		
	30	50	70
125	...	$187.28	...
100	...	123.72	$66.07
75	$103.54	44.17	34.91
50	46.23	21.66	...

These vary from $187 per four-week period in the most generous plan to less than $22 in the least generous. (In addition, of course, substantial variation occurs within plans because of differences in family size and earned income.)

Changes in average payments for continuous husband-wife families also vary by plan, from the first to the third year. These changes are shown below (in percent):

Guarantee level (percent)	Tax rate (percent)		
	30	50	70
125	...	8.9	...
100	...	9.1	13.9
75	−4.5	−10.3	15.1
50	−2.6	3.2	...

In the three plans with a guarantee equal to or above the poverty line, payments increase between 9 and 14 percent. Payments in the low-guarantee plans vary more, but three of the five show decreases in payments—including both plans with the lowest (30 percent) tax rate.

Experimental Time

We had expected before the experiment began that the best results from the experiment would be obtained during the middle part of the experimental period. At the outset, participants still might be learning how to report income and how their payments would vary with changes in income. Toward the end of the experiment, anticipation of the termination of payments also might affect labor supply, producing unknown kinds of endgame effects. Where we present results separately by years, results for the middle year generally should be the most reliable. Often we use the central two years—that is, quarters three through ten. For some purposes we average observations over the entire period.

Experimental time, of course, does not have the same meaning in each site in terms of calendar time because each site entered and left the experiment at a different date. To control for trends in the economy, calendar time sometimes is entered into the analysis in addition to experimental time.

The Findings

Findings are summarized below for three groups of participants: married men, married women, and the family as a whole. Within each grouping, attention is given to differences by ethnic group. The analyses of the three groups were done simultaneously by different members of the research team. Although the methods used for each group have important features in common, there are also important differences, and results are not always directly comparable from one group to another.

Male Heads

As we expected, the differences in work behavior between experimental and control families for male heads of continuous husband-wife families were very small. But contrary to our expectations, they do not all show a clear and significant pattern; indeed, they show a discernible pattern only after a great deal of refined analysis. The results, in the crude form of unadjusted means, are reproduced below for the central two years of the experiment, quarters three to ten:

Variable	Controls	Experimentals	Experimentals on high and medium plans
Participation rate (percent)	93.7	94.7	95.5
Employment rate (percent)	87.0	86.4	86.8
Unemployment rate (percent)	6.7	8.3	8.7
Hours worked per week	33.6	33.1	32.9
Earnings per week (dollars)	84.1	89.9	89.4
Earnings per hour (dollars)	2.50	2.72	2.72

Experimental families show a slightly higher participation rate than controls, a lower employment rate, and a correspondingly higher unemployment rate. The unemployment rate difference carries over into hours worked per week. On the two measures of earnings, however, experimentals do better than controls, a result that may reflect greater misreporting—of net rather than gross earnings—by controls.

The higher unemployment rate of male experimentals does not result from higher job turnover: actually, an unambiguous effect of the experimental treatment is to reduce job turnover.[8] Our analyses suggest an increase in the duration of unemployment in the experimental group for heads of household who become unemployed. For younger, better-educated heads, the analyses also suggest an improvement in occupational status and job satisfaction after changing jobs. Thus, at least some members of the experimental group may have looked for work longer and been more selective about the job they accepted.

BASIC REGRESSION COMPARISONS. The next step in the analysis of male heads is to construct a set of simple multiple regressions, with the labor supply measures as dependent variables. These are done separately for each time period and ethnic group, with control variables for such things as age, education, preenrollment hours of work, weeks worked in the year before the experiment, site, family size. The coefficients of interest are those giving the size of the differential between experimental and control groups for several dependent variables. Except for the suspect earnings measure, where the differential is positive, none of these coefficients are statistically significant even at the 10 percent level for the critical central two years. There are significant (at the 5 percent levels) negative coefficients for the treatment variables in the regressions for hours worked in the last year by whites and for hours and employment of Spanish-speaking heads in the first year. The coefficients for blacks are never significant and usually positive.

These regressions have several limitations. In the experimental group, they include families who received the very low payments provided by the two least generous plans, which were dominated by welfare and had high attrition. These regressions also do not allow for differential response at different income levels. Therefore, the next step in the analysis is to construct a set of regressions that control for normal wages and normal income as a fraction of the poverty level, that permit nonlinear wage effects, and that analyze the experimental plans separately in three groups, of high, medium, and low generosity.

These regressions do little better than the first set in disclosing significant

8. See Seymour Spilerman and Richard E. Miller, "The Effect of Negative Tax Payments on Job Turnover and Job Selection," in *Final Report of the New Jersey Experiment*, vol. 1, sec. 2, chap. 7.

effects of the treatment. There are some significant negative coefficients for experimental treatment for white employment and hours, but most often for the low-payment plans where one would least expect them. The coefficients for blacks remain insignificant except for earnings, and almost entirely positive. Coefficients for the Spanish speaking are preponderantly negative, but never both negative and significant.

ESTIMATES OF MORE ELABORATE RESPONSE FUNCTIONS. The remaining analysis for male heads discards the suspect earnings variable as a measure of supply and eliminates the two least generous experimental plans, which were dominated by welfare. Dropping of these plans means, however, that there are few observations at the 70 percent tax rate, which reduces our ability to measure the effects of varying the tax rate.

The new analysis also attempts to deal more directly with another problem that may cause underestimates of the size of the response to payments. In the regressions discussed above, there is no explicit way of allowing for the fact that some of the experimental families are above the breakeven point of their plans and therefore receive no payments and do not face high marginal tax rates. Nevertheless, these families are counted in the experimental group. The normal income variable in the set of regressions discussed above allows for differential response at different normal incomes but does not specifically identify families above their breakeven points. In the remaining analysis of male heads, therefore, a variable designated θ is introduced that measures the distance between a family's normal income and its breakeven point. This variable is scaled in hours of work at the male head's normal wage. It is equal to 0 if the family is a control family or if it is an experimental family whose head could forgo twenty hours or more of work per week without having the family's normal income fall below the breakeven point. It is equal to 2 when normal income is at the breakeven level and to 4 when it would take twenty hours' more work at the normal wage to reach breakeven. The mean value of θ for all experimental families is approximately 5. At this level of θ, a family needs thirty more hours of work at the male head's estimated normal wage to reach its breakeven point.

The experimental response function interacts each of the plan parameters—guarantee and tax rate—multiplicatively with θ and with θ^2, thus estimating a nonlinear response function that typically changes sign over different values of θ. The significance of the response functions is then evaluated by an F-test in which the null hypothesis is that there is no experimental response.

In the central two years, the null hypothesis for labor force participation and employment cannot be rejected for white or black heads; but it is rejected at the 1 percent level for the Spanish speaking, for whom the treatment decreases rates of labor force participation. For hours, the null hypothesis is rejected at the 5 percent level for white and the 1 percent level for Spanish-speaking heads, but it cannot be rejected for blacks. For white and Spanish-speaking heads, the size and pattern of the response can be seen in looking at a relatively generous plan—guarantee of 100 percent and tax rate of 50 percent, the 100–50 plan—and at a typical value of θ, namely 5. The estimated reduction in hours per week at this point in the response surface is 2.4 hours for white heads and 7.3 hours for Spanish-speaking heads. The reductions are larger for higher values of θ: that is, for poorer families.

The two hours effects summarized here seem to emerge in different ways. For the Spanish-speaking heads, a 9 percentage point decrease in the employment rate is estimated for the central two years at $\theta = 5$ for the 100–50 plan. This accounts for much of the decrease in hours. It suggests that Spanish-speaking heads were unemployed more when in the experimental group, which is verified by analyzing unemployment rates directly. For whites, however, the employment response at these values is positive and very small. Their entire hours effect is a reduction in hours per week for those at work. This is confirmed in separate estimates of the hours response for those who are employed, when the response is significant at the 1 percent level for white heads, but is not significant for the other two ethnic groups. Further investigation of the data is needed to determine whether the change in hours for whites arises from less overtime work, a reduction in multiple job holding, or some other source.

The hours response for white heads is strongest in the last year, during which it is significant at the 1 percent level and is estimated at -7.3 hours per week at $\theta = 5$ for the 100–50 plan. For Spanish-speaking heads, the time pattern is opposite. The negative hours responses in the first year and the central two years become predominantly positive and even significant at the 5 percent level in the last year.

Some information also is gained by looking at the results for the central two years in terms of the plans. For Spanish-speaking heads the estimates are ordered by tax rates, as we would expect, with higher tax rates producing substantially stronger disincentives. For whites the reverse is true: the largest disincentives are estimated for the plans with the lowest tax rates. In neither case is there a strong or consistent ordering by guarantee levels— indeed, the most generous plan (125–50) shows the smallest effects.

By far the most surprising result of the analysis for male heads is the complete failure to find any significant effect for black male heads in any of the analyses, despite the fact that black husband-wife families received larger average payments than similar families in the other two ethnic groups. Indeed, the estimated supply response for blacks is not only insignificant but also preponderantly positive. This kind of finding for blacks is not limited to male heads; it recurs in the analysis of other components of the household.

We certainly did not anticipate this outcome; moreover, we have no plausible explanation for it after the fact. The earnings data suggest that something peculiar happened to the black control group, but we do not know why. Although there is always some possibility that the result arises from sampling variability, we should note that black continuous husband-wife families represent more than a third of the total, a larger group than the Spanish speaking, for whom negative supply effects were found.

Married Women, Husband Present

The supply response of married women with husband present can be seen fairly clearly from the simple descriptive statistics below, which show, separately for experimentals and controls, the labor force participation rates of wives at the preenrollment interview and averages for four interviews during the next three years:

		Average, four quarterly interviews (percent)		
Group	*Preenroll-ment*	*First year*	*Second year*	*Third year*
Experimental	16.0	14.0	15.2	18.0
Control	13.4	16.3	16.5	18.5

One of the first things to note is that the participation rates are very low—less than half the 1971 rates of all married women in the U.S. population as a whole. This is in part because the average family size in the experiment is very large, and consequently we have an overrepresentation of families with small children. In part it is an unfortunate consequence of the decision to truncate the sample by family income, a decision that leads to an underrepresentation of working wives even among large families. In retrospect, it might have been preferable to truncate on the basis of husband's income or, better still, husband's wage rate. The same decision probably accounts in part for the rather sharp rise over time in participation rates of control wives, since at the outset we overrepresent families in which the wife is temporarily out of the labor force. The difference in the average rates at preenrollment is a result of the experimental design model, which assigned more of the higher-income families to the experimental group. The effect of the treatment is shown by the drop in the participation rate of experimental wives during the first two years of the experiment. By the third year the rate for experimental wives is above the preenrollment rate but still slightly below the rate for wives in the control group.

REGRESSION COMPARISON. Controls are entered in the regression analysis for wives for the presence of children by detailed age, for the health of both husband and wife, and for education, age, and previous work experience. Two methods of entering the treatment parameters are used. We shall summarize here the results for one that defines treatment by a dummy variable with the value of 1 when the family is in the experimental group and 0 for controls, a variable for average payments based on preenrollment income, and a variable that gives the tax rate of the experimental plan if the payments are positive—that is, if the family was below breakeven at preenrollment. The results of this analysis are summarized in Table 1. The effects shown are from regressions in which the treatment effect applies to

Table 1. Labor Supply Response of Wives in Continuous Husband-Wife Families, by Ethnic Group, Quarters Three to Ten

Percentage points

	Dependent variables	
Ethnic group	Labor-force participation rate[a,b]	Hours of work in survey week[a,c]
All	−0.03[d]	−0.61[e]
White	−0.08[f]	−1.82
Black	−0.002[e]	+0.60[d]
Spanish speaking	+0.05[e]	+0.05

Source: Derived from data from the New Jersey Graduated Work Incentive Experiment.

a. Significance levels of treatment variables on F-test are shown in notes d, e, and f. The F-test for the white subgroup applies to the three treatment variables and tests for an overall effect that is significantly different from zero. The F-tests for the two minority ethnic groups apply to their respective interactions with these same three treatment variables, and the significance levels are with respect to differences from the white subgroup.

b. Control group mean = 0.17.

c. Control group mean = 4.00.

d. Significant at 1 percent.

e. Significant at 5 percent.

f. Significant at 10 percent.

wives in families below breakeven level and is evaluated at the mean level of payments and a tax rate of 50 percent. The coefficient for all wives is the weighted average of three ethnic effects in a regression in which treatment and ethnicity interact.

The analysis shows significant negative effects on labor force participation rates for all experimental wives. These rates are defined as the proportion of quarterly surveys in which the wife was in the labor force during the survey week. When the results are disaggregated by ethnic group, they are seen to arise almost entirely from the behavior of white wives; the effects of the treatment on the participation rates of black and Spanish-speaking wives are close to zero and sometimes positive. When the dependent variable is hours, the results generally are similar but somewhat weaker. The estimated effect for black wives is positive and significantly different from that of white wives. Once again, we have no plausible explanation for the strong differences in results by ethnic group.

Where the regressions include treatment variables that distinguish among experimental plans, the pattern of results by the parameters of the plans is consistent with expectations. The estimated negative response is consistently larger the higher the level of payments, and the differences usually are significant. Moreover, with levels of payments held constant, it is generally larger the higher the tax rate, though this effect is usually small and never significant.

ALTERNATIVE INTERPRETATION. The size of the estimated effects on labor supply are subject to two rather different interpretations. In the central two years (quarters three through ten) the average estimated reduction in labor force participation for all wives, as shown in Table 1, is 3 percentage points; for white wives, it is 8 percentage points. These are not large absolute changes, but given the low rates from which they start, they are very large relative changes. The mean participation rate for all control wives in quarters three through ten is only 17 percent. The estimated percentage reduction in labor supply for all experimental wives is 20 percent and for white wives a startling 50 percent.

The results thus indicate that a temporary negative income tax program would cause a substantial percentage reduction in the proportion of working wives in large low-income families, at least among white wives. How such a result is evaluated in terms of social priorities will depend on one's views about the value of having mothers care for their children. In addition, these estimated effects probably are larger than those to be expected in an otherwise similar but permanent income maintenance program. For the control families, no more than 19 percent of wives were in the labor force in any one quarter, but 41 percent were in the labor force in at least one of the thirteen quarters, counting preenrollment. In other words, this is a group that enters and leaves the labor force frequently. The experimental treatment creates a strong incentive to concentrate periods out of the labor force during the life of the experiment. A permanent program therefore could be expected to have a somewhat smaller impact.

Labor Supply of the Family

The family as analyzed here includes male heads, wives, and all other members of the household sixteen years of age and over. The sample still is restricted to continuous husband-wife families. For this analysis, no estimates are available at this time that are restricted to the central two years; all estimates cover the full three years of the experiment. As mentioned earlier, earnings as a dependent variable has more relevance for the whole family than for its components, since it provides a natural way of weighting hours by value. Therefore, it will be discussed in this summary despite the possible reporting bias. Normal earnings are used as a control variable and are estimated from control families only. The independent variables used to estimate normal earnings include site, race, age, union membership, industry, occupation, family size, and preenrollment earnings.

Table 2 shows two sets of estimates of percentage response for the family as a whole, from different analytical models. All the estimates shown are for plans with a 50 percent tax rate. In the first set, the estimates are from pooled regressions in which an observation is entered for each family in each quarter, and experimental time is entered on the righthand side. In the second set, the twelve quarters for each family are first averaged, and regressions are run on the averages. In the first, the control for income is normal income divided by the poverty line; the tax and guarantee effects are linear. In the second, there are separate estimates for experimental effects above and below breakeven, and the tax effects are nonlinear. The regressions in this set include the predicted variance of family income across time as an independent variable. This variable, constructed in much the same way as predicted normal income, is included for two reasons. First, families with variable income may have weaker attachments to the labor force, and therefore the payments may have more effect on their behavior. Second, variation in income gives the family experience with the effect of

**Table 2. Labor Supply Response of the Family as a Whole,
Based on Alternative Models, by Ethnic Group**[a]

Percent

	Ethnic group[b]		
Model and variable	Whites	Blacks	Spanish speaking
Regressions pooled from eighth quarter			
Hours	−8	−3	−6
Earnings	−12	+9	−2
Regressions calculated from averages for twelve quarters			
Hours	−16	+1	−2
Earnings	−8	+13	−28

Source: Same as Table 1.

a. Includes male heads, wives, and all other household members 16 years of age and over in continuous husband-wife families. The estimates cover the full three years of the work incentives experiment. The tax rate is 50 percent.

b. Estimated coefficients are jointly significant at the 1 percent level for whites and blacks, at the 5 percent level for the Spanish speaking.

the negative tax plan on the level of payments. The variance measure is highly significant in the regression for white earnings.

The hours and earnings effects for whites in both sets of regressions are consistently negative and range from 8 to 16 percent. Moreover, the estimated effects for whites also are consistently negative in the second set at the 30 and 70 percent tax rates (not shown in the table). For blacks, both sets of earnings effects of experimental treatment are large and positive; the hours effects are small and differ in sign. For the 30 and 70 percent tax rates, the positive hours effects in the second set are larger than those shown for the 50 percent tax rate. For Spanish-speaking families, all the estimates are negative. The second set of estimates for hours for the 30 and 70 percent tax rates, however, are positive rather than negative, as for the 50 percent tax rate shown in Table 2.

Thus, for whites the results for the family as a whole are consistent with those from the separate analyses of male heads and wives: that is, in showing appreciable and significant negative effects on labor supply. For blacks, the results again show predominantly anomalous positive responses, though not consistently so for hours. For Spanish-speaking families, the effects are negative, though they generally are smaller and less significant than for whites.

If we regard the hours estimates as somewhat more reliable than the earnings estimates because of the possible bias in reporting earnings, a rough summary measure of the effects on labor supply at the 50 percent tax rate might be obtained by averaging the six hours estimates shown in Table 2. This suggests an overall reduction of labor supply of about 6 percent. But further analysis of the effects for the family as a whole is needed—to determine, for example, whether estimates for the central two years agree with those for the full three years.

Conclusions

In general, the estimated effects of the experimental treatment on labor supply are in accord with our expectations. The major surprise is the absence of any negative effect on the labor supply of black households. For white and Spanish-speaking families and for the group as a whole, the effects are negative, usually significant, but not large. They consist of a reduction in hours of white male heads, an increase in the unemployment rate of Spanish-speaking male heads, and a large relative reduction in the labor force participation rate of white wives.

If one calculates the cost of a negative income tax program on the assumption of no supply response, then these results strongly suggest that the estimated cost will be too low. The added cost produced by the supply response is, however, a rather small portion of the total cost—not more than 10 percent and probably closer to 5 percent. The estimates suggest that in effect a substantial part of this will represent added benefits for mothers whose withdrawal from paid employment is likely to be offset by increased employment at home. There is a further suggestion that tax rates higher than 50 percent may lead to a more pronounced negative supply response and consequently a larger increment to total cost. Whatever the percentage change in income, a higher tax rate requires that more of that change be made up in benefits.

Although nothing in the results contradicts our expectation that the reduction in labor supply will be greater with higher tax rates and with higher guarantees, these expectations are not clearly confirmed. Further analysis of the data is needed to determine whether a sharper picture of the tax and guarantee effects will emerge.

If the results we found by ethnic group were applied to the national low-income urban population, using national ethnic weights, the importance of our results for whites would rise and the importance of the results for the

Spanish speaking would fall. It is not at all clear that results for Puerto Ricans in New Jersey say anything at all about Mexican Americans in the Southwest.

We place less weight on our results for blacks for a different reason. They are strange results that appear to arise from the unusual behavior of the black control group, whose labor supply and, especially, earnings fell relative to other control groups for reasons we do not understand. That the experimental treatment effects for blacks are often statistically significant gives no assurance that they are not biased.

The patterns of labor supply response that we have found are not as clear as we had expected. Yet in many ways they are clearer and more sensible than the results in much of the nonexperimental literature. Certainly they call into serious question the very large effects estimated in some of the nonexperimental studies. The burden of proof would now appear to be on those who assert that income maintenance programs for intact families will have very large effects on labor supply.

HENRY J. AARON

Cautionary Notes
on the Experiment

Between the start and finish of the New Jersey–Pennsylvania income maintenance experiment, the state of economic knowledge about the impact of income and wage rates on work incentives increased enormously. Some of this knowledge was gained through the planning and execution of the experiment itself; even more resulted from the numerous studies carried out on survey data. As a result, any evaluation of the experiment will be based on different and better information than was available to its designers.

Those persons who executed the experiment, however, also were involved in analyses of survey data. As a result, an observer not intimately involved with either the experiment or research based on surveys cannot escape the feeling that any questions or objections that he may raise probably have occurred to someone already and have been disposed of. The following comments are advanced, therefore, with a considerable diffidence that is magnified by the complexity of the experiment itself.

The experiment originated because advocates of large-scale income support for poor intact families realized that prospects for such aid were meager unless it could be shown that the recipients would not stop working en masse. The primary motivation for the experiment, therefore, was political, and it was for political purposes that the Office of Economic Opportunity agreed to spend $8 million. The skills of numerous statisticians, economists, and other social scientists were required, however, and at many points scientific and political goals appeared to conflict—for example, in designing the experimental plans and choosing the sample.

This conflict is especially apparent in the analysis and presentation of results. For political purposes, simple models, simply explained in prose unencumbered by qualifications, are most effective. For scientific purposes, complex models may be necessary, and all relevant qualifications must be stated. Samuelson has warned us to beware of economists who write too well.[1] Viewed in these terms, the various reports on the experiment thus far available may be scientifically useful—an issue discussed below—but they are of limited short-run political value. With a few exceptions, including several nontechnical papers in this volume, the published papers on the New Jersey negative income tax experiment are not fully comprehensible to any but well-trained economists.

Even for this latter group, the various reports suffer from uneven style, employ diverse models that cannot be compared, and in general reflect a kind of scholarly laissez-faire that makes integration and evaluation of the findings quite difficult. Professors afflicted by students who make the tired claim that the content of their work was good even if the style was weak will appreciate that these comments are not merely editorial. At this point the claims of science and politics converge.

Furthermore, the experiment took place in four cities close to one another, lasted three years in each city, and reached 1,357 families, of whom only 725 received benefits under one of the eight negative income tax plans, and of these only 425 survived to join the ranks of the continuous husband-wife sample. Four of the eight plans had fewer than fifty continuous husband-wife recipients—divided among four distinct sites and three disparate ethnic groups.

Nearly everyone agrees (a) that if all other analytical problems are correctly resolved, the brief duration of the experiment is likely to lead to estimates of the sensitivity of labor supply to guarantee levels that are too low and to estimates of the sensitivity of labor supply to tax rates that are too high; (b) that the peculiarities of the sites make extrapolation of the results to other sites hazardous; (c) that the thinness of the sample and the brevity of the experiment make it impossible to observe the impact of a negative income tax on the mores of entire groups; (d) that, following from (c), the estimated responses to both the guarantee and the tax rate may be understated, which conflicts in part with (a), above; and (e) that the thinness of the sample, the use of four sites, and the unexpected diversity of ethnic responses make the coefficients individually unreliable. These acknowledged problems will not—and should not—prevent people from treating the results of the experiment as another piece of evidence on the

1. Paul A. Samuelson, "Economists and the History of Ideas," *American Economic Review*, vol. 52 (March 1962), p. 6. He qualified the warning by noting that economists seldom give readers any cause to heed it.

impact of negative income taxes, but they will reduce the weight attached to this evidence.

Impact of Welfare

The fates were most unkind to the experiment in causing New Jersey legislators in January 1969 to introduce the Unemployed Parents segment of the Aid to Families with Dependent Children (AFDC-UP) program. They magnified the unkindness by making the system perhaps the most generous in the nation.[2] They then compounded their malice, now to the poor as well as to the experimenters, by cutting the guarantee by nearly 40 percent and sharply reducing the number of families served. In addition, a shortage of white families led to extension of the experiment to Scranton, Pennsylvania, a city blessed with numerous poor white families and a quite different welfare system from either of the variants in New Jersey.

New Jersey was chosen as the site for the experiment in part because the absence of the AFDC-UP program would permit a clearer test of the consequences of a negative income tax experiment than would have been possible in its presence. The experimental treatments also were designed on the assumption that AFDC-UP would not be available.

Comparison of Welfare and the Negative Income Tax

The relatively generous welfare plan instituted in 1969 completely dominated two of the eight experimental plans, the 50–50 and the 75–70 plans.[3] The welfare benefit exceeded the negative income tax benefit for all families eligible for welfare. In addition, many other families on these plans had incomes above the breakeven level. In fact, more than 90 percent of the experimental families assigned to the 50–50 plan had incomes above the breakeven level in eleven of the twelve quarters, to the 75–70 plan, in eight of the quarters. This fact led authors of many of the papers on the experi-

2. Massachusetts offered a higher guarantee than New Jersey but reached only one-sixth the proportion of low-income families served in New Jersey. California served a marginally larger proportion of low-income families than did New Jersey, but its guarantee was nearly 40 percent smaller than New Jersey's. See Irwin Garfinkel, "The Effects of Welfare on Experimental Response," in Harold W. Watts and Albert Rees (eds.), *Final Report of the New Jersey Graduated Work Incentive Experiment* (University of Wisconsin—Madison, Institute for Research on Poverty, and Mathematica, 1974), vol. 2, pt. C, chap. 2, p. CII-11.

3. Ibid., Table 7.

ment to exclude from the analyses those families assigned to these plans. The stated reason for the exclusion was that, for the most part, families assigned to these treatments were not subject to much meaningful stimulus, although the grounds for excluding them seem weak in light of the many regressions in which negative income tax benefits were related to normal rather than actual income. Elsewhere, several authors briefly considered the impact of welfare on the experiment,[4] and one paper was devoted entirely to this issue.[5] In the simplest case, where the negative income tax is at least as generous as welfare at all income levels, one would expect that in otherwise identical jurisdictions, the presence of welfare would lead to unambiguously smaller estimated effects of the negative income tax on the supply of labor than would occur in its absence. The reason is that some persons in the control group will work fewer hours when welfare is available than they would work when it is not available. To this extent, the difference in labor supply among families receiving the negative income tax and control families will be reduced.

Unfortunately, the story is far more complex. First, consider the classification of families on the basis of experimental status and eligibility for welfare shown in the following matrix:

	Experimental group		
Eligibility status	Negative income tax greater than welfare at normal income	Welfare greater than negative income tax at normal income	Control group
Eligible for welfare			
Took welfare	A	B	C
Took negative income tax (did not take welfare)	D	E	...
Not eligible for welfare	F		G

First, groups A and E—representing a kind of irrational behavior—would not exist if all families claimed benefits under whichever system paid larger benefits. Some families probably fall in these categories because they chose the less generous negative income tax payment to avoid the stigma of

4. See Glen G. Cain and others, "The Labor Supply Response of Married Women, Husband Present, in the Graduated Work Incentive Experiment," and Robinson G. Hollister, "The Labor Supply Response of the Family," in *Final Report of the New Jersey Experiment*, vol. 1, pt. B, chaps. 3 and 5(a), respectively.
5. Garfinkel, "Effects of Welfare."

welfare; others may have chosen a less generous welfare payment because they did not wish to endanger their eligibility for welfare, medicaid, or other benefits contingent upon welfare. The income level at which the relative sizes of the negative income tax and welfare should be compared is unclear if the labor supply of the household is materially affected by either program; at normal income, welfare may exceed the negative income tax payment, but the relation may be reversed at the income earned after labor supply has adjusted fully to the transfer offer.

Second, of households whose incomes fell below the breakeven level, roughly one-fourth of those under the 50–50 and more than one-third of those under the 75–70 experimental plans did not receive welfare (see Table 1, column 5). This circumstance may have occurred either because the family was categorically ineligible—category F or G—because the family owned a car worth more than $500, or because the family, intentionally or

Table 1. Percentage Distribution of Families among Negative Income Tax Plans, by Welfare and Breakeven Status[a]

	All experimental families				*Families below breakeven[c]*	
Plan[b]	*On welfare* (1)	*Above break-even* (2)	*On welfare or above break-even* (3)	*On negative income tax plan* (4)	*Actually on welfare* (5)	*Eligible for welfare* (6)
50–30	21	28	49	51	29	42
50–50	18	76	94	6	75	59
75–30	8	9	17	83	9	23
75–50	12	47	59	41	23	28
75–70	18	72	90	10	64	61
100–50	12	15	27	73	14	35
100–70	13	41	54	46	22	32
125–50	7	6	13	87	7	22
All experimental families	12.1	...	...	...	...	...
Control families	23.2	...	...	...	...	...

Source: Garfinkel, "Effects of Welfare," Tables 1 and 7.

a. Unweighted average of twelve quarters.

b. The figures in the first column are the percent of the poverty line that is guaranteed; in the second, the negative income tax rate, in percent.

c. As estimated from data on all households in two quarters, one immediately preceding, one immediately following the cut in New Jersey welfare benefits. Numbers in column 5 are based on actual data and may exceed those in column 6 because insufficient data were available for precise determination of eligibility (column 6).

unintentionally, did not apply for benefits to which it was entitled—category D or E. In the first two cases the household is exposed to the planned experimental incentive. Families in A or E did not behave rationally—according to the restricted definition of that term used by economists. Families in the first category presumably should be included in the experimental calculations. Whether to include the second group is less certain. On balance, it would seem that they too should be included, since irrational behavior will not be banished by a negative income tax.

Third, welfare offers superior benefits to many households on negative income tax plans other than the two least generous ones. The ratio of the number of families on welfare to the number of families who were eligible for negative income tax benefits under the other six formulas ranged from 7 to 29 percent (see Table 1, column 5). Some New Jersey families receiving welfare under all plans except those with the highest breakeven levels—the 75–30 and 125–50 plans—may have had incomes over the negative income tax breakeven point. The guarantee under the initial AFDC-UP plan in New Jersey, $4,164 for a family of four, or 105 percent of the poverty threshold, exceeded the guarantee under seven of the eight negative income tax plans. The Pennsylvania guarantee, $3,756, or 95 percent of the poverty threshold for a family of four, exceeded the guarantee under five of the eight negative income tax plans.

To complicate matters still further, the actual tax rates to which families were subject, under the negative income tax plans as well as welfare, differed from the nominal rates, as shown in Table 2. The initial New Jersey AFDC-UP program dominated six of the eight negative income tax plans completely and a seventh for four-person households whose income was less than $7,540. In fact, however, most households under these plans received negative income tax payments rather than welfare. How many of such households were categorically ineligible for welfare and how many missed higher benefits to which they were entitled is unclear. Only the 125–50 plan clearly dominated initial New Jersey AFDC-UP. The relation between welfare and the negative income tax differed among the plans in operation in New Jersey, before and after the cut in welfare, and in Pennsylvania.

Finally, the actual guarantee under welfare is greater than shown in Table 2, since welfare status brings automatic eligibility for food stamps and medicaid and may entitle the family to certain special welfare allowances, job training, or other services. On the other hand, some benefits whose value varies with income—for example, subsidized housing—were available to families not on welfare.

Table 2. Real and Nominal Welfare and Negative Income Tax Guarantees, Tax Rates, and Breakeven Levels

Program	Welfare guarantee (dollars)	Nominal tax rate	Nominal breakeven (dollars)	Eligibility level (dollars)	Actual tax rate[c]	Actual breakeven (dollars)	Income level at which welfare equals negative income tax (dollars)[a,b]		
							New Jersey precut	New Jersey postcut	Pennsylvania
Welfare									
New Jersey precut	4,164	0.67	6,575[b,d]	4,248	0.47	9,220[b]	...	...	...
New Jersey postcut	2,592	0.67	4,589[b,d]	3,310	0.47	6,235[b]	...	...	...
Pennsylvania	3,756	0.67	5,966[b,d]	3,756	0.34	11,407[b]	...	...	...
Negative income tax									
50–50	1,984	0.50	3,968	3,968	0.46	4,313	[e]	[e]	[e]
50–30	1,984	0.30	6,613	6,627	0.29	6,841	[e]	5,258	[e]
75–70	2,976	0.70	4,251	4,246	0.64[d]	4,650	[e]	268	[e]
75–50	2,976	0.50	5,952	5,952	0.46	6,470	[e]	[f]	[e]
75–30	2,976	0.30	9,920	9,920	0.29	10,262	7,540	[f]	[e]
100–70	3,968	0.70	5,669[d]	5,674	0.64[d]	6,200	[e]	6,104	299
100–50	3,968	0.50	7,936	7,936	0.46	8,626	[e]	[f]	747
125–50	4,960	0.50	9,920	9,920	0.46	10,783	[f]	[f]	9,013

Sources: The first five columns are from Garfinkel, "Effects of Welfare"; column 6 (welfare) = [column 1 + (column 5 × disregard in note b] ÷ column 5; column 6 (negative income tax) = column 1 ÷ column 5; the last three columns are derived from data in the preceding columns.

a. Column shows crossover point for New Jersey precut, New Jersey postcut, and Pennsylvania, respectively.

b. Based on a $360 set aside in New Jersey precut and Pennsylvania, and $720 set aside in New Jersey postcut.

c. Reported by Garfinkel, "Effects of Welfare," p. CII-18, but not explained. Garfinkel's actual tax rates under the 70 percent negative income tax plan were adjusted upward by the author.

d. Author's estimate.

e. At all income levels welfare is above the negative income tax.

f. At all income levels the negative income tax is above welfare.

Clearly, therefore, the experimental stimulus generated by the negative income tax plans is not shown adequately by the guarantee and tax rate—or by the tax rate and payment level at normal income. Instead, the stimulus for families eligible for welfare is equal to (a) the difference between the negative income tax guarantee and welfare guarantee, and (b) the difference between the effective negative income tax rate and the effective welfare tax rate; or, for families ineligible for welfare, to (a) the difference between the negative income tax rate and the tax rate they otherwise would face, and (b) the difference between the negative income tax payment and benefits for which they otherwise would be eligible. In either case the stimulus provided by each negative income tax plan is not unique but varies widely depending on potential, as well as actual, welfare status of the family; on family size (since the ratio of the welfare guarantee to the poverty threshold varies by family size, whereas the negative income tax guarantee does not); and on work-related expenses (since welfare reimburses families for more work-related expenses than does the negative income tax). In addition, families under the negative income tax and welfare may be subject to a variety of benefits and tax rates that interact with the welfare and negative income tax guarantees and tax rates, and consequently the true stimulus is even more tenuously related to the nominal parameters of the negative income tax plans and even more specialized to each household than the foregoing characteristics indicate. What this all means is that each household is confronted by a highly complex stimulus represented by a function that may increase and then decrease and that exhibits quirks and discontinuities. Within each negative income tax plan were numerous such families with widely different functions. That families were aware of these functions—or that they understood the experimental stimulus—is doubtful.

Analytical Problems

The introduction of welfare clearly contaminated the experiment in a manner the investigators had hoped to avoid. The critical question is: "how serious was the contamination?" The answer depends on precisely how the objective of the experiment is phrased. Was the objective to find out (a) how a negative income tax would affect the supply of labor in a state with no preexisting welfare system, (b) how a national negative income tax would affect the supply of labor, or (c) how variations in the guarantee or the tax rate would change the impact of the negative income tax on the supply of labor?

Garfinkel, in his paper on the sensitivity of the results to the presence of welfare, addresses the first two questions. He demonstrates that, despite the contamination from the welfare system, the average effects on labor supply that would have been observed in New Jersey without AFDC-UP would not have been drastically larger than those actually estimated. This conclusion follows from regressions in which it is assumed that control families receiving welfare would have worked the same amount had welfare not been available as did those not receiving welfare (after controlling for relevant socioeconomic characteristics). Because welfare may have reduced the labor supply of eligible control families, the difference between the labor supply of control and experimental families is smaller in the presence of welfare than in its absence. According to his calculations, the reduction in hours worked would have been less than 13 percent even if welfare had not been present, in comparison with an average reduction of 7.9 percent actually observed.[6]

The problems in transferring the results of the experiment to the rest of the nation are extremely serious, but the great diversity in welfare practices is not one of them if the other difficulties are surmountable. This conclusion follows from the upper limit (mentioned above) on the increased effects on labor supply if no welfare system had existed in New Jersey. Thus, Garfinkel, by answering the first question, also answered the second as far as the variability of welfare is concerned.

But the third question—how variations in the guarantee or tax rate would change the impact of the negative income tax on the labor supply—cannot be answered on the basis of analysis so far presented. Indeed, estimates of the effects of variations in both the guarantee and the tax rates are biased so seriously toward zero as to be essentially meaningless. Such estimates are dependent on the association for each family or worker between (a) the change in the guarantee and in the tax rate associated with the negative income tax and (b) the labor supply of the family or worker after the influence of other variables has been removed. The crucial question concerns the effect of the negative income tax plan on the guarantee and tax rates faced by each family. For families not eligible for welfare, the

6. See Garfinkel, "Effects of Welfare," Table 9, assumption 2; 13 percent is the ratio of the unweighted average reduction in hours divided by weighted average hours from Albert Rees, "An Overview of the Labor-Supply Results," *Journal of Human Resources*, vol. 9 (Spring 1974), Table 8. The value 7.9 percent is the weighted average reduction in hours from Rees, Table 8, with number of continuous husband-wife families as weights.

change in the guarantee and tax rate was equal to that defined by the negative income tax plan to which the household was assigned. But widely varying percentages of families under the different plans with incomes below the breakeven point claimed welfare benefits instead of accepting negative income tax payments (see Table 1, column 5). Furthermore, 23 percent of all control families received welfare payments. Compared with control families who were ineligible for welfare, they too faced sizable guarantees and tax rates. Thus, it is far from clear what the effective guarantees and tax rates under each plan really were and what kind of guarantees and tax rates control families faced.

Net Benefits and Tax Rates

The problem stands out more starkly in the comparison of the payment amounts under each plan with payments under welfare. Figure 1 shows the relation between income and actual benefits under two negative income tax plans (100–70 and 75–30) and welfare in New Jersey before and after the cut in benefits. Figure 2 shows the difference between these negative income tax plans and the New Jersey welfare levels. It is not clear why any family eligible for welfare would have accepted benefits under the negative income tax plan before the cut. The striking contrast is observed by comparing benefits under each negative income tax plan with welfare payments after the cut. As is apparent, a recipient under the 75–30 plan faced a meager increment in his guarantee and increasing benefits (that is, an earnings subsidy) as his earnings rose. The recipient under the 100–70 plan faced a somewhat larger increment in his guarantee and an increment in his tax rate of about 18 percent.

These sharp contrasts require a number of comments.

First, these comparisons are relevant only for those households eligible for welfare. For ineligible families, the stimulus is shown correctly by lines C and D in Figure 1 and by the guarantees and tax rates in Table 2.

Second, the experimental stimulus is highly nonlinear, and net payments and tax rates are discontinuous: that is, the ratio of changes in net benefits to changes in income (the tax rate) varies from one income level to another and the variation occurs abruptly at certain income levels.

Third, compared with the welfare alternative, the payment differential rises with income over certain ranges, from which it may be inferred that the experimental stimulus reduces the tax rates confronted by some families over some income ranges.

Figure 1. Benefit Levels under Alternative Plans, by Family Earnings

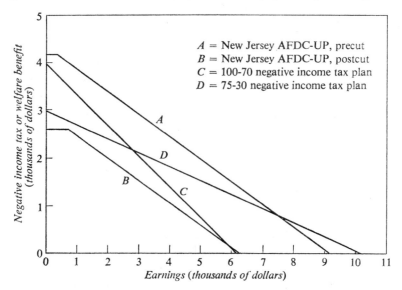

Fourth, not only does each family confront a very complex experimental stimulus, but also each negative income tax plan contains numerous such functions, varying with family size and wage rate—to say nothing of numerous other peculiarities that can cause welfare payment levels and implicit tax rates to vary at each earnings level.

Fifth, all of these problems are aggravated for the roughly three-quarters of experimental families subject to the change in AFDC-UP enacted by New Jersey in the midst of the experiment and deeply aggravated for all families who received food stamps, public housing, or other cash or in-kind benefits with tax rates and guarantees of their own. What all of the foregoing means is that each negative income tax plan is a composite of numerous subplans, where the term "subplan" refers to the schedule of net experimental payments faced by a particular family. It is quite likely that some subplans under different negative income tax plans more closely resemble one another than some subplans under a single negative income tax plan.

The impact of these observations on statistical analysis is quite disturbing. At first glance, it appears that at least one can still represent the eight experimental plans by dummy variables that would permit one to say that, for example, the 100–50 plan decreases hours by X percent and the 100–70

Figure 2. Difference in Benefit Levels, by Income Class

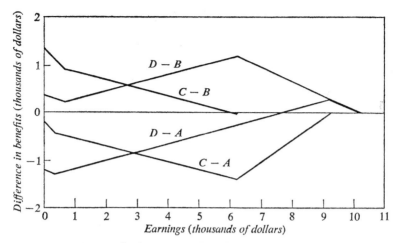

$C - A$ = 100-70 negative income tax plan minus New Jersey AFDC-UP, precut
$C - B$ = 100-70 negative income tax plan minus New Jersey AFDC-UP, postcut
$D - A$ = 75-30 negative income tax plan minus New Jersey AFDC-UP, precut
$D - B$ = 75-30 negative income tax plan minus New Jersey AFDC-UP, postcut

plan decreases hours by Y percent. One would then be able to say that going from a 50 to a 70 percent nominal tax would reduce hours by $Y - X$ percent, even though one would not know what actual differential in tax rates had caused that effect. Unfortunately, such an inference is not legitimate, because the actual differential depends not only on the nominal differential but also on the characteristics of the households assigned to each plan—for example, their size, welfare eligibility, normal wage, and so on. In particular, families were not assigned randomly to various negative income tax plans in the experiment; rather, families with relatively high expected incomes were assigned to the more generous plans in order to hold down costs.

The consequences of the availability of welfare and of nonrandom assignment are summarized in Table 3. This table shows, for all experimental families over two quarters, the estimated guarantee levels and tax rates derived from regressions of the differential between the negative income tax benefit and welfare on income. The regressions have several striking characteristics: the fits are extremely loose; the actual guarantees are all smaller than the nominal guarantees, especially for the least generous plans; and the actual tax rates are smaller than the nominal tax rates, and some

Table 3. Estimated Average Guarantee Levels and Tax Rates Relative to AFDC-UP[a]

Plan	Estimated guarantee (percent of poverty threshold)	Estimated tax rate (change in net benefits associated with an increase in earnings of $100)	$\bar{R}^2$
50–50	−50	35	0.25
	(4.76)	(3.14)	
50–30	−40	36	0.38
	(5.18)	(5.42)	
75–70	9	−23	0.07
	(1.01)	(2.06)	
75–50	12	−2	−0.01
	(2.32)	(0.49)	
75–30	29	3	−0.00
	(5.98)	(0.98)	
100–70	41	−23	0.13
	(5.23)	(3.35)	
100–50	39	−8	0.03
	(6.78)	(1.87)	
125–50	74	−14	0.09
	(15.99)	(4.38)	

Source: The guarantees and tax rates are the coefficients from the regression $D = a + bY$, where D is the difference between the negative income tax benefit and the welfare benefit to which a family was eligible at the observed income level, Y. Data cover two quarters, one just before and one just after the cut in welfare by New Jersey. Thus, each family is represented twice. Regressions include only those observations for which either welfare or negative income tax benefits were positive.

a. The numbers in parentheses are t-statistics.

are actually positive, indicating that an increase in earnings increases net benefits. All of these characteristics are explained by the fact that each plan contained two types of households, those eligible and those not eligible for welfare.[7] Points representing the latter households indicated guarantees and tax rates in rough accord with nominal values. Points representing families eligible for welfare were widely scattered and tended to be along a line with quite different intercept and slope. The results were lines with peculiar intercepts (guarantees) and slopes (tax rates) and loose fits. Because fewer families were eligible for welfare under the more generous plans, these estimated slopes and tax rates varied less from nominal values than those under less generous plans.

The fact that each negative income tax plan is a composite of so many

7. Sufficient data for an accurate determination of welfare eligibility were not available from experimental records. In fact, the most important variable was ownership of an automobile more valuable than welfare regulations permitted recipients to own.

and such complex subplans may help explain why differences among the estimated effects of the various guarantees, payments, and treatment levels are so small and so frequently insignificant. In particular, each plan contains such a wide range of effective tax rates that the average tax rates within each plan are almost randomly associated with nominal rates; on the other hand, differences in guarantee levels shine through the haze generated by welfare. These findings might explain why the effects of the tax rates on work effort are so small and, in some cases, counter to expectations; they might explain also why the effects of guarantees are stronger and more plausible. It is also quite possible that the true differences in the effects of variations in tax rates and guarantees are negligible. In that case the conclusions of the reports would remain accurate, even if the parameterization of the treatments were not.

In summary, the introduction of AFDC-UP exposed families to a wide variety of net guarantees and tax rates. Although this fact does not preclude estimates of the outer range on labor supply effects, it does obscure the effects of variations in tax rates and guarantee levels on labor supply. The experiment did not answer the question of how much difference tax rates and guarantees make on labor supply.

Sample Selection, Normal Income, and Normal Wages

The experiment was conducted on families whose income during preenrollment did not exceed 150 percent of the poverty threshold. Families whose income fell below that standard only because of such extraordinary events as protracted illness were eliminated. On the other hand, there is no indication that families whose incomes exceeded the threshold for such extraordinary reasons as unusual amounts of overtime were included. Despite some effort to exclude families whose normal incomes were clearly above the cutoffs, it seems fair to say that eligibility was based on income at preenrollment. This decision, it seems, was largely imposed on the experiment by the Office of Economic Opportunity.

Sampling Strategy

Two alternative procedures for selecting the sample, it is now apparent, might have been used. First, eligibility might have been determined on the basis of the husband's income or wage rate at preenrollment. Second, eligibility might have been based on family characteristics other than income or wage rates that correlate with normal income. In other words, eligibility might have been based on expected normal income estimated from some normal earnings function, such as that used by Robert Hall or Michael Boskin in studies based on survey research.[8] Such estimates clearly could have referred to the normal income of the husband, of the couple, or of the entire family.

The decision to base eligibility for the experiment on a preenrollment family income of less than 150 percent of the poverty threshold is now generally acknowledged to have had the unfortunate effect of excluding nearly all families in which the wife worked more than a negligible amount. As a result, the estimates of labor force response by women are based on a sample that excludes the kind of workers who supply the bulk of female labor. This peculiarity in the sample can only reduce the faith one can place in the relevance of the experimental results to the labor supply of female family heads or working wives. Whether it led to overestimates or underestimates of the changes in female labor supply is less clear, but overestimates seem more likely.[9]

Nonexperimental Influences on Income

The method of sample selection raised a number of analytical problems that in turn induced the investigators to adopt statistical procedures to isolate variations in labor supply induced by the experiment from variations caused by other circumstances.

In normal experimental procedure, a sample of experimental subjects and controls is chosen. The experimental subjects receive some treatment that is thought to alter their behavior. The controls do not. This behavior may be related systematically to other variables. In that case the experimentals and controls are chosen so that the behavioral impact of those other variables can be estimated and controlled before the impact of the

8. Robert E. Hall, "Wages, Income, and Hours of Work in the U.S. Labor Force," and Michael J. Boskin, "The Economics of Labor Supply," in Glen G. Cain and Harold W. Watts (eds.), *Income Maintenance and Labor Supply: Econometric Studies* (Markham, 1973).

9. Because only those wives with very marginal attachment to the labor force appear in the sample, even a small reduction in the remuneration for work and small additions to family resources might lead to complete withdrawal from the labor force. On the other hand, reported reductions in labor supply may exceed actual reductions because casual labor is easy to conceal.

experimental treatment is measured. In some situations completely randomized assignment to control and experimental groups achieves this objective optimally, but in the experiment it did not.[10] Under one procedure, the behavioral impact of nonexperimental variables is estimated on the control group; the resulting estimates then are applied to the control group and behavioral deviations in the experimental group that are nonrandomly related to experimental treatments are attributed to the treatment.

If this procedure had been used here, the impact on labor supply of such factors as age, education, number and age of children, race, and so on would have been estimated on the control group—and, perhaps, experimental households at preenrollment. These estimates would have been used to calculate the expected labor supply of experimental men, women, and families. Deviations in the labor supply of experimental units that are not randomly distributed among all households would be attributed to the negative income tax, and those nonrandom deviations among experimental families would be attributed to the various income tax plans.

But with one exception, this procedure was not used.[11] Two related problems with it exist. Estimates of the relation between labor supply and variables other than the negative income tax may be biased because the sample is truncated on preenrollment income and badly biased because the level of truncation is low.[12] The problems created in studies based on cross-sectional survey data by truncation of the sample at a low income level are fatal. They are less serious in the experiment for two reasons. First, the experiment includes data covering more than three years, so that transitory deviations in labor supply will tend partially to even out. But protracted

10. See Charles E. Metcalf, "Consumption Behavior Under a Permanent Negative Income Tax: Preliminary Evidence," *Final Report of the New Jersey Experiment*, vol. 3, pt. D; and John Conlisk and Harold Watts, "A Model for Optimizing Experimental Designs for Estimating Response Surfaces," in American Statistical Association, *Proceedings of the Social Statistics Section* (1969), pp. 150–56.

11. The exception is the set of averaged estimates of changes in family hours and earnings; see Hollister, "Labor Supply Response of the Family."

12. For example, assume income is a simple linear function of education and random fluctuations. If one estimates this relation on a sample limited to those with low income, the sample will include nearly all families with low education and a few families with relatively high education who are having bad years. Additional schooling will seem to have a smaller impact on income than in fact it does because the sample is limited by truncation to include only those households whose education is not currently associated with higher incomes. This problem is discussed lucidly by Glen G. Cain and Harold W. Watts, "Toward a Summary and Synthesis of the Evidence," and Irwin Garfinkel, "On Estimating the Labor Supply Effects of a Negative Income Tax," both in Cain and Watts (eds.), *Income Maintenance and Labor Supply*.

variations in the relation between these variables and labor supply that do not average out in three years or permanent variations randomly distributed among households will remain. The resulting estimates of the impact on labor supply of different variables may deviate from estimates that would be generated for the population at large, but they may be unbiased estimates for the truncated population (apart from lingering transitory deviations). Second, because a control group exists, it does not really matter whether the contribution of education, for example, to labor supply is estimated incorrectly. All that matters is that the estimate is biased in the same direction and by the same amount for the experimental and control groups. In that case one will have controlled the impact of other influences correctly within the sample and the consequences of the negative income tax treatment should stand forth.

A further difficulty with this procedure remains. The explanatory power of all normal earnings functions that exclude labor supply variables from the righthand side is very low, even when coefficients are significant.[13] Thus, almost all the observed variance in income is attributed to random noise or, in the experiment, to negative income tax treatment. To reduce random variation in income associated with each household observation, the major papers employ estimates of normal income, $\hat{y}$, and normal wages, $\hat{w}$, for each household. The procedure used in estimating $\hat{w}$ is summarized in the following three equations:

$$(1) \qquad\qquad w_{it} = w_{it}^* + \bar{w}_{it} + u_{it},$$

$$(2) \qquad\qquad \bar{d}_i = \sum_{t=1}^{n} \frac{u_{it}}{n}, \text{ and}$$

$$(3) \qquad\qquad \hat{w}_{it} = w_{it}^* + \bar{d}_i,$$

where w_{it} is the actual wage rate of worker i in quarter t; w_{it}^* is the wage predicted for worker i at time t on the basis of personal characteristics other than his negative income tax or control assignment; $\bar{w}_{it}$ is the impact on his wage rate of his negative income tax assignment (defined as zero for controls); u_{it} is an error term; $\bar{d}_i$ is the mean error for worker i in the n quarters ($6 \leq n \leq 13$) for which information was available; and $\hat{w}_{it}$ is the normal wage rate. The procedure used in estimating y was similar, although the detailed application differed.[14]

13. See, for example, Garfinkel, "Estimating Labor Supply Effects."
14. In particular, y^* and $\bar{y}$, predicted income and experimentally induced change in income, respectively, were estimated by an interactive procedure. The text does not indicate whether this procedure converges to the same estimates regardless of where the

The key aspect of the estimation of these equations is that data used to estimate equation (1) include not only experimental families at preenrollment and controls at all quarters, but also experimental families during the life of the experiment. Because $\hat{w}$ and $\hat{y}$ are the basic variables used in subsequent analysis of the effect of various negative income tax plans on wages, earnings, hours, employment, and labor force participation, it is quite obviously vital that $\hat{w}$ and $\hat{y}$ remove the effects of the experiment from $\hat{w}$ and $\hat{y}$ in an unbiased way, in the sense that the coefficients of other variables that affect labor supply should not absorb experimental effects. If these coefficients include experimental effects, then the normal wage and income of control families—and thus estimates of their normal labor supply—will reflect experimental effects. The control families would cease to be controls.

One area of concern stands out. Families were not randomly assigned to experimental treatments. Rather, relatively high-income families disproportionately received relatively generous negative income tax plans. This step was taken because it decreased transfer costs, increased the number of observations that could be obtained within a given budget constraint, and enabled greater statistical reliability.[15] This procedure would seem to introduce some systematic relation between whatever characteristics determined preenrollment and subsequent wage rates (or income) and parameters of the negative income tax plans. It seems likely, therefore, that coefficients of variables appearing in the w^* (or y^*) equations would absorb some of the effects of the more generous negative income tax plans.

The same matter can be put another way. Suppose that w_{it}^* in equation (1) is estimated two ways. In each case the same variables and functional form are used, but coefficients are estimated on two sets of data: for control families at preenrollment and throughout the experimental period and for experimental families at preenrollment only; or for all families at preenrollment and throughout the experimental period. Before the latter set is used, it should be shown that when families are assigned nonrandomly to experimental treatments, the two sets of residuals yield estimates of $\hat{w}$ having the

---

iterations begin, nor does it indicate that estimates of y^* will be uncontaminated by experimental influences. It is vital that the published reports include considerable support for the estimates of $\hat{w}$ and $\hat{y}$, because the entire report rests heavily on these two variables. For details on the functional forms and estimating procedures, see Harold W. Watts, Dale J. Poirier, and Charles Mallar, "Concepts Used in the Central Analysis and Their Measurement," in *Final Report of the New Jersey Experiment*, vol. 1, sec. 1, pt. B, chap. 1. The explanation of the estimation of $\hat{y}$ is far less complete than that of $\hat{w}$.

15. See Metcalf, "Consumption Behavior," and Conlisk and Watts, "A Model for Optimizing Experimental Designs."

same expected values. If they do, then reasons of efficiency or some other statistical advantage might tip the balance in favor of this set. If they do not, then some proof of its advantages over the former set seems to be called for, but it is not provided. If this criticism is valid, then variables related to normal income but unrelated to the negative income tax may have absorbed some of the labor supply responses that properly should have been attributed to the negative income tax. I have not tried to estimate how important these effects may be. Although this problem exists in principle, it may not be important in practice, a possibility suggested by a comparison of the two sets of results reported by Hollister.[16]

A second aspect of the estimates of $\hat{w}$ and $\hat{y}$ is disturbing. Because of the truncation of the sample, estimates of the contributions of nonexperimental variables to $\hat{w}$ and $\hat{y}$ are different from those which an untruncated sample would yield. The reasons for this difference were set forth above. It is less clear whether the coefficients of the independent variables are biased estimates for this sample, and whether the estimates of normal wages and income for this sample are biased. There is some reason for concern, since some of the estimated relations are implausible—for example, that normal wages of white males with eight years of schooling and black males with twelve years of schooling rise after age forty-five and normal wages of all females with eight years of schooling rise after age forty-five, whereas earnings of black and white females with twelve years of schooling decline after age forty-five. Moreover, the authors of various studies go out of their way to dissuade readers from attaching any significance to the coefficients of the independent variables.[17] I frankly do not understand how an equation

16. Hollister's averaged estimates are derived from equations in which normal income and wages are based on data on the control group only, whereas his pooled estimates are derived from equations based on data from both the control group and experimental families. The reduction in hours because of the experiment is larger for whites and for blacks in the pooled than in the averaged estimates. The reverse is true for Spanish-speaking families. On the other hand, a certain capriciousness in the underlying coefficients raises serious doubts about the results: an increase in the guarantee increases hours for whites (insignificantly) but reduces them (significantly) for black and Spanish-speaking families. An increase in the tax rates reduces hours insignificantly for whites, but increases them significantly for both black and Spanish-speaking families. See Hollister, "Labor Supply Response of the Family."

17. "It should be kept in mind that the main objective here is to derive a better basis for stratifying families by income class than is available using pre-enrollment values. The emphasis is not on obtaining highly significant or readily interpretable coefficients." Watts and others, "Concepts Used," p. BI-67.

"The regression prediction [of normal income] is of untested validity as a measure of

whose coefficients are not to be taken seriously, at least for the group on which they are estimated, can be used to estimate normal income and wages. If goodness of fit has been sought regardless of the plausibility of coefficients, then the possibility grows into likelihood that these equations capture experimental effects as well as normal income and wages.

Although these variables may have little impact on the final results, the ultimate test of the results is the plausibility of the estimated experimental effects. According to the estimates of $\bar{w}$, the effects of the negative income tax on wage rates have a most uneven and implausible pattern. For Spanish-speaking males the effect is first positive, reaching a maximum in the second quarter, then declines, turning negative by the fifth quarter and reaching a minimum in the ninth quarter. For white men the effect is always positive, but it reaches a maximum in the fourth quarter. For black men, the effect is always positive, rising sharply through the first four quarters, then leveling off and rising more slowly, finally reaching its maximum in the twelfth quarter. For white women the negative income tax appears to depress wage rates through the first six quarters, an effect that is eroded gradually thereafter, until at the twelfth quarter the effect is slightly positive. The negative income tax is associated with a swift rise in wage rates for Spanish-speaking women—35 percent after four quarters, but eroding to negligible dimensions after twelve quarters. The wage rates of black women follow a roller-coaster pattern: up 12 percent after two quarters, down 2 percent (a gross decline of 14 percent) after eight quarters, and finishing up about 7 percent at the end of the experiment. The behavior of these differentials raises the possibility—almost the certainty—that the average relations are in error, since the pattern of wage rate responses over time defies all reason. It remains possible, however, that the impact of these variables on estimated effects of guarantees and tax rates may be modest.

In summary, it seems likely that a combination of factors—truncation of the sample, correlation between income at preenrollment and experimental plan, and the method of estimating normal income and wages—has produced estimates of normal income and wages that may well include the

---

normal income." Cain and others, "Labor Supply Response of Married Women," pp. BIIIa–52–53.

"My objective was to develop an equation which would best predict what the families' earnings would have been in the absence of the experiment; since there was no intention to interpret the meaning of individual coefficients in the estimating equation there seemed to me less need than is normally the case to develop carefully the justification for the variables included and the form in which they were included." Hollister, "Labor Supply Response of the Family," Appendix IV, p. 1.

experimental effects they are meant to exclude. This outcome, together with the misspecification of experimental stimulus alleged in the preceding section, would seem to understate estimates of response to the negative income tax treatments.

Extrapolation

The value of the experiment for policy lies in its usability in estimating the real costs of a nationwide negative income tax plan.[18] The reports contain no such estimates and indeed warn readers against facile use of the results for that purpose. The reports correctly remind readers that responses to a permanent negative income tax available to all of the poor may differ from responses to a temporary negative income tax available to only a few. In addition, research done at the Urban Institute suggests wide interstate variations in the character of labor markets and in the effects on population groups of public policies that alter unearned income or net wages.[19] It is quite possible that an organization of negative income tax recipients, similar to the National Welfare Rights Organization, would spring up that might alter attitudes and behavior.

But there are further difficulties in extending the results to a national plan even if one is willing to assume that labor markets in New Jersey are typical of those elsewhere. If one wishes to use the point estimates, one must still reweight the sample for the national distribution of ethnic groups. In addition, since the size of the experimental stimulus in the experiment depends on the potential welfare status of experimental households, it would be necessary to take account of variations in welfare programs from levels prevailing in Pennsylvania and New Jersey. Finally, there is some indication in the reports that changes in labor supply are greater the farther normal income and wages fall below breakeven levels;[20] to the extent that

18. Clearly the experiment will be valuable for other purposes as well, primarily as a demonstration and an administrative trial run in putting a negative income tax into operation and as a unique source of data that may help reshape views on the supply of labor. These purposes alone may well have justified the expense and effort.

19. See P. M. Greenston and C. D. MacRae, "Labor Markets, Human Capital, and the Structure of Earnings," Working Paper 3606-02 (Urban Institute, July 1974; processed); and P. M. Greenston, C. D. MacRae, and D. T. Riordan, "Categorical Earnings Subsidies: Market Effects and Program Costs," Working Paper 3606-06 (Urban Institute, July 1974; processed).

20. Cain and Watts, "Toward a Summary and Synthesis of the Evidence," Table 9.1 and Figure 9.3; and Watts, "Labor Supply Response of Married Men," in *Final Report*

this is true, the translation of the experiment into national estimates would require estimates of normal income and wages for all families, a process that cannot depend on the estimated coefficients from this study because of the truncation of the sample. For all of these reasons the mechanical estimation of real costs of a national negative income tax from average values discovered in the experiment may be seriously in error.

The final question inevitably emerges: do the results of the experiment make sense in light of economic theory and other studies? At present the experimental findings concerning changes in the supply of labor in response to a negative income tax fall at the bottom end of the wide range of estimates put forth in previous studies. The mean experimental guarantee and tax rate (89–51)[21] corresponds rather closely with the $3,000–50 percent plan for a family of four used by Cain and Watts in comparing cross-sectional studies. The best summary measure of the change in labor supply is that there was a 4 to 5 percent reduction in hours worked by males,[22] a 25 to 50 percent reduction by women, and roughly a 6 percent reduction by families.[23] These resemble the estimates of Orley Ashenfelter and James Heckman; Michael Boskin; Garfinkel and Stanley Masters; and Alfred Tella, Dorothy Tella, and Christopher Green, all of whom found reductions in labor supply by males of 6 to 13 percent and for females of 27 to 38 percent.[24]

But the underlying income and substitution effects in the experiment vary by disturbing amounts among races and normal income groups. In addition, the characteristics of the welfare system, as noted earlier, may have tended to bias estimated responses toward zero, especially responses to tax rates. For these reasons I am inclined to think that reanalysis of the experimental data is likely to produce somewhat higher estimates of sub-

---

of the New Jersey Experiment, Table 13, p. BIIa-35. In some cases the results seem to depart farther from theoretical expectations the farther normal income falls below breakeven.

21. Among continuous husband-wife families. The mean plan at the outset was 86–51.

22. Watts, "Labor Supply Response of Married Men," p. BIIa-46. This estimate refers to the middle of the experiment. Among the very poor the reduction approaches 20 percent.

23. Hollister, "Labor Supply Response of the Family," p. BVa-16.

24. See summary calculations of Sandra Christensen, "Evidence of the Work Behavior of the Poor" (U.S. Department of Health, Education, and Welfare, manuscript in preparation), based on Cain and Watts, "Toward a Summary and Synthesis," Tables 9.1 and 9.2, pp. 332–37.

stitution effects and possibly somewhat greater overall responses than have
emerged so far.

Comment by Michael J. Boskin

Certain analytical approaches and empirical informa-
tion that are taken for granted today were neither so readily available nor
so widely accepted nearly a decade ago. At the time the experiment was
first discussed in government circles, I was a sophomore studying the
principles of economics. Therefore, much of what I write is with the benefit
of hindsight and is meant more as an attempt to evaluate what can be
learned from the experiment rather than any critique of its designers and
analysts.

These comments are divided into two parts. First, I discuss Henry
Aaron's comments on the attempts to measure the effects of a negative
income tax on market labor supply. Although I agree with most of his
comments, I shall add a few of my own, especially on the need to imbed
the analysis of labor supply in a richer description of household behavior.

Second, I turn to some comments on the appropriateness of the concept
of labor supply used for purposes of the experiment and point to some
important questions that the experiment was not designed to answer but
that ought to weigh heavily in professional judgments on the effects of
income maintenance programs.

Interpretation of the Labor Supply Effects

Aaron raises several important points that cast doubt on the validity of
the conclusion that a negative income tax plan would have very small
effects on labor supply. First, a series of problems makes extrapolation to
the entire population hazardous. The truncation of eligibility for the experiment—by preenrollment income—screens the sample on the basis of the
dependent variable upon which the experiment concentrates attention,
labor supply. Families with wives working substantial amounts of time
thus were systematically excluded from the analysis. Hence, the results are
not very useful in examining the impact of a negative income tax on the
labor supply of wives or female family heads, the labor force groups likely
to be most sensitive to wage and income effects on labor supply.

Second, Aaron's most telling criticism is that the guarantees and tax rates have not been calculated after taking into account the effects of welfare. Indeed, in some cases the net effects of the guarantees and tax rates are the reverse of the nominal ones. Within each subplan, the net effects varied markedly and even changed sign for different households—according to location, family size, and the like.

Most of the analyses of the data report the difference in the average number of hours worked between the control group and the group enrolled in any of the negative tax subplans. Hence, these results aggregate wage, cross-wage, and income effects of varying magnitude and sign.

The aggregation bias introduced is potentially severe, so that the small differences across subplans with different tax rates are difficult to interpret until an examination is made of the labor supply and the net effective tax rates and guarantee levels for each family. This may make little difference, since most previous studies of the labor supply of husbands suggest a quite inelastic labor supply.

Aaron also mentions the problem of the brief duration of the experiment. Even if all the other problems were overcome, I would still be skeptical of interpreting the results of the experiment as permanent responses. The experiment interrupted families in the course of their life-cycle decisions regarding labor supply, savings, and human capital investment. The net effect of a permanent negative income tax plan on lifetime wealth is of a totally different order of magnitude for low-income families than the corresponding effect for a three-year program. If one adopts the view that low-wage males have an investment in training or in a reputation as a stable worker, they are much less likely to reduce labor supply under a temporary negative income tax than a permanent one.

Even if the temporary-permanent distinction can be overcome—for example, we sometimes interpret cross-sectional regression results as reflecting permanent responses—we cannot estimate the effect of a negative income tax on household labor supply by examining only the change in current hours of work related to changes in current wages and income. We need to imbed the labor supply decision in a fuller analysis of household behavior that deals with saving and accumulation of human capital.

It may well be that the negative income tax plans do have a substantial labor supply disincentive in terms of planned future work effort—for example, earlier retirement. Part of the response to the experiment was to accumulate consumer durables or other assets. Increased current saving and reduced future labor supply are perfectly consistent with an optimal life-cycle consumption-saving and work-leisure plan. The results of the experiment would be better understood in the context of a complete model of individual household behavior that analyzes labor supply, consumption, and saving decisions simultaneously; such an analysis would incorporate balance sheet information, not just information on current measured hours of work, wages, and income.

Consider a model of lifetime utility maximization—in which utility is a function of the consumption of goods and leisure in each period and the stock of assets at the end of the planning horizon—subject to a budget constraint limiting expenditures by the wealth of the family. The consumer-worker thus develops a lifetime plan of consumption, labor supply, and saving in each period as a function of real wage rates after taxes in each period and of the initial stock of assets. The coefficients in an equation for a single year—say, the current period—reflect the effect of a permanent negative income tax plan on wage rates in every future period and wealth—or nonwage income in every future period. In addition, the changes in wage rates and nonwage income in each period caused by the plan affect the planned labor supply in subsequent periods. Estimating the effects of a permanent program on labor supply from an equation relating current labor supply to current wages and nonwage income obviously implies a potentially severe and possibly unreasonable set of restrictions on the coefficients of the equations in such a larger model.

An experiment of relatively short duration provides virtually no information about two other long-run responses. First, if indeed there is a labor supply response to a permanent negative income tax, it is likely that it would manifest itself at least partly as an increased demand by workers for part-time jobs. It might then become profitable for firms to increase the supply of such jobs in quantity and variety. This long-run response would reinforce the initial work disincentive on the other side of the market.[25] Second, any peer group or neighborhood effects wherein the individual labor supply disincentives are reinforced by the decreased labor supply of other low-income workers are unlikely to show up in an experiment that is confined to three years, spread over several sites, and limited to a small percentage of the low-income labor force in each locale. We simply do not know how important these effects would be in response to a generous permanent negative income tax.

I am making two points. First, the brief duration of the experiment would have rather different implications depending upon whether the pro-

25. Martin Feldstein of Harvard University has stressed the potential importance of this effect to me.

gram parameters were treated as transitory or permanent phenomena. Second, the measurement of the effects of the program may ignore important events occurring at a point in time beyond the three-year observation limit. In this context, even the most sophisticated analyses of the data dealing with such important problems as divergent tastes, the piling up of hours of work at zero, and the like may provide a good description of only a small part of the whole story.

The Concept of Labor Supply

Let me now turn to the problem of the concept of labor supply—hours of work in the marketplace—that dominated the design and analysis of the experiment. Some of the most important potential effects of a negative income tax on work effort were not dealt with by the designers and analysts of the experiment.

The overwhelming concern was to examine the impact of income maintenance on hours of work and earnings in the very short run. This was probably caused by the political reality noted by Aaron that "prospects for such aid were meager unless it could be shown that the recipients would not stop working en masse."

At least two other aspects of labor supply deserve attention. Many taxpayers and politicians clearly dislike the idea of an income maintenance program that supports loafing. In light of this, it is unfortunate that the experiment did not include a detailed analysis of time spent out of the market. We know from other survey sources that large amounts of time spent not working in the market are spent in (presumably productive) work in the home. Raising children is probably the most important and time-intensive of these household activities, which implies that a negative income tax may affect the behavior of more than one generation.

A second defect in the measures of labor supply used is the lack of attention to investment in human capital. Some attention was paid to the educational attainment of teenagers, but investment in job search, training, and migration are relatively ignored.

In predicting the effects of establishing a permanent negative income tax, the concern of economists and, perhaps with the appropriate persuasion, of politicians should focus also on labor supply in this longer-run sense. I suspect that if a substantial amount of any decrease in market labor supply or increase in income a negative income tax might induce were devoted to caring for and raising children or investing in training or job search, it would not have been necessary to focus the experiment on short-run market labor supply in the first place. This outcome certainly could imply long-run effects of the negative income tax different from those which the experiment suggests and could have important implications for the steady-state number of families dependent upon income maintenance.

Finally, it should be emphasized that the cost to society of an income maintenance program is not the amount transferred from taxpayers to tax receivers; it is the sum of the resources devoted to promoting, opposing, and administering the program plus any deadweight loss from distortions of work-leisure and consumption-savings decisions. Nor does it include any decline in output resulting from a decreased market labor supply. Market labor supply has a social opportunity cost that reflects the value of time spent outside the market to the person doing so, perhaps measured by something close to the after-tax wage.

Although I have focused on some limitations of the experiment—several of which are inherent in any program subject to perhaps inevitably severe budgetary and political constraints—I am pleased to report that it has added some potentially important information about the economic behavior of poor families to our rather meager store of knowledge. Indeed, much of the information obtainable from the data is still to come. It is also worth noting that we learned a great deal about the phenomena of experimentation and program administration in the sphere of public policy. It was, after all, the first truly large-scale social experiment, and its lessons have had, and will continue to have, an important external benefit: the improved quality of other social experiments. This learning-by-doing aspect of the technology of social experimentation in itself, I believe, would have justified the expenditure of the funds.

ROBERT E. HALL

Effects of the Experimental Negative Income Tax on Labor Supply

The negative income tax experiment in New Jersey and Pennsylvania has provided much new evidence on the decisions of poor families about their supplies of labor. Even though the income and substitution effects of the negative income tax act in the same direction—making work both less remunerative and less necessary—the average family in the experiment reduced its hours of work only slightly when subject to the tax and transfer provisions of the negative income tax.

I shall discuss three lessons that economic students of labor supply have learned.

First, the finding of small effects has an impact on the way theoretical models of labor supply are specified. I argue that a good theory of labor supply must take account of the diversity of behavior of apparently identical workers, as well as of their average behavior. A theory of the representative individual is inadequate to predict the effect of a negative income tax because of its differential appeal to those whose ability or propensity to work is low.

Second, I examine the relation between the effect of the negative income tax in the experiment with predictions from econometric studies of labor supply in cross sections. The theory of the first part of the paper suggests that a naive application of the cross-sectional studies will overstate the effect of the negative income tax. I argue that adjustment for these biases makes the cross-sectional results consistent with the experiment, at least within sampling error.

Third, I examine the data from the experiment from a point of view somewhat different from that of the extensive empirical analysis carried out by the economists associated with it. Although the basic effect of the experiment is small, the statistical reliability of the estimate is sufficiently high to make it implausible that there is actually no effect at all. Statistically insignificant regression coefficients in the elaborate models of other studies have left this question somewhat up in the air. The fact that the effect is statistically significant does not mean that it is large, only that the experiment was sufficiently well designed to detect a small effect.

A major theme of the paper is that permanent unobserved determinants of labor supply vary among families. Econometrically, these induce a positive correlation between the average hours of work of the subjects before and during the experiment. The presence of this correlation suggests an important respect in which the design of the experiment could have been improved. As conducted, the experiment failed in two ways to take full advantage of the opportunity to let the subjects serve as their own controls. First, too few observations were made of the subjects' preexperimental hours of work. Additional quarters of data would have provided a better baseline from which to measure the response of each individual. Second, if half of the subjects had received the negative income tax first and had been interviewed for a number of quarters after its termination, it would have been possible to dispense with the controls altogether. A proposed revision of the experiment following both of these suggestions could have gathered the same amount of information with only a little over one-sixth the number of subjects.

A major surprise in studies of the data from the experiment is the apparent finding of large differences in the responses of the three ethnic groups distinguished in it: whites, blacks, and the Spanish speaking. Other investigators seem to take this finding at face value, concluding that there are important ethnic differences in labor supply functions. I question this conclusion on the grounds that attrition in the black and Spanish-speaking samples is so large as to make the data unusable without a thorough analysis of the interaction between the response to the negative income tax and the departure of families from the sample. Among the experimental subjects, 46 percent of the black and 56 percent of the Spanish-speaking families were excluded from the category of "continuous husband-wife sample" that is used extensively by others. Problems in the data may well explain their puzzling findings of large ethnic differences.

Theory

A discussion of the negative income tax experiment must begin with a fairly complete development of the economic theory of the response to a negative income tax. The paper by Albert Rees and Harold W. Watts has provided a good graphical discussion of the theory. Here—and in much greater detail in appendix A to this paper—I develop an analytical version of the same theory in which an important issue can be treated explicitly: families must decide whether or not to be covered by the negative income tax. They may escape its tax and forgo the income guarantee simply by earning more than the breakeven level of income. The theory must pay close attention to the endogeneity of participation in the negative income tax. Within the experiment, 13 percent of the families who were offered the generous plan paying a guarantee of 125 percent of the poverty level and taxing earnings at 50 percent opted against the plan by earning more than the breakeven level.[1] Practically all families, 94 percent, opted against the least generous, or 50–50, plan. Slightly more than one-quarter of the families who were offered the 100–50 plan decided against it. Surprisingly, the writings by the economists associated with the experiment omit any theoretical treatment of the issue of the choice that families make: whether to earn above or below the breakeven level and thus whether or not to be covered by the negative income tax.[2]

Closely related to the issue of the endogeneity of participation in the negative income tax is the need to treat the diversity of responses to the negative income tax and other economic opportunities among an apparently homogeneous population of families. Virtually all discussions of the response to the negative income tax are framed in terms of a representative family and suggest that the average response in the population is the same as the response of that family. But the negative income tax has a differential appeal to families whose ability or propensity to work is small. In many cases the representative or median family will not respond at all to a negative income tax, but an important minority will decide to earn less, so the average response is negative. In appendix A, I deal with this issue by formulating a model in which an unobserved variable indexes attitudes and

1. See Henry J. Aaron, "Cautionary Notes on the Experiment," in this volume.
2. As Zvi Griliches remarked at the conference, it is misleading to talk as if all of the experimental subjects were paying the tax and receiving the guarantee when in many cases only a small fraction were covered by the negative income tax.

abilities for work. The distribution of the variable among the members of the population implies a distribution of hours of work when no negative income tax is available and permits a prediction of the distribution of responses to a negative income tax when it becomes available. I discuss two models within this framework. In model 1, families differ in the fraction of their total resources they devote to purchases of goods. Some families work a good deal, purchase a large volume of goods, and spend relatively little time at home. These families have little or no response to the negative income tax. Others work less, purchase less, and spend more time at home. In model 1, these families have a large response to the negative income tax.

The parameters of model 1 are fitted informally to data on average hours of work (about thirty-five a week) and to the dispersion of hours of work (a standard deviation of about eighteen a week). For a family with a wage of $2.00 an hour that is offered a negative income tax with a guarantee of $80 a week and a tax rate of 50 percent, it makes a number of predictions. First, all families opt to participate in the negative income tax; not even the hardest-working family finds it desirable to earn above the break-even level of $160 a week, or eighty hours of work. Second, only 45 percent of the families continue working after the negative income tax becomes available. Because they pay the tax of 50 percent on their earnings and have higher incomes nonetheless, they reduce their work by almost twenty-four hours per week. The remaining families stop work altogether, representing an average reduction of about twenty-two hours of work a week—those who stop work are also those who worked less than average before the negative income tax. The average reduction within the whole population is 22.4 hours a week. Model 1 confirms the worst fears of the opponents of the negative income tax: the program causes wholesale withdrawal from the labor force as a large fraction of the population retires and lives on the guaranteed income alone.

In my view, however, the experiment has conclusively laid to rest any fears of a response of hours of work to the negative income tax of the magnitude predicted by model 1. The defect of model 1 is its assumption that families with relatively low hours of work in the absence of the negative income tax are those which spend a large fraction of their resources on time at home. When the negative income tax expands total resources, they spend the same fraction of the increase on time at home and consequently work considerably less. Model 1 assumes that the labor supply functions of a fraction of the population are highly income elastic, which must be false in view of the results of the experiment.

Model 2 embodies an alternative view of diversity among families. It assumes that they differ in the number of hours a week over which they have discretion in choosing between work in the market and work and other activities at home. All families are assumed to have a relatively low propensity to spend increases in resources on additional time at home. Model 2 gives about the same distribution of hours of work among families as model 1 but predicts a much smaller response to a negative income tax. Families with wages of $2.00 an hour opt unanimously in favor of a plan with a guarantee of $80 a week and a tax rate of 50 percent, and all of them continue to work. Average hours of work fall by 2.4 when the negative income tax becomes available, a reduction that seems consistent with the findings of the experiment. According to model 2, only 84 percent of families with wages of $3.00 an hour would opt in favor of the same negative income tax plan. Average hours of work would fall by only 1.6 a week. A program whose guarantee was only $40 a week would attract just 54 percent of families with wages of $2.00 an hour. Those opting for the program would reduce their hours of work by 1.2 a week, so the average would fall by half that amount, 0.6 hour a week.

Model 2 seems to give a reasonable prediction of the distribution of responses to the negative income tax, as well as a reasonable prediction of the average response. Future research will attempt to fit an econometric model along the lines of model 2 to the data from the experiment. For now, the main econometric contribution of this study of the theory of the response to the negative income tax is emphasis on the importance of the distribution of unobserved determinants of the labor supply of the families in the experiment.

Predicting the Effect of a Negative Income Tax from Cross-sectional Studies

Interest in the potential impact of a negative income tax has stimulated considerable research on labor supply functions over the past few years. In this section I will look briefly at the predictions of a cross-sectional regression study of hours of work in the light of the findings of the experiment.[3] Although I will use my own results, I should emphasize that most of the studies are in substantial agreement about the response of hours of work to changes in wages and income.[4] I repeat my point, however, that in principle regression studies are incapable of predicting the effect of the negative income tax because they are unable to deal with the opportunity to opt out of the program. The best they can do is to predict the effect of a mandatory tax and transfer program with the same parameters as the negative income tax. They will invariably overstate the effect of the program, and the overstatement will be most severe for families whose alternative sources of income are large enough that only a fraction decides to participate.

Table 1 presents estimates of the effect of a program with a guarantee of $80 per week and a tax rate of 50 percent. The first two rows give estimates of the response of hours of work to wages and income, derived from my earlier study—which involved putting them on a weekly rather than annual basis and converting from income per adult to family income. It is important to understand the measure of income used in the study: full-time income = unearned income + (38.5 · husband's wage) + (38.5 · wife's wage).[5]

The family considered in Table 1 has a full-time income of $154 per week arising solely from the value of the family's time. The negative income tax imposes a tax of 50 percent, or $77 per week, on the family and also gives it $80 in transfers. Measured by full-time income, the family is ahead by only $3 per week. In fact, the negative income tax has an income effect much larger than this, because the tax actually applies only to work in the market; time spent at home escapes taxation. In the husband's labor supply function, there is a cross-income effect from the implicit lowering of the wife's wage caused by the tax: that is, tax rate · wage · (38.5 − wife's actual hours). This appears in row 4 of the table and is the main ingredient in the total income effect in row 5. A similar though much smaller adjustment is made for wives.

Husbands show no strong evidence in favor of a positive wage elasticity in my study, so the effect of the negative income tax operates entirely

3. Sandra Christensen currently is preparing a more complete survey of cross-sectional evidence on the impact of a negative income tax.

4. See Robert E. Hall, "Wages, Income, and Hours of Work in the U.S. Labor Force," in Glen G. Cain and Harold Watts (eds.), *Income Maintenance and Labor Supply: Econometric Studies* (Markham, 1973), pp. 102–62.

5. The logic of the use of this measure of income is discussed in ibid., pp. 104–07.

Table 1. Effects of a 50 Percent Negative Income Tax on Income and Hours of Work of Husbands and Wives, by Color, from Cross-sectional Regression[a]

	Husbands		Wives	
Effect	White	Black	White	Black
1. Wage effect (hours/week per dollar/hour)[b]	0	0	12.7	11.5
2. Income effect (hours/week per dollar/week)[b]	0.110	0.045	0.075	0.115
3. Change in full-time income (dollars per week)[c]	3	3	3	3
4. Adjustment for cross-income effect (dollars per week)[d]	23	21	0	5
5. Adjusted change in income (dollars per week)[e]	26	24	3	8
6. Income effect of the program (hours per week)[f]	2.9	1.1	0.2	0.9
7. Wage effect of the program (hours per week)[g]	0	0	9.5	8.6
8. Total effect (hours per week)[h]	2.9	1.1	9.7	9.5

a. Assumptions: husband's and wife's wages, $2.50 and $1.50 per hour, respectively, with no other income; husband's hours, 38.9 for whites, 34.1 for blacks; wife's hours, 7.6 for whites, 10.8 for blacks; negative income tax guarantee, $80 per week; tax rate, 50 percent.

b. Derived from Robert E. Hall, "Wages, Income, and Hours of Work in the U.S. Labor Force," in Cain and Watts (eds.), *Income Maintenance and Labor Supply*, Table 3.5, pts. A–D, pp. 133–34.

c. $80 − 0.5[(38.5 · 2.50) + (38.5 · 1.50)].

d. Spouse's wage times (38.5 minus spouse's hours) times 0.5.

e. Row 3 plus row 4.

f. Row 2 times row 5.

g. Row 1 times 0.5 times wage.

h. Row 6 plus row 7.

through the income effect. The effect for whites is just under three hours a week and just over one hour for blacks. Both figures are larger than most estimates derived from the experiment, although both sets of evidence agree that whites are more likely to reduce their hours of work in response to the negative income tax than are blacks. In view of the tendency for regression results to overstate the response, I find no reason to think that the cross-sectional and experimental results are in conflict.

For wives, the regression prediction is unreasonable on its face, implying negative hours for whites and essentially complete withdrawal for blacks. The regression model in my study—and in all others known to me—fails to take account of nonnegativity by attenuating the response to wage reductions as they gradually push a larger fraction out of the labor force altogether. The data from the experiment are much more suitable for this type of analysis than those obtained from surveys, since they deal with individuals facing much lower effective wages.

Econometric Appraisal of the Effect of the Negative Income Tax within the Experiment

Econometric methods can answer two somewhat distinct questions about the experiment. Did the program have any effect at all? If so, precisely how large was it and how did it vary among different groups in the sample? Most of the attention of the investigation associated with the experiment has been devoted to the second question, in part, apparently, because it never occurred to them—or to anyone else—that the first question was a live issue. The models and methods used have been sophisticated and complex. In my view, however, they are not well suited to answering the first question. As all experienced users of statistical methods are aware, the more complex the model, the greater is the dispersion in the estimates of its parameters, and the more likely is the acceptance of the null hypothesis that any one of them is zero. In statistical terms, complexity reduces the power of some tests. I think that Harold Watts and his coauthors mislead their readers slightly in summarizing their results by stating: "Overall, it would not require a determined skeptic to claim that there is no evidence of any disincentive at all for husbands."[6] In this section I will argue that, on the contrary, there are small but clearly positive reductions in average hours of work among those offered the experimental negative income tax. The methods I use will be fairly simple and directed toward the first of my two questions.

I will begin with the following numbers (which are calculated from all data reported in the "Vargn" file for the experiment), representing average weekly hours of white husbands:

	Experimental group	*Control group*
Before experiment	34.1	34.8
During experiment	31.8	34.4

From these numbers I will try to derive a simple estimate of the average effect of the program on the labor supply of the experimental subjects.

6. Harold W. Watts and others, "The Labor-Supply Response of Husbands," *Journal of Human Resources*, vol. 9 (Spring 1974), p. 199.

Statistical analysis requires the specification of the expected values of the observed statistics in terms of unknown parameters and a specification of their variances and covariances. For now, I will take the simplest possible model of the expected values:

$$E(H_{S,B}) = E(H_{C,B}) = E(H_{C,D}) = \mu, \text{ and}$$
$$E(H_{S,D}) = \mu + \beta,$$

where H is average hours; S refers to the experimental group and C to the control group; and B refers to the observations before the experiment took place and D to those made during the experiment.

The statistical problem, then, is to find an estimator b of β, the average effect of the program. The basic question is whether to compare the hours of the subjects during the experiment to their own hours before the experiment or to the hours of the controls during the experiment. There is also a subsidiary question of whether or how to use the data from the controls before the experiment. One polar choice is to measure the effect by the change in the hours of the subjects only; this yields what I will call the difference-in-means-of-subjects estimator, or DMS:

$$b_{DMS} = H_{S,D} - H_{S,B}$$
$$= -2.3 \text{ hours per week.}$$

This estimator is unbiased.[7] The other polar choice is to use data from the experimental period only, giving the difference-in-means-during-the-experiment estimator, or DMD:

$$b_{DMD} = H_{S,D} - H_{C,D}$$
$$= -2.6 \text{ hours per week.}$$

Again, this estimator is unbiased.[8]

Finally, a compromise, the equal-weighting estimator, EW, gives a weight of one-third to each of the three observations on groups not subject to the program:

$$b_{EW} = H_{S,D} - \tfrac{1}{3}(H_{S,B} + H_{C,B} + H_{C,D})$$
$$= -2.6 \text{ hours per week.}$$

This estimator also is unbiased.[9]

Which estimator is best? The usual answer is the one with minimum variance. Derivation of the variances of these estimators requires some preliminary examination of the stochastic character of the underlying data.

7. $E(b_{DMS}) = \mu + \beta - \mu = \beta$.
8. $E(b_{DMD}) = \mu + \beta - \mu = \beta$.
9. $E(b_{EW}) = \mu + \beta - \tfrac{1}{3}(\mu + \mu + \mu) = \beta$.

The theory of family labor supply presented earlier in this paper suggested that the wide dispersion in hours of work among apparently homogeneous families was the consequence of the dispersion of an underlying more or less permanent unobserved index of tastes, attitudes, and abilities among the families. In practical work, this model of labor supply must be amended by adding a transitory component representing the effects of short-run fluctuations in employment opportunities, especially overtime and layoffs, and in the ability to work. A simple model then has the form:

$$H_{it} = \mu + \eta_i + \epsilon_{it},$$

where H_{it} is hours of work of family i in time t; μ is the average over all families; η_i is a permanent unobserved shift for family i with mean zero across all families (in the models of appendix A, η_i is a multiple of θ, shifted downward to have mean zero); and ϵ_{it} is the transitory shift at time t. I make the simple stochastic assumptions that the permanent and transitory components are uncorrelated and that the transitory component does not exhibit serial correlation.[10] Further, I assume that families are stochastically independent of each other. Of these assumptions, the only one open to serious question is the lack of serial correlation of the transitory component. I shall present evidence on this point shortly.

The stochastic model just outlined is familiar to all students of panel data on individuals. It has been used extensively in analyzing data from the negative income tax experiment by Harold Watts, although he uses an elaborate regression specification in place of my μ.

In appendix B to this paper, I derive the variances and covariances of the four means implied by this stochastic model. I calculate the variances of the three estimators—*DMS*, *DMD*, and *EW*—and then derive the minimum variance or efficient estimator, called *GLS*, and calculate its variance. In all of these calculations, a critical parameter, λ, appears; it is defined as the fraction of the total variance in the data contributed by the permanent component. If λ is close to zero, the efficient estimator is similar to *DMD*—most information comes from the comparison of subjects and controls during the experiment. But if λ is positive, the situation is rather different. The efficient estimator takes maximal advantage of the correlation between the average hours of the subjects before and during the experiment by

10. The assumptions are as follows:

$$\text{var}(\eta_i) = \delta^2, \text{ and var}(\epsilon_{it}) = \sigma^2;$$
$$\text{cov}(\eta_i, \epsilon_{it}) = 0, \text{ for all } t, \text{ and cov}(\epsilon_{it}, \epsilon_{it'}) = 0, \text{ if } t \neq t'.$$

making the subjects serve as their own controls. When λ is much above 0.25, the efficient estimator is more like *DMS*. Data from the controls receive little weight, and indeed the question arises whether the experiment should have had controls at all.

Evidence on Variances and Covariances of Hours of Work in the Experiment

The next step is to establish the relevance of the stochastic model and to estimate the value of λ for the data at hand. Table 2 presents estimates of the variances and covariances for the whole sample. The model predicts equal covariances for all lags, but it is no surprise that the covariances tend to be smaller for longer lags. Still, the evidence in favor of an important permanent component is strong. For both men and women, the covariance of hours in adjacent quarters is substantially less than the variance—about one-half for men and two-thirds for women. The covariance for hours two quarters apart drops by much less. The covariance seems to approach constant levels of 110 for men and 60 for women, and falls some more at the longest lag. It is reasonable to approximate this variance-covariance

Table 2. Variances and Covariances of Hours at Work of Husbands and Wives[a]

Description	Husbands	Wives
Variance	330	143
Covariance[b]		
Lag, j		
1	174	100
2	145	89
3	138	82
4	132	75
5	122	71
6	117	68
7	109	63
8	112	61
9	104	59
10	99	56
11	93	52
12	72	41

Source: Derived from data in "Vargn" files of the New Jersey Graduated Work Incentive Experiment. See text and appendix B of this paper for the method of derivation.

a. Includes all individuals who were husbands and wives in the first interview.

b. Covariance of H_t and H_{t-j}, where H_t is hours of work in time t and J is quarterly lag.

structure with the simple permanent transitory model with $\delta^2 = \text{cov}(H_t,$ $H_{t-6})$ and $\sigma^2 = \text{var}(H_t) - \delta^2$. This gives $\lambda = 117/330 = 0.35$ for men and $\lambda = 68/143 = 0.48$ for women.

Estimates and Standard Errors for White Husbands

The following tabulation presents, for white husbands, the three alternative estimates already discussed (*DMS*, *DMD*, and *EW*), the efficient estimate (*GLS*), and their standard errors (in parentheses):

	Weight for preexperimental data		Estimated effect (hours per week)
	---	---	---
Estimator	Experimental group (ω)	Control group (γ)	(b)
DMS	1	. . .	-2.3 (1.0)
DMD	0	0	-2.6 (1.1)
EW	0.33	0.50	-2.6 (0.9)
GLS	0.56	0.08	-2.4 (0.8)

In all cases, the standard errors are calculated from formulas in appendix B, taking account of the permanent component of the variance. Only in the case of the *DMD* estimator is the standard error the same as the usual standard error of the difference of two uncorrelated means.

All four estimators agree in rejecting the null hypothesis of no disincentive effect of the experimental negative income tax. It is essentially impossible that random variation in hours of work could account for the observed reduction in hours of the experimental subjects.

The standard errors give a ranking of the four estimators. Poorest is the comparison between subjects and controls during the experiment (*DMD*), and third is the comparison of subjects before and during the experiment (*DMS*). If there were no permanent effect, *DMD* would have been substantially better than *DMS* because there are twelve times as many observations on controls during the experiment as there are on subjects before the experiment. *DMS* would have had a crushing advantage over *DMD* if the design of the experiment had divided the thirteen observations more equally between those before and those during the experiment. The second-best estimator is *EW*: it is advantageous to give some weight to the controls. Best of all is the *GLS* estimator, which improves on *EW* by assigning more weight to the preliminary data for the subjects and less to the preliminary data for the controls.

A Model with Changes in Hours over Time

A major objection to the results just presented is their dependence on the assumption that nothing changed the mean hours of work of the subjects except the negative income tax. The conclusion that data on controls are not as useful as data on subjects derives from the lack of a need for information about the probable behavior of the subjects during the experiment. In this section I reconsider the previous results under a model with a time effect, χ:

$$E(H_{S,B}) = E(H_{C,B}) = \mu;$$
$$E(H_{C,D}) = \mu + \chi; \text{ and}$$
$$E(H_{S,D}) = \mu + \chi + \beta.$$

The general class of unbiased estimators in this model is:

$$b = H_{S,D} - \omega H_{S,B} - (H_{C,D} - \omega H_{C,B}).$$

Note that $H_{C,B}$ entered b with a negative sign in the efficient estimator without a time effort, but enters here with a positive sign. Further, it is no longer possible to reduce the variance introduced by $H_{C,D}$ by multiplying it by a weight less than unity. The best that can be done is to subtract a fraction of $H_{C,B}$, which is positively correlated with $H_{C,D}$.

The DMD estimator is a member of this class, with $\omega = 0$. If there is a permanent component in the stochastic element, however, a more efficient estimator uses a positive ω to reduce the variance of $H_{S,D} - \omega H_{S,B}$ and of $H_{C,D} - \omega H_{C,B}$.[11] With a single observation before the onset of the program, as in the experiment, the optimal procedure is to take quasi-differences with a weight for the earlier observation equal to the correlation, λ, of hours of work in different periods. In a regression framework, this corresponds to including initial hours of work as a righthand variable, a procedure used extensively by the investigators associated with the experiment.

The data for white husbands previously studied shows no evidence of a time effect. On the other hand, the data on the average weekly hours of

11. The optimal ω can be shown to be equal to:

$$\omega = \frac{\lambda}{\lambda + \dfrac{1-\lambda}{T_B}} [= \lambda, \text{ if } T_B = 1],$$

where T_B is the number of observations obtained before the experiment.

their wives suggests rather strongly that they increased during the experiment:

	Experimental group	Control group
Before experiment	3.8	2.7
During experiment	3.9	4.5

Why should there be a time effect? First, the labor force participation rate of women in the entire U.S. economy was rising fairly rapidly during the experiment. Second, the subjects and controls were chosen deliberately because they were the poorer members of a much larger population. Some families were included because of the temporary withdrawal of the wife from the labor market. Both controls and subjects tend to work more as the experiment progresses and they return to their normal patterns of work. The disincentive effect of the negative income tax tends to counterbalance this increase, so the experimental effect must be inferred indirectly from the data on both subjects and controls.

Results for white wives, assuming time effect, for the two estimators that are unbiased in the presence of a time effect are shown below, where *DMD* represents differences in means of subjects and controls, experimental period, and *GLST*, efficient weights subject to constraint of unbiasedness with time effect, and the figures in parentheses are standard errors:

Estimator	Weight for preexperimental data (ω)	Estimated effect (b)
DMD	0	-0.5
		(0.8)
GLST	0.47	-1.5
		(0.6)

The simple comparison of subjects and controls (the *DMD* estimator) gives an effect in the expected direction, but of small magnitude. The estimator that makes optimal use of the sample data, *GLST*, not only has a smaller standard error, but estimates a larger effect. The null hypothesis of no response to the negative income tax is rejected by the *GLST* results at any reasonable level of significance.

Among white families, the simple methods of this paper demonstrate statistically unambiguous evidence of small disincentive effects of the negative income tax on the labor supply of both husbands and wives. The fact that the effects are statistically significant does not mean that they are large, only that the design of the experiment and the variance-components estimators measure the effects with sufficient precision to detect even a small effect.

Black and Spanish-speaking Families

The results for black and Spanish-speaking families are more difficult to interpret. The relevant means of the average weekly hours of work for black and Spanish-speaking husbands and wives—tabulated from all data reported in the experiment's "Vargn" file—are shown below:

	Experimental group		Control group	
	Before	During	Before	During
Black husbands	31.8	31.2	31.9	28.5
Black wives	5.6	6.0	6.2	6.3
Spanish-speaking husbands	32.9	31.7	36.7	32.9
Spanish-speaking wives	3.3	2.0	3.1	4.4

Taken at face value, the data for husbands in both groups suggest, paradoxically, that labor supply hardly changed for those offered the negative income tax program, whereas it decreased substantially for the control group. The results for wives are more reasonable: black wives show no effect and Spanish-speaking wives in the control group show an effect of about the same magnitude as white wives. In the experimental group, however, a considerable decline occurred, whereas white wives changed hardly at all. I have serious reservations, however, about the validity of the data for the black and Spanish-speaking families. In spite of intense effort, the administrators of the experiment found great difficulty in collecting data from these ethnic groups. The following data on the percentages of families lacking continuous structure and data throughout the experimental period illustrate the problem:[12]

	Experimental group	Control group
White	22	34
Black	46	45
Spanish speaking	56	61
Total group	41	45

12. Computed from Harold W. Watts, Dale J. Poirier, and Charles Mallar, "Concepts Used in the Central Analysis and Their Measurement," in Harold W. Watts and Albert Rees (eds.), *Final Report of the New Jersey Graduated Work Incentive Experiment* (University of Wisconsin—Madison, Institute for Research on Poverty, and Mathematica, 1974), vol. 1., sec. 1, pt. B, chap. 1.

In the critical experimental group, just over one-fifth of the white families failed to report fully usable data, either because the husband or wife left the household or because interviewing stopped before the end of the experiment. This level of attrition is troublesome but probably not capable of obscuring the basic effect of the program. But for black families, nearly one-half of the data are not fully usable, and for Spanish-speaking families, more than one-half of the data are absent or contaminated. The situation is no better for the less important control group: an astonishing 61 percent of the data for the Spanish speakers are not fully usable.

The high rate of attrition in the sample and its implications have not escaped the attention of the proprietors of the experiment. Jon K. Peck[13] has studied the relation between family characteristics at the first interview and subsequent attrition and confirms the differential among ethnic groups reported above. The analyses of the impact of the negative income tax on labor supply in the other chapters of the final report seem to ignore the implications of the high rates of attrition. In particular, I suspect that biases on this account are an important part of the explanation of the paradoxical response of black husbands reported by Harold Watts and associates.[14] Nowhere do Watts and his coauthors mention what a small fraction they are able to use of the potential number of observations for black families, although they confess some mystification at the behavior of the sharply truncated black control group.

I do not know why attrition should cause the hours of the experimental group to rise over time and the hours of the control group to fall, but I am reluctant to calculate estimates of the effect of the negative income tax when the surviving part of the sample involves so much self-selection. A thorough treatment of the relation between attrition and response to the negative income tax is needed.

Benefits of Additional Observations before Onset of the Program

Permanent unobserved differences make the experimental subjects their own best controls. As the data for white husbands below illustrate, with the same effort in collecting data the experiment could have reduced the variance of almost all of the estimators by delaying the onset of the program by five quarters:

13. Jon K. Peck, "The Problem of Attrition," in ibid., vol. 2, pt. C, chap. 1.
14. Watts and others, "The Labor-Supply Response of Husbands," pp. 181–200.

Variance

Estimator	As conducted $(T_B = 1, T_D = 12)$	Proposed modification $(T_B = 6, T_D = 7)$
DMS	0.54	0.17
DMD	0.75	0.83
EW	0.45	0.41
GLS	0.33	0.16
GLST	0.48	0.30

Particularly noteworthy is the low variance of the *DMS* estimator in the modified design. If time effects are ignored, the controls make almost no contribution to reducing the variance of *b*; *GLS*, which weights the controls optimally, has a variance only slightly below that of *DMS*. The experiment could have been run with half the data collected if it had been designed to avoid the need to estimate a time effect. It seems to me that this could have been done easily by dividing the experimental subjects into two groups, one of which would have six quarters of control observation followed by six quarters of the program, and the other group the reverse. Then the time effects in the *DMS* estimator would be canceled and it would be unbiased. The variance of *b* estimated by *DMS* in the modified experiment would be 0.17, compared with the variance of the optimal estimator for the experiment as conducted, 0.48. It is a remarkable implication of these calculations that the same amount of information about the overall effect of the program that is available from the existing body of data for some 1,200 families could have been gathered by observing fewer than 200 families.

Regression Analysis and More Powerful Tests of the Hypothesis of No Experimental Effect

The defect of the methods considered in this paper is their use of a fixed parameter, β, to represent the effect of the program on the hours of work of the subjects. In fact, the subjects received benefits according to a variety of guarantee levels and tax rates and differed in predictable ways in their likely response to the program. This information can be used to advantage in statistical analysis of the data from the experiment. A slight extension of my previous model is:

$$E(H_{S,D} \mid w, Y_0, \tau, B_0) = \mu(w, Y_0) + \rho\beta(w, Y_0, \tau, B_0),$$

where $\mu(w, Y_0)$ is the expected labor supply in the absence of the program for a family with wage w and income Y_0; $\beta(w, Y_0, \tau, B_0)$ is the expected effect of the program; and ρ is a parameter to be estimated, interpreted as the fraction of the expected effect that is actually observed. Harvey Rosen[15] has studied the effect of the personal income tax on the hours of work of married women within this framework and has found that ρ is close to unity.

Harold Watts has attempted something rather similar in defining his θ variable, which takes on large values for susceptible families and small values for those who are unlikely to respond to the program. Watts's procedure is ad hoc, but a variable in the same spirit can be calculated from the theory of the first section of this paper. It is exactly the $E(H_N) - E(H_P)$ function defined, for example, for model 2 in Table 4. Under this definition of $\beta(w, Y_0, \tau, B_0)$, tests of the null hypothesis $\rho = 0$ are more powerful tests of whether the negative income tax has any effect at all, and tests of $\rho = 1$ test whether it has the magnitude predicted by economic theory.

Conclusions for Future Research

A close look at the data from the experiment has resolved some of its mysteries. There is, after all, a measurable decline in the hours of work of white families when they are offered a negative income tax. With an appropriate statistical technique, the magnitude of the decline can be estimated with reasonable precision. For blacks and Spanish speakers, the data will not support the same kind of analysis because attrition in the samples was so high. Several lessons for future research and experimental design have emerged from my study.

First, statistical work needs to take full account of the permanent and transitory components of individual behavior.

Second, when an explicit model of labor supply is fitted to data from the experiment, it should recognize the endogeneity of participation in the negative income tax. This requires an explicit model of the diversity of preferences.

Third, future experiments should gather as much data as possible on their subjects before and after the negative income tax or other treatment is administered. The most efficient estimators of the effect of the experiment let the subjects serve as their own controls.

15. Harvey S. Rosen, *The Impact of U.S. Tax Laws on the Labor Supply of Married Women* (Ph.D. dissertation, Harvard University, 1974).

Fourth, it is worthwhile to devote a great deal of effort to keep in touch with all experimental families. An experiment with 100 subjects and 10 percent attrition is more useful than one with 1,000 subjects and 50 percent attrition.

Appendix A: Theory of the Response to a Negative Income Tax

The theory needs to deal with three complications: the diversity of attitudes about work and consumption within the population; the opportunity to choose whether or not to be covered by the program; and the fact that hours of work cannot be negative. The analysis of this section is the working out of a simple story about family decisions. The family starts by formulating a work-consumption plan on the assumption that it is not covered by the program. Then it formulates an alternative plan on the assumption that it pays the tax and receives the transfer from the program. Finally, it decides whether or not to participate by choosing the plan that yields the greater satisfaction. There is a strong presumption that the second plan, which assumes participation, will involve less market work than the first plan. The program reduces the incentive to work by taxing earnings and stimulates the use of time at home by providing income to purchase goods. I distinguish three kinds of response to the program:

—The family would not work in the absence of the program. Then it is certain to participate and will not work under the program either.

—The family would work if it did not participate, but would not work if covered by the tax and transfer. Then the program causes families to withdraw from the labor force if by spending all of their time at home and using the transfer to buy goods they achieve a higher level of satisfaction than by spending less time at home and using earnings to buy goods.

—The family works whether or not it is covered. It decides in favor of the program if the combination of more time at home and smaller purchases of goods—financed by the earnings after the tax and the transfer income—is more satisfying than the alternative. If the program makes it possible to reduce work and yet spend more on goods, then it is certain that the family will participate. The effect of the program is to reduce the hours of work of those families who opt to participate.

My next step is to provide a general analytical apparatus to describe family decisions. The basic tool is the indirect utility function, which measures the level of satisfaction achieved by the family when it faces a reward, w, for each hour of work, and has income, Y, from sources other than earnings. Call it $g(w, Y)$. Then the level of satisfaction (u) conditional on not participating is:

$$u_N = g(w, Y_0),$$

where Y_0 is the family's unearned income from interest, pensions, and the like. The alternative of participating yields:

$$u_P = g[(1 - \tau)w, B_0 + (1 - \tau)Y_0],$$

where τ is the tax rate imposed by the program and B_0 is its transfer component, or income guarantee. A family opts for the program if u_P exceeds u_N, but otherwise not. For future use I note here that the labor supply function can be extracted from the indirect utility function by differentiating it:

$$H_N = \frac{\partial g(w, Y_0)/\partial w}{\partial g(w, Y_0)/\partial Y_0}, \text{ and}$$

$$H_P = \frac{\partial g[(1 - \tau)w, B_0 + (1 - \tau)Y_0]/\partial w}{\partial g/\partial Y_0}.$$

The actual labor supply depends on the family's decision about the program:

$$H = H_N \text{ if } u_N > u_P, \text{ or } H = H_P \text{ if } u_P > u_N.$$

So far I have dealt explicitly with the decision about participation and implicitly with the nonnegativity of labor supply—the indirect utility function takes account of the family's inability to reduce hours of work below zero. The problem of nonnegativity will arise explicitly when I assign a particular functional form to the indirect utility function.

Next I want to deal with the issue of diversity among families. Unexplained variation in hours of work is quite large even when an extensive set of explanatory variables is available. For example, even the best regression for hours of work has a residual standard error of about half the average level of hours. The casual development of a theory of the representative family, together with an unexplained additive random deviation, would not be suitable for the range of issues raised in the negative income tax experiment. Rather, the existence of diversity in the determinants of hours of work ought to be built into the theory from the start.

I propose a theory along the following lines. Suppose θ is an index of family attitudes about work and abilities to work. Everything else held constant, families with low values of θ choose to work more than those with high values. The distribution of θ among the population accounts for the apparent randomness in hours of work. In the absence of the negative income tax, there will be a critical value of θ, say θ_N, such that families with θ exceeding θ_N will not work at all. The probability that a family drawn at random from the population will work is just the fraction having θ below θ_N. Note that θ_N depends on the observable characteristics of the family, especially its wage and nonlabor income. Similarly, among families participating in the program there is a threshold, θ_P, beyond which they will not work. Because I assume that labor supply is inversely related to θ, it is evident that θ_P is less than θ_N—some families would choose to work if the program were not available but would choose not to work if they participated. No family would do the opposite; working under the program but not working otherwise.

There is another threshold, say θ^*, dividing families who opt in favor of the program from those who do not. Again, from the assumption that families with low values of θ favor work, those whose θ is less than θ^* will remain off the program, whereas those above θ^* will take advantage of it. A negative income tax is inherently more attractive to families that are less willing or less able to work. In terms of an indirect utility function now considered as a function of θ as well as w and Y, say $g(w, Y, \theta)$, the threshold θ^* is defined succinctly by:

$$g(w, Y_0, \theta^*) = g[(1 - \tau)w, B_0 + (1 - \tau)Y_0, \theta^*].$$

Under the assumption that the program is always attractive to nonworkers, θ^* must be less than or equal to θ_N. The three groups I distinguished earlier now can be restated as:

Group 1, $\theta > \theta_N$,

Group 2, $\theta_P < \theta < \theta_N$, and

Group 3, $\theta < \theta_P$.

The fraction of the population falling in each of the three groups is the fraction having values of θ in each of the corresponding intervals. Two distinct cases need to be considered in deriving the response of the three groups to the negative income tax. Case 1, in which θ^* is less than θ_P (some participants work), and case 2, in which θ^* is greater than θ_P (no participants work). The responses then are:

	Case 1 $\theta^* < \theta_P$	Case 2 $\theta_P < \theta^* < \theta_N$
Group 1 $(\theta > \theta_N)$	All participants, none work	All participants, none work
Group 2 $(\theta_P < \theta < \theta_N)$	All participants, none work	Those above θ^* participate and do not work; those below θ^* work and do not participate
Group 3 $(\theta < \theta_P)$	All work; those above θ^* participate; those below do not	All work; none participate

Labor supply functions can be derived immediately from this matrix: expected hours of work in absence of program equals [fraction of population in group 2] · [average hours in group 2] + [fraction of population in group 3] · [average hours in group 3]; expected hours of work when program is available, in case 1 ($\theta^* < \theta_P$), equal [fraction of population in group 3 with $\theta < \theta^*$] · [average hours of these nonparticipants] + [fraction of population in group 3 with $\theta > \theta^*$] · [average hours of these participants], and, in case 2 ($\theta_P < \theta^* < \theta_N$), equal [fraction of population in group 2 with θ less than θ^*] · [average hours of these] + [fraction of population in group 3] · [average hours in group 3].

The difference between these is the expected effect of the program: expected reduction in hours of work, in case 1, equals [fraction of population in group 2] · [average hours in group 2 when the program is not available] + [fraction of population in group 3 with $\theta > \theta^*$] · [average reduction in hours of these participants]; and, in case 2, equals [fraction of population in group 2 with θ above θ^*] · [average hours of these when program is not available].

In case 1, the program causes some families to withdraw from the labor market (those in group 2) and others to reduce their hours (part of group 3). In case 2, on the other hand, withdrawal is the only effect. The magnitude of either effect depends on the distribution of the population among the groups as well as on the response within each group. I emphasize that no simple application of conventional labor supply equations can answer the questions of the expected impact of a negative income tax.

Within this general framework, a number of steps are required to create an operational model:

—First, specify decisions in terms of an indirect utility function $g(w, Y, \theta)$.

Identify θ as a parameter of attitudes and tastes. Be certain that $g(w,\ Y,\ \theta)$ correctly incorporates the constraint that hours of work cannot be negative.

—Second, derive the labor supply functions $L_N(w,\ Y,\ \theta)$ and $L_P[(1 - \tau)w,\ B_0 + (1 - \tau)Y,\ \theta]$ conditional on not participating and on participating, respectively. Derive the thresholds θ_N and θ_P from them.

—Third, derive the participation threshold θ^* from:

$$g(w,\ Y,\ \theta^*) = g[(1 - \tau)w,\ B_0 + (1 - \tau)Y_0,\ \theta^*].$$

—Fourth, specify the distribution $f(\theta)$ of θ within the population.

—Fifth, calculate expected labor supply in the absence of the program as:

$$E(H_N) = \int_0^{\theta_N} L_N(w,\ Y,\ \theta)f(\theta)\ d\theta.$$

—Sixth, calculate expected labor supply in the presence of the program as:

$$(\text{Case 1})\quad E(H_P) = \int_0^{\theta^*} L_N(w,\ Y_0,\ \theta)f(\theta)\ d\theta$$

$$+ \int_{\theta^*}^{\theta_P} L_P[(1 - \tau)w,\ B_0 + (1 - \tau)Y_0,\ \theta]f(\theta)\ d\theta.$$

$$(\text{Case 2})\quad E(H_P) = \int_0^{\theta^*} L_N(w,\ Y_0,\ \theta)f(\theta)\ d\theta.$$

—Seventh, calculate expected impact of the program as $E(H_N) - E(H_P)$.

First Application

My first attempt to create a model was unsuccessful, but its failure was instructive, so I will describe it briefly. The model starts from the assumption that both the income and wage elasticities of the demand function for nonwork are unity. That is, if $\bar{H}$ is the total amount of time to be divided between work (H) and nonwork $(\bar{H} - H)$, then:

$$\bar{H} - H = \theta\frac{R}{w},$$

where R is total family resources (what Gary Becker calls full income)[16]

16. Gary S. Becker, "A Theory of the Allocation of Time," *Economic Journal*, vol. 75 (September 1965), pp. 493–517.

and θ is the fraction of total resources allocated to nonwork. In this model, variations in this budget share account for the dispersion in hours of work among an apparently homogeneous group of families. Now total family resources are the sum of the total value of its time, $w\overline{H}$, and its nonlabor income Y_0:

$$R = w\overline{H} + Y_0.$$

Thus its labor supply function is:

$$H = \overline{H} - \theta \frac{Y_0 + w\overline{H}}{w}$$

if positive; otherwise:

$$H = 0.$$

It is easy to derive the thresholds θ_N and θ_P:

$$\theta_N = \frac{w\overline{H}}{Y_0 + w\overline{H}} \text{ and}$$

$$\theta_P = \frac{(1 - \tau)w\overline{H}}{B_0 + (1 - \tau)(Y_0 + w\overline{H})}.$$

Note that both lie between 0 and 1 and that θ_N exceeds θ_P, as required. The indirect utility function is:

$$g(w, Y_0, \theta) = \theta^\theta (1 - \theta)^{1-\theta} \frac{Y_0 + w\overline{H}}{w\theta} \quad \text{if} \quad \frac{Y_0}{w} \leq \frac{1 - \theta}{\theta} \overline{H}$$

$$= \overline{H}^\theta Y_0^{1-\theta} \quad \text{if} \quad \frac{Y_0}{w} \geq \frac{1 - \theta}{\theta} \overline{H}.$$

The kink is caused by the constraint of nonnegativity. Satisfaction does not depend on the wage rate for families with values of θ sufficiently large that they do not work at all. In case 1:

$$\theta^* = \frac{\log\left[\dfrac{Y_0 + w\overline{H}}{B_0 + (1 - \tau)(w\overline{H} + Y_0)}\right]}{-\log(1 - \tau)}, \text{ if positive, and 0 if not.}$$

This threshold behaves in the expected way, rising with w and Y_0 (the plan is less attractive to families with more resources of their own), rising with τ (higher tax rates are less attractive) and falling with B_0 (higher guarantees are more attractive). For high enough B_0, θ^* would become negative by the first formula. This occurs when:

$$Y_0 + w\bar{H} \leq B_0 + (1 - \tau)(w\bar{H} + Y_0)$$

or

$$B_0 \geq \tau(w\bar{H} + Y_0).$$

That is, the lump sum B_0 exceeds the amount of tax paid even for a family that devotes all of its time to market work. In this case all families will opt for the program. Taking $\theta^* = 0$ in this case will account for it correctly.

For this model, case 2 is irrelevant for all reasonable values of the parameters, so I omit its consideration.

The next step is to find a distribution that will account for the dispersion observed in hours of work. The beta density, $f(\theta) = 6\theta(1 - \theta)$, does well in fitting the observed standard error of hours, although it does not account for the tendency for hours to bunch around forty a week. I doubt that this is important here. Note that the model does predict that a positive fraction of the sample—those with θ below the appropriate threshold—will have zero hours of work. In this respect, the model is in the Tobit family of probability models.[17]

Putting all these assumptions into the recipe at the end of the previous section, I get:

$$E(H_N) = 6 \int_0^{\theta_N} \left(\bar{H} - \theta \frac{Y_0 + w\bar{H}}{w}\right)\theta(1 - \theta)\, d\theta$$

and

$$E(H_P) = 6 \int_0^{\theta^*} \left(\bar{H} - \theta \frac{Y_0 + w\bar{H}}{w}\right)\theta(1 - \theta)\, d\theta$$

$$+ 6 \int_{\theta^*}^{\theta_P} \left(\bar{H} - \theta \frac{B_0 + (1 + \tau)(Y_0 + w\bar{H})}{(1 - \tau)w}\right)\theta(1 - \theta)\, d\theta.$$

It is easy but not illuminating to carry out these integrations. I will pass directly to the results shown in Table 3. The first three columns compare families facing wages of $1.50, $2.00, and $3.00 an hour, holding constant the other determinants of labor supply. The first row of calculated responses shows the expected or average labor supply in the absence of the negative income tax. Both its level and its response to the wage rate are in

17. James Tobin, "Estimation of Relationships for Limited Dependent Variables," *Econometrica*, vol. 26 (January 1958), pp. 24–36.

Robert E. Hall

Table 3. Response to a Negative Income Tax, Model 1: Effect on Hours of Work of Variations in Labor Supply Determinants

	Combinations of parameters							
Item	*(1)*	*(2)*	*(3)*	*(4)*	*(5)*	*(6)*	*(7)*	*(8)*
Labor supply determinants								
Wage (dollars per hour) (w)	1.50	2.00	3.00	2.00	2.00	2.00	2.00	2.00
Nonlabor income (dollars per week) (Y_0)	10	10	10	50	10	10	10	10
Guarantee (dollars per week) (B_0)	80	80	80	80	40	120	80	80
Tax rate (percent) (τ)	50	50	50	50	50	50	30	70
Attitude thresholds								
Switch on to program (θ^*)	0	0	0.25	0.15	0.42	0	0	0.19
No work, participants (θ_P)	0.40	0.47	0.57	0.42	0.63	0.38	0.55	0.35
No work, nonparticipants (θ_N)	0.92	0.94	0.96	0.75	0.94	0.94	0.94	0.94
Calculated responses								
Expected hours, no program [$E(H_N)$]	34.2	35.0	35.8	26.4	35.0	35.0	35.0	35.0
Expected hours, with program [$E(H_P)$]	9.5	12.6	18.8	10.8	24.1	8.6	16.3	9.1
Effect of program (hours) [$E(H_N) - E(H_P)$]	24.7	22.4	17.0	15.6	10.9	26.4	18.7	25.9
Percent of families opting for program	100	100	84	94	63	100	100	91
Percent of families continuing to work[a]	35	45	45	31	31	32	57	19
Average reduction in hours of those continuing to work	27.0	23.6	22.2	7.5	6.4	28.8	19.3	36.5
Percent of families stopping work[a]	63	54	39	47	31	67	42	71
Average reduction in hours of those stopping work	24.1	21.9	18.3	17.3	4.5	25.8	18.4	26.7

Source: Model 1, discussed in the text.

a. Percent of families who continue to work plus percent of families stopping work is less than 100 because some families do not work in the absence of the negative income tax.

accord with evidence from empirical studies of hours of work of groups who are not eligible for income supplements. Even though the model embodies a rather wage-elastic demand function for nonwork, the derived wage elasticity of average labor supply is very low. Further, the derived standard error of hours of work, eighteen hours a week, is close to that found in the data from the experiment and in other studies of weekly hours. Judged by its prediction of average hours, the standard deviation of hours and the response of average hours to wages model 1 seems quite satisfactory.

But the third row of calculated responses shows that the model greatly overstates the response to the negative income tax. In the benchmark case— $w = \$2.00$, $Y_0 = \$10.00$, $B_0 = \$80.00$, and $\tau = 50$ percent—all families opt in favor of the program. A little under half of them (45 percent) work but reduce their hours by an average of 23.6 relative to hours of work in the absence of the program. The rest (54 percent) would work an average of 21.9 hours in the absence of the program but do not work at all in its presence. The average reduction is 22.4 hours a week, far in excess of anything suggested by the results of the experiment for a plan with these parameters.

The responses to changes in nonlabor income shown in column 4 give an indication of the trouble. Families with $40 more a week in nonlabor income reduce their labor supply from 35.0 to 26.4 hours a week. Model 1 clearly has an excessive response of hours of work to increases in income. A glance at the labor supply function, $H = \bar{H} - \theta(Y_0 + w\bar{H})/w$, shows why. Families with large values of θ not only supply smaller amounts of labor to the market but also are more responsive to changes in Y_0. These families reduce their supply by a large amount under the negative income tax. But the results of the experiment are inconsistent with large responses in even a small minority of the population. Model 1 cannot be made to give correct predictions by reducing the dispersion of θ, because its predicted dispersion in hours of work would then be too low. It is clear that model 1 is unsatisfactory because its explanation of diversity of hours of work is incorrect. Families that supply few hours cannot be as income elastic as model 1 assumes.

Second Application

Model 2 overcomes this problem by explaining diversity in hours of work through differences in the maximum number of hours available for work. In common with model 1, it assumes unitary income and wage elasticities of the underlying demand function for nonwork. Its labor supply function for a family of type θ is:

$$H = (1 - \theta)\bar{H} - \alpha \frac{Y_0 + w(1 - \theta)\bar{H}}{w},$$

where $(1 - \theta)\bar{H}$ is the amount of time that the family has available to allocate between work on the market and work and other activities at home. Figure 1 shows the difference between the two models.

Figure 1. Labor Supply as a Function of Nonwage Income in Models 1 and 2

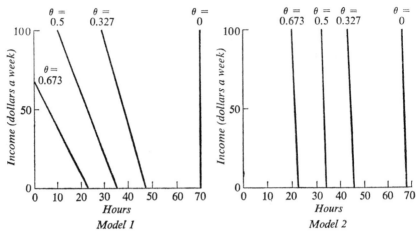

Note: $\theta = 0.327$ is the first quartile of the distribution of θ; $\theta = 0.5$ is the median; and $\theta = 0.673$ is the third quartile.

The points of zero labor supply for model 2 are:

$$\theta_N = 1 - \left(\frac{\alpha}{1-\alpha}\right)\left(\frac{Y_0}{w\bar{H}}\right)$$

and

$$\theta_P = 1 - \left(\frac{\alpha}{1-\alpha}\right)\left(\frac{B_0 + (1-\tau)Y_0}{(1-\tau)w\bar{H}}\right).$$

The crossover point dividing families who opt for the program from those remaining off it is:

$$\theta^* = 1 - \left(\frac{1}{w\bar{H}}\right)\left(\frac{B_0}{(1-\tau)^\alpha - (1-\tau)} - Y_0\right).$$

In realistic cases, this formula needs no modification on account of non-negativity. Table 4 reports the response of hours of work to variations in wages and income and in the guarantee and tax rates of the negative income tax. These responses are much closer to those found in the experiment, even though models 1 and 2 share the same unitary wage and income elasticities of demand for time at home. As in model 1, the ordinary labor supply function, $E(H_N)$, is not very wage elastic. The average family raises its hours of work by only 0.1 a week as the wage rises from $1.50 to $3.00. On the other hand, neither is model 2 very income elastic: as income rises

Table 4. Response to a Negative Income Tax, Model 2: Effect on Hours of Work of Variations in Labor Supply Determinants

Item	Combinations of parameters							
	(1)	(2)	(3)	(4)	(5)	(6)	(7)	(8)
Labor supply determinants								
Wage (dollars per hour) (w)	1.50	2.00	3.00	2.00	2.00	2.00	2.00	2.00
Nonlabor income (dollars per week) (Y_0)	10	10	10	50	10	10	10	10
Guarantee (dollars per week) (B_0)	80	80	80	80	40	120	80	80
Tax rate (percent) (τ)	50	50	50	50	50	50	30	70
Attitude thresholds								
Switch on to program (θ^*)	0	0	0.25	0.17	0.48	0	0	0.21
No work, participants (θ_P)	0.95	0.96	0.97	0.95	0.98	0.94	0.97	0.94
No work, nonparticipants (θ_N)	1.00	1.00	1.00	0.99	1.00	1.00	1.00	1.00
Calculated responses								
Expected hours, no program [$E(H_N)$]	33.7	33.8	33.8	33.2	33.8	33.8	33.8	33.8
Expected hours, with program [$E(H_P)$]	30.6	31.4	32.5	31.0	33.2	30.2	32.1	30.3
Effect of program (hours) [$E(H_N) - E(H_P)$]	3.1	2.4	1.3	2.2	0.6	3.6	1.7	3.5
Percent of families opting for program	100	100	84	93	54	100	100	89
Percent of families continuing to work	99	100	84	92	54	99	100	87
Average reduction in hours of those continuing to work	3.2	2.4	1.6	2.4	1.2	3.6	1.7	4.0
Percent of families stopping work	1	0	0	1	0	1	0	1
Average reduction in hours of those stopping work	2.1	1.6	1.0	1.4	0.8	2.4	1.1	2.6

Source: Model 2, discussed in the text.

from \$10 to \$50 a week, average hours in the absence of the negative income tax fall by only 0.6, in contrast to 8.6 hours in model 1. The weaker effect of income on labor supply in model 2 makes it predict much smaller responses to the negative income tax. In the benchmark case—$w = \$2.00$, $Y_0 = \$10$, $B_0 = \$80$, and $\tau = 50$ percent—average hours fall by 2.4, from 33.8 to 31.4, when the plan becomes available. All families opt in favor of the plan, and none of them stop work. In the high-wage group, the average effect is smaller, only 1.3 hours, partly because 16 percent of the families opt against the program and do not reduce their hours at all, and partly because the response of those under the negative income tax is smaller. The difference in the responses of high- and low-income families is similar.

Model 2 predicts a particularly small response, 0.6 hour on the average, to a plan with a guarantee level of only $40 a week. Again, part of the population decides against the plan (46 percent), and the remainder reduce their hours by a relatively small amount (1.2 hours). On the other hand, the plan with a high guarantee achieves universal acceptance and even drives 1 percent of the families out of the labor market altogether. Finally, the last two columns of Table 4 show how the response to the negative income tax depends on the tax rate. The low tax rate, 30 percent, corresponds to a more generous plan yet causes a reduction of 1.7 hours a week, compared with 2.4 hours for the benchmark rate of 50 percent. The high tax rate of 70 percent causes 9 percent of the families to opt against the program, so that although those on the program reduce their hours of work by 4.0 hours a week, average hours in the population fall by only 3.5 when the plan becomes available. The unattractiveness of high tax rates tends to counterbalance their discentive effects on labor supply.

Both model 1 and model 2 would fit fairly well the earlier cross-sectional data on the mean and dispersion of hours of work. Among low-wage families, the defective income elasticity of model 1 would not cause trouble because so few of the families have significant nonwage income. The experiment has provided the first opportunity to observe the response of hours of work to large amounts of income. The small size of the response requires the use of a theoretical model of labor supply that does not attribute large income responses even to a minority of families. Model 2 is such a model and demonstrates that the findings of the experiment are not contradictory to the economic theory of the household.

Appendix B: Derivation of Variances and Covariances of Means and Variances of Estimators

The first step is to derive the variances and covariances of the four basic statistics implied by the variance-components model. I define:

$\lambda = \dfrac{\delta^2}{\delta^2 + \sigma^2}$, the fraction of the total variance contributed by the permanent component;

$N_S = 225$, the number of experimental subjects reporting valid data;

$N_C = 200$, the number of controls reporting valid data;

$T_B = 1$, the number of observations before the experiment; and $T_D = 12$, the number of observations during the experiment.

Then it is not hard to show, first:

$$\text{var}(H_{S,B}) = \frac{\delta^2 + \sigma^2}{N_S}\left(\lambda + \frac{1 - \lambda}{T_B}\right);$$

and, second:

$$\text{cov}(H_{S,B}, H_{S,D}) = \frac{\delta^2 + \sigma^2}{N_S}\lambda.$$

That is, the statistics $H_{S,B}$ and $H_{S,D}$ are positively correlated because they share the common variation arising from permanent unobserved differences among families. As λ, the fraction arising from the permanent component, becomes larger, so does the correlation. A well-chosen estimator will take advantage of this positive correlation to reduce the variance of the estimated effect of the experiment.

Similar calculations show that:

$$\text{var}(H_{S,D}) = \frac{\delta^2 + \sigma^2}{N_S}\left(\lambda + \frac{1 - \lambda}{T_D}\right), \text{ and}$$

$$\text{var}(H_{C,B}) = \frac{\delta^2 + \sigma^2}{N_C}\left(\lambda + \frac{1 - \lambda}{T_B}\right);$$

$$\text{cov}(H_{C,B}, H_{C,D}) = \frac{\delta^2 + \sigma^2}{N_C}\lambda, \text{ and}$$

$$\text{var}(H_{C,D}) = \frac{\delta^2 + \sigma^2}{N_C}\left(\lambda + \frac{1 - \lambda}{T_D}\right).$$

From this information about the stochastic relation among the means, I can calculate the variances of the various estimators:

$$\begin{aligned}
\text{var}(b_{DMS}) &= \text{var}(H_{S,D}) + \text{var}(H_{S,B}) - 2\,\text{cov}(H_{S,D}, H_{S,B}) \\
&= \frac{\delta^2 + \sigma^2}{N_S}\left(\lambda + \frac{1 - \lambda}{T_D} + \lambda + \frac{1 - \lambda}{T_B} - 2\lambda\right) \\
&= \frac{\delta^2 + \sigma^2}{N_S}\left((1 - \lambda)\frac{1}{T_D} + \frac{1}{T_B}\right).
\end{aligned}$$

Note the cancellation of the two λ terms from the variances by the λ from the covariance. The variance of b_{DMS} arises solely from the variances of the transitory components, which contribute the terms $(1 - \lambda)/T_B$ and $(1 - \lambda)/T_D$ to the variances. These terms are not canceled by the covariance.

If both T_B and T_D are large, the variance of b_{DMS} can be made very small even in an experiment with a limited number of subjects.

The estimator b_{DMD} fares less well with this stochastic specification because it fails to cancel the variance from permanent components through the use of data from before the experiment:

$$\text{var}(b_{DMD}) = \text{var}(H_{S,D}) + \text{var}(H_{C,D})$$

$$= (\delta^2 + \sigma^2)\left(\frac{1}{N_S} + \frac{1}{N_C}\right)\left(\lambda + \frac{1-\lambda}{T_D}\right).$$

Similar calculations apply to the compromise estimator b_{EW}, but the resulting formula is too complicated to justify discussing it here.

None of the three estimators discussed so far is optimal in the sense of minimizing variance. The general class of linear unbiased estimators can be written as:

$$b = H_{S,D} - \omega H_{S,B} - (1 - \omega)[(1 - \gamma)H_{C,D} + \gamma H_{C,B}].$$

The parameter ω represents the major decision about the weight for the preexperiment data for the subjects against the weight for the controls, both before and during the experiment. It will turn out that the more important the permanent component of the difference among families, the larger will be ω. The parameter γ represents the subsidiary decision of how to distribute the total weight assigned to the controls between the data for before and during the experiment. For a given fixed choice of ω and γ, the variance of b is:

$$\begin{aligned}
\text{var}(b) = {}& \text{var}(H_{S,D}) + \omega^2 \, \text{var}(H_{S,B}) - 2\omega \, \text{cov}(H_{S,D}, H_{S,B}) \\
& + (1 - \omega)^2[(1 - \gamma)^2 \, \text{var}(H_{C,D}) + \gamma^2 \, \text{var}(H_{C,B}) \\
& + 2\gamma(1 - \gamma) \, \text{cov}(H_{C,D}, H_{C,B})].
\end{aligned}$$

It is not difficult to show that the optimal weight to assign to the data for the controls before the experiment is: $\gamma = T_B/(T_D + T_B)$. Given optimal weighting of the controls, some additional algebra shows that the optimal weight for the data for the subjects before the experiment is:

$$\omega = \frac{\dfrac{\lambda}{N_S} + \dfrac{1}{N_C}\left(\lambda + \dfrac{1-\lambda}{T_B + T_D}\right)}{\dfrac{1}{N_S}\left(\lambda + \dfrac{1-\lambda}{T_B}\right) + \dfrac{1}{N_C}\left(\lambda + \dfrac{1-\lambda}{T_B + T_D}\right)},$$

if $\lambda = 1$, $\omega = 1$, and the best estimator is the *DMS* estimator. High values of λ are associated with high ω weights for the preexperiment data for subjects. As long as λ is positive, ω also approaches unity as T_B, the number of observations before the experiment began, becomes large. On the other hand, if there are no permanent differences ($\lambda = 0$) and all of the samples are of equal size ($N_S = N_C$ and $T_B = T_D$), then $\omega = \frac{1}{3}$, $\gamma = \frac{1}{2}$, and $b = H_{S,D} - \frac{1}{3}[H_{S,B} + H_{C,D} + H_{C,B}]$, the EW estimator discussed earlier. Finally, if $\lambda = 0$ and $T_B = 1$, ω approaches zero as T_D becomes large: in the absence of a permanent error component, the DMD estimator is close to minimal variance where the number of periods during the experiment is large relative to the number before the experiment. If, however, λ is positive, the efficient estimator gives weight to the preliminary data $H_{S,B}$ no matter how large T_D may be. Data on the experimental subjects before the experiment are extremely useful in reducing the variance of the estimated effect of the program within the experiment.

Comment by Zvi Griliches

Hall's paper outlines a theoretical model with individual differences in behavior built into it; recomputes the statistical significance of the mean effect of the experiment; and comments on the desirable design of such experiments. In my comments, I shall try to follow this outline.

The Theoretical Model

There are two reasons for worrying about individual behavioral differences in such data. First, and most important, they dominate the data. Despite a large number of variables included in the analysis, at the individual level the fits are poor and the bulk of the observed variance remains unexplained. Tacking on a routine additive disturbance to the estimated equation does not do justice to the problem. Second, and quite important for the econometric analysis of the results, a model is needed that would explain participation rates in the negative income tax experiment. One cannot simply regress labor supply behavior on the guaranteed income levels and tax rates because for a significant fraction of the subjects the tax rate is not binding if they are above the breakeven point. Moreover, this switching point is endogenous and has to be built into the model explicitly—unless the experiment had been so designed that participation rates were always 100 percent.

Hall presents two versions of a simple model that tries to capture the phenomenon of variations across individuals. In the first, the random variable is directly the relative preference for leisure. In the second, which gives a bit more realistic results, the individual variability is introduced through the variability of available or uncommitted hours. It is assumed that the week is shorter for some people than others, that people have different amounts of available hours to allocate between leisure and work.

The econometrics of the second model would be relatively simple if the effective tax rate were not endogenous to the experiment. The labor supply equation can be written as $H = A_i - \alpha y_0/w$, where H is hours worked, y_0 is nonlabor income, w is the after-tax wage rate, α is a parameter fixed across the whole population, and A_i is an unobservable but estimable individual parameter connected to the distribution parameter as follows: $A_i = (1 - \alpha)(1 - \theta_i)\bar{H}$, where $\bar{H}$ is the ceiling value of total available hours. Econometric problems arise because the actual effective tax rate is endogenous and because H cannot take on negative values, converting this into a Tobit type problem. The latter point is discussed ably and in some detail by Hall.

I have two points to make about this model, one constructive and one critical.

First, this model is reminiscent of the ones actually estimated by Watts and his associates, who also allow, in effect, separate constant terms for each individual. But Hall's model is more powerful and hence also easier to refute because it predicts nonparticipation rates, making them conditional on the true A_i (or θ_i). Because such an equation could be estimated for the entire working sample, one could get estimates of α and the individual A_i. One could then insert these estimated values into the participation formula and see whether in fact they explain who does or does not participate in the program. Alternatively, one could estimate the hours equation and participation equation jointly, since the same parameters appear in both.

Second, I am not certain that I like the assumed form of the labor supply function for a given θ_i. Note that in both models the response of hours worked to wages depends on the availability of nonlabor income. Zero response to the wage rate occurs in both models 1 and 2 if nonlabor income is zero, irrespective of the level of earnings. Similarly, the elasticities of hours worked with respect to nonlabor income and with respect to the wage rate are opposite in sign but equal, and their absolute magnitude depends on the ratio of nonlabor income to labor earnings, implying lower elasticities as earnings increase and as nonlabor income decreases. The first may be reasonable if an asymptote in hours worked is approached, but in the second, the strong dependence of the labor supply elasticity on the level of nonlabor income seems too specific and may lead to perverse results. (Nonlabor income is far from a homogeneous entity and may be related to the θ_is.)

In the next section Hall shows, in spite of the caveats in the text, that the cross-sectional surveys do in fact predict an average response for men on the order of magnitude observed in the experiment, supporting both the earlier estimates and the experiment. On the other hand, there is a substantial discrepancy for women, which in fact is predicted by the model outlined by Hall.

Statistical Significance of the Experiment

The third section of Hall's text ingeniously recomputes the mean experimental response and the associated standard errors and shows that in fact there was a statistically significant average response in the experiment. I have several comments and queries about it.

First, should not an attempt be made to reconcile these results with those of Watts and others to determine the sources of the difference?

Second, given the rather rich econometric theory of the earlier sections, I am a bit disappointed that it is not carried over into the estimation of the mean effect. In particular, I would have liked to see an estimate of the effect of the experiment on the participators alone: that is, those families that actually have been affected by the experiment and are taking money from it, and excluding those who found themselves above the breakeven point. To do so, however, would have required the estimation of the complete model outlined by Hall earlier, since participation itself is endogenous to the model. My guess is that Hall's mean effect estimates—as well as those of Watts—are underestimates of the "effective effects."

Third, the estimated effects are not so small after all. For white males a reduction of 2.6 hours a week represents a 7 percent reduction in total labor supply. For participators, for those who actually were affected by the experiment, the effect probably is double that figure—which is not insignificant.

Fourth, I am not so certain what this means, however, because the actual amount of money transferred to the subjects was rather small. If I read the numbers correctly in Rees and Watts, of the experimental families whom they analyzed, about half got less than $15 a week, and fewer than a hundred families received an average payment of as much as $45 a week in payments. That is not very generous, and it may not be so surprising that larger effects were not observed.

Design of the Experiment

The problem of attrition in the experiment clearly is serious and requires further study. Hall suggests that more data should have been collected before the onset of the experiment. Let me expand this to suggest that more data should have been collected after the experiment. From the point of view of Hall's model, whether the additional observations are from $t - h$ or $t + h$ does not really matter. It would have been relatively cheap, I think, to have kept interviewing the same people for another year after the completion of the actual experiment, and perhaps we should return and resurvey them again.

Let me end with a few scattered comments. More analyses of these data certainly are needed. They should be analyzed in relation to actual benefits received, not merely plans under which enrolled. Something more than simply averaging could be done with the time structure of the model. Wages, hours, and husband and wife labor force behavior should be analyzed jointly, not one at a time. In retrospect, it would be desirable, I think, to have a postmortem analysis of the original design of the experiment. What were the particular places at which it went wrong?

Finally, we should thank the designers and executors of the experiment for having gone through with it and shown us that it can be done—that behavior can be studied in this way. With all its imperfections, I think that the experiment is something we can all be proud of. Next time we might do it better, but there might not have been a next time and we might not have known how to do it better without the care and effort invested in this endeavor.

Comment by Jacob Mincer

It may be nice to sit on top of a pyramid, but the view of the ground below is rather distant, and it might actually be difficult to get down at all. This is the feeling I get in attempting to survey the findings of the experiment through the successive layers of past progress reports, the thirty papers that make up the final report, and the papers prepared for this conference. Although I read only a small fraction of all this material, I take the liberty to comment on the results of the experiment, as well as to remark on Robert Hall's excellent paper.

Design and Data Problems

There is some danger that the analyses of the experiment's findings might be colored by attitudes toward the need for welfare reform and toward the desirability of experimental research in the social sciences, including economics. Let me confess that my attitudes about these matters are quite positive, although I insist that they do not at all inhibit my critical comments. It is much easier, of course, for an onlooker to be detached than for those present at the creation. So it is possible that the perceived political urgency of the experimental program led to a less than perfect design: too little time and attention to preexperimental observation, too short a duration of the experiment, and some problems with data quality. Perhaps the realization of some of these shortcomings did not require an actual experience with the experiment. The experimental design, according to Hall, could have been improved by a factor of 6 to 1 at no additional cost, if half of the sample were studied preexperimentally half the time, the other half postexperimentally half the time. This, of course, would have cut the effective duration of the experiment in half, but Hall considered only the statistical efficiency of face value estimators.

One troublesome problem is the inadequate quality of the earnings and wage-rate data. The interesting questions on the possible effect of the experiment on wage rates, which Rees enumerates, are largely unanswerable because of the differentially inaccurate understanding of the concept by the experimental and control groups. This loss of opportunity to gather much cleaner data on wage rates than the usual surveys provide is bothersome, because it will hamper possible reanalyses or other kinds of analyses of the data generated by the experiment.

The deterioration of data, mainly by attrition, appears to be so massive that it leads Hall to discard the findings on blacks and the Spanish speaking, reducing the sample size to one-third. Multiply this by the 6-to-1 estimate of loss in efficiency due to design and the staggering loss in potential information is more than 90 percent.

Undaunted by the more than decimated efficiency of the experiment, Hall argues that the experiment provided a good deal of new evidence about the labor supply response of poor families to a negative income tax. This is probably true, if what we wanted to learn is the short-run response of a particular part of the population to a temporary flow of cash grants. I say temporary cash grants, without adding the proviso "work-conditioned receipts," because no evidence was produced on effects of differential marginal tax rates.

It is unfortunate that 0 percent and 100 percent marginal tax plans were not studied. If the evidence is to be taken at face value, the experimental results are either silent on this important question or they do not disparage categorical 100 percent tax welfare systems. Aside from the nominal high tax feature (100 percent before 1967, 66⅔ percent thereafter), much of the opposition to AFDC (for which intact families are not eligible) is based on its tax on family integrity and its consequent plausible association with family disintegration. Regrettably, though perhaps inevitably, the experiment was not designed to study this problem. Yet the important labor supply effects probably are related to family dissolution, but they escape the observers who focus on the behavior of the deserted mothers.

Of course, the question of how well actual work behavior and actual family dissolution can be inferred from reported behavior is partly a question of law enforcement, for which the experiment was not designed and certainly not suitable.

Other Biases

Aside from questions of design, attrition, and varying quality of data, the basic problem in interpreting the experimental results is the short duration of the experiment. The purpose of the experiment, as defined by its managers, was to find out what would be the responses of the families of the working poor to a legislated, permanent negative income tax program, which would replace the current system. Do we get the answer to this question from the three-year experiment? Hall's answer is not explicitly positive, though perhaps implicitly, when he finds that after some adjustments made on his own nonexperimental cross-sectional estimates of labor supply parameters, the latter become consistent with experimental effects for men, at least within sampling error. It is not clear whether the same conclusion would obtain if Hall's recipe for adjustments were used on other available nonexperimental estimates. Although I would agree that these are not of uniform quality and I do not object to Hall's healthy respect for his own work, this exercise is not likely to serve as a final answer.

If consistency with nonexperimental results were the measure of validity of the experimental results, there would be no need for experiments. Short of this happy state, we must judge the validity of the experimental results by a number of indications emerging from the experiment. Among these there are suggestions of perceptions, misperceptions, and selectivity biases on the part of the experimental subjects that militate against an unambiguous reading of the experimental results as a prognostication of the effects of a permanent program. I proceed to a discussion of doubts about the validity of such prognostication.

SELECTIVITY PROBLEMS. The managers of the experiment found it very difficult to locate intact working families who were poor by the standards of the experiment. Consequently, the selected families have the unusual composition of above-average numbers of children, below-average labor force attachment of secondary workers, and temporarily low incomes. The labor force attachment of male heads in such families is particularly strong, and the mothers have strong incentives to drop out of market work when they can afford it. The prior existence of an AFDC program for which intact families were not eligible—not to be confused with the AFDC-UP program instituted later—suggests an additional selection bias toward family stability and strong work motivation of the fathers in the families eligible for the experiment.

In addition, the truncation of low current family income three months before the experimental period predicts a subsequent regression toward the mean and consequently increases in income during the experiment. This bias is mitigated to the extent that it is shared by the controls, but the attrition and replacement of controls makes this escape doubtful. If the black and Spanish-speaking sample comes from a New Jersey population with higher permanent income than the whites in Scranton, and the major attrition was in the New Jersey controls, the differences in results are better understood as statistical artifacts than as ethnic mystique.

SHORT SPAN OF EXPERIMENT. "Nothing is as permanent as the temporary," a French proverb, may well apply to politics but not to the consumption function—and even less so, I would judge, to labor supply functions. Cain notes that male heads of families "have a firm attachment to a job that requires them to work a fixed number of hours" a week on a full-time basis, and to expect them to make major changes in their schedules, knowing that at the end of three years they will have to return to their old schedules, is not realistic. By contrast, the options of women to work inter- mittently and less than full time permit wives "to show a greater responsive- ness to the experimental incentives."[18]

The response of husbands to a permanent program probably is under- stated—but by how much? It is the assessment of magnitudes, not just direction of responses, that was the purpose of the experiment. The re- sponse of wives may be overstated, though this is not clear, given the small number of working wives and the truncation bias that may have prevailed despite the controls.

It is rather clear from the consumption data presented by Metcalf that the households were acutely aware of the transitoriness of the grants they were receiving. The marginal propensity to consume food out of the ex- perimental payments was only one-half to one-third as large as the marginal propensity to consume out of normal income. The experimental payments were viewed the same way as transitory components of income, whereas public assistance subsidies were treated as permanent. The same and per- haps an even stronger conclusion emerges from the data on purchases of appliances. Their timing was rather quick in response to the payments and more sensitive to the subsidies than to other variable components of in- come. This is to say that the windfall nature of the experimental payments was clearer than that of the other sources of income.

INTRUSION OF STATE WELFARE PROGRAMS. The introduction of an AFDC-UP program after the start of the experiment obscured the com- parisons between control and experimental families, probably reducing the differentials. It seems to me that the appearance of these state programs may have presented an opportunity to contrast effects of what are viewed as permanent programs with those of the temporary experimental program. It is shown by Garfinkel that the lower the guarantee and the higher the marginal tax rate, the greater the withdrawal of experimental families into state welfare.[19] And, of course, many more control than experimental families went on welfare. Moreover, families on welfare tended to work and earn substantially less than those not on welfare. According to Garfinkel's Table 3, heads of families who went on welfare for less than half the period—that is, six quarters or less—worked five hours a week less, and those on welfare for more than half the period worked nine hours less than those who did not go on welfare. Compare this with the experimental

18. Glen G. Cain and others, "The Labor-Supply Response of Married Women, Husbands Present," *Journal of Human Resources*, vol. 9 (Spring 1974), p. 203.
19. Garfinkel, "The Effects of Welfare," Table 3.

differential of a reduction of only one or two hours a week. But we are not told the work behavior of the same families before the AFDC-UP was instituted. The matter deserves closer attention.

PERCEPTION OF THE "RULES OF THE GAME." It is my understanding that after about a year in the rural experiment—and I recall a similar progress report on the urban experiment—25 percent of the families thought that their subsidies would be reduced if they quit or lost a job. I am not sure whether this response represented ignorance of the rules of the game on the part of participants or a conviction prevailing despite the overt rules that proper response to the experimental payments must be in the socially appropriate direction that the experiment set out to demonstrate. Whichever the interpretation, ignorance or attitude, the effects were to diminish the observed disincentive effects.

Some Conclusions

First, at best, we have learned the short-run responses of a particular population group to short-run negative income tax type programs. I find it impossible to extrapolate from these findings to predict general and long-term effects of a bona fide and rather sweeping institutional change. Second, urgent policy research is likely to be more vulnerable to haste, impatience, pressure, and Hawthorne effects than are basic research studies. And, unfortunately, policy research is more likely to be funded. Thus, purely scientific progress in experimental economics is likely to be slow unless grantors of funds recover their respect for basic research. I should add, however, that despite the potentially thin line that existed in the New Jersey project between a political demonstration project and a scientific experiment, the work appears to have been conducted with impeccable standards of scientific objectivity.

Where do we go from here? As far as reanalyses of the generated data are concerned, it would be useful to follow up the families if they can be located. Closer attention to age and to job mobility may shed more light on some of the questions that were posed in the experiment. To a person of sixty-two years, a three-year program is more permanent than it is to a person of thirty. The turnover observed in the group probably is not aimless, and if so, the brevity of the experiment is the more serious a problem.

I hope these comments concerning the interpretation of the outcome of the New Jersey experiment are not taken as an expression of doubt about the potential of experimental economics. I have no doubt about the promise of this tool, which is new in the social sciences but has proven its power in the traditional sciences, including agriculture and medicine. Of course, the feasibility and payoff must differ depending on the research question. It does seem to me that the problem of gauging long-run macrosocietal adjustments from necessarily limited samples and periods is inherently difficult. Despite these reservations, I believe the experiment is to be applauded as a milestone in the history of economic research.

PETER H. ROSSI

A Critical Review
of the Analysis of
Nonlabor Force Responses

The purpose of this paper is to provide an overview and critique of those aspects of the New Jersey–Pennsylvania income maintenance experiment that dealt with behavior of the participating families aside from that relating to labor supply. This residual category covers variables of considerable heterogeneity, including changes in family composition, patterns of consumption, health and health care, and a set of social psychological variables designed to measure attitudes and values among participants.

The main concern of the experiment clearly lay in the labor force responses: the design of the experiment and the distribution of resources within the research team reflect this concern. Enough interest lay in non-labor force aspects of a negative income tax program for the Office of Economic Opportunity to incorporate such concern into the experiment's goals. There are several reasons for including these interests, since policy issues surrounding income maintenance do not end with questions about labor force response. Existing welfare programs supposedly had such perverse incentives built into them as a pronatalist bias and a reward for family dissolution.[1] There was also some concern with what might be called the color television problem, a belief that an increase in the income of the poor would lead only to expenditures on luxuries.

Furthermore, the existing welfare system supposedly had negative consequences upon its clients in terms of social psychology. Welfare stigmatized and degraded its clients with means tests for eligibility and constant

1. This was particularly the case under eligibility rules for AFDC, which restricted coverage largely to households comprising only mothers and their dependent children.

supervision of client households, forcing them to lowered self-esteem and apathy.[2] Finally, a new income maintenance plan would have some effects upon the jobs taken by low-income persons, either by making low-paying jobs bearable or by subsidizing job searches. Each of these problems merited inquiry.

Nonlabor Force Aspects of Poverty

In a more comprehensive vein, there was concern over the supposed pathology of the poor. On almost any indicator of social pathology— crime, juvenile delinquency, mental illness, most organic diseases and disabling physical conditions, low levels of intellectual performance, family instability, and related conditions—the poor show greater incidence and prevalence rates. From the early days of the public health movement to the latest twist in social casework, each new social welfare measure characteristically has claimed for itself the ability to lower the levels of such indicators among the poor, at least in the long run. A negative income tax plan reaching the policy agenda would be unlikely to be an exception: advocates would claim for it miraculous curative properties, and opponents probably would insist that these very pathologies and causes of poverty were unlikely to be cured by income augmentation alone.

The policy questions have their counterpart in issues in the social sciences. Many of the supposed benefits or perversities that might result from a negative income tax program can be restated in terms of the controversy over the idea of a "culture of poverty." According to Oscar Lewis, who coined the term,[3] poor people in an open society develop a culture—or subculture—characterized by a value system that stresses, among other things, an immediate rather than long-term time orientation: a preference, for example, for immediate sensory gratification as opposed to rewards

2. Oddly enough, few scholars asked whether any negative income tax plan, including the ones tested in this experiment, would have the same defects. It may not be necessary to have a means test to be eligible for payments, but it is necessary to submit some statement of earnings and other income. The possibility of fraud and the likelihood that some fraud would be detected would mean that eventually any negative income tax scheme would come to resemble the existing welfare system in its administration. Indeed, it is difficult to see the differences between welfare and the negative payments plan when we consider that a constant monitoring of income was involved in both, along with investigations of possible fraud and other factors.

3. Oscar Lewis, *La Vida: A Puerto Rican Family in the Culture of Poverty—San Juan and New York* (Random House, 1965).

stemming from achievement, status, and the like. Lewis lists seventy traits that characterize the culture of poverty. As a subculture, the culture of poverty is inherited by each succeeding generation through early childhood socialization, so that poor families or individuals rarely can rise above their origins. The holding power of such a subculture over the poor is so strong that Lewis believed that little could be done for the poor short of mass psychiatric treatment.

The alternative to the culture of poverty advanced by other social scientists conceded that to a greater or lesser degree the poor resembled the description advanced by Lewis. But these characteristics, they stressed, arose continually in response to the conditions of poverty rather than being passed on from generation to generation as a subculture. Rather, they felt, improving the conditions of the poor would lead to a disappearance of the signs of personal and social disorganization that everyone agreed existed among the poor. For some who held this view, an income strategy was an appropriate remedy; for others, a jobs strategy was held to be the more effective nostrum.

Except for those who held to the notion of a culture of poverty, sociologists and social psychologists dealing with poverty all had some expectations that a negative income tax would have some nonlabor force effects. Exactly what sorts of effects, how strong such effects would be, and what exposure time to such a program would be required for effects to manifest themselves were all questions to which the rudimentary theory of social science could provide no answers.

Although static equilibrium theory was silent on many points about expected labor force responses to a negative income tax plan, it at least predicted both the existence and direction of the response. In contrast, sociology and social psychology provided theories that were formulated vaguely and provided contradictory predictions. From the culture of poverty hypothesis one would predict, if anything, that no response would occur in labor force or other terms. From the competing theory, one also might predict "no response" or "some response," depending on how long a run was thought to be necessary to reverse the effects of poverty.[4] The

4. To allay any impression that the culture of poverty theory dominates the noneconomic social sciences' view of poverty, I hazard the guess that most such social scientists reject the theory. Most who worked on the income maintenance experiment certainly did. The prominence given to this formulation is more a function of its monopoly position than of its persuasiveness: it is virtually the only contender for the status of a theory of poverty.

extent to which this is so is demonstrated in almost all of the papers that arose out of a series of monthly conferences on poverty held over a two-year period by the American Academy of Arts and Sciences.[5]

Previous empirical researches on the characteristics of the poor were of little help. Although the literature had many descriptions of the quality of life among the poor and of relevant characteristics, it tended to be dominated by qualitative rather than quantitative researches. Well-designed quantitative studies of the poor have appeared only in the last few years. At the time the New Jersey–Pennsylvania experiment was being designed, definitive research on the poor was quite slight in volume.[6] Even more important, most statements in the literature concerning the characteristics of the poor were based on studies that were badly flawed in one way or another. For example, one repeatedly cited allegation about the poor is that they are unable to defer gratification. The original source for this characterization is a small-scale study of high school students who were asked, in effect, whether they would save or spend a small sum of money ($5) if it were given to them. In this study, the differences between poorer and richer students were not great, although statistically significant, nor did the study take into account differences between poorer and richer students in cash on hand.[7]

Another problem with the literature has been the absence of a clear definition of who, exactly, were the poor, as well as vague indexes of association. Thus, findings that amounted to correlations of 0.05 to 0.20 on samples that largely missed households below the poverty line were magnified into characteristics that purported to differentiate sharply between the relatively affluent and the poor.

In short, empirical social research of any minimum substance that could illuminate the characteristics of poor individuals or households was simply

5. See Daniel P. Moynihan (ed.), *On Understanding Poverty: Perspectives from the Social Sciences* (Basic Books, 1968).

6. A contemporary literature review is Zahava D. Blum and Peter H. Rossi, "Social Class Research and Images of the Poor: A Bibliographic Review," in Moynihan, *On Understanding Poverty*.

7. The persistence of research findings of this sort against the contradictions of better research can be seen most flagrantly in Edward C. Banfield, *The Unheavenly City: The Nature and Future of Our Urban Crisis* (Little, Brown, 1970). Banfield raised the alleged characteristic of short-range time perspectives and inability to defer gratification to the status of the distinguishing mark of the urban poor. See Peter H. Rossi, "The City as Purgatory," *Social Science Quarterly*, vol. 51 (March 1971), pp. 817ff. The high school study referred to is reported in Louis Schneider and Sverre Lysgaard, "The Deferral Gratification Pattern," *American Sociological Review*, vol. 18 (April 1953), pp. 142–49.

missing. In its absence, qualitative accounts of little probity tended to dominate the image of the poor in the literature of the social sciences: an image of the poor as impulsive, lacking in foresight and ambition, alienated, anomic, and possessing a fragile ability to sustain family relationships or participate in the larger society.

Role of the Noneconomist in the Experiment[8]

It is paradoxical that economists should have played the major role in designing and fielding the income maintenance experiment. Sociologists have relied heavily on the collection of primary data in the form of sample surveys, and psychologists are perhaps the heaviest users of experimental designs among the social scientists. With notable exceptions, however, economists have tended not to collect their own primary data nor to use controlled experiments as even a minor part of their research repertoire. Yet in the early history of the experiment—from the first proposal from Heather Ross to the OEO through the early design phases—sociologists and psychologists were almost conspicuous by their absence. Only after the experimental design had been sufficiently set to proceed with field work in Trenton were these two groups involved.

Of course, the experiment might have been no better designed or the field work carried off no more efficiently had sociologists and social psychologists been more centrally involved early in the experiment. Social psychologists often use controlled experiments in their research, but their usual experiment tends to be designed for use in the laboratory, with volunteer subjects recruited from among students in basic courses. Few, if any, social psychologists have had direct, appreciably broad-scale experience in the conduct of field experiments. Sociologists and social psychologists both use sample surveys in their work, but few have had direct experience in the conduct of extensive field operations. Furthermore, although the War on Poverty was more than four years old, few survey organizations had completed the surveys of the poor population commissioned by the OEO, and thus little experience had been gained with surveys of the poor.

8. Much of the information contained in this section was obtained in personal interviews with members of the research groups at the Institute for Research on Poverty and at Mathematica, Inc. The interviews were conducted as part of a project, funded by the Russell Sage Foundation, to evaluate the New Jersey–Pennsylvania income maintenance experiment.

Those sociologists and social psychologists who were brought in as part of the research teams at the University of Wisconsin and Princeton University had had little experience in either experimental design or large-scale field operations. Earlier participation on the part of these individuals probably would have added little materially to the design or the field operation.[9]

The principal investigators at neither Mathematica nor the Poverty Institute were experienced in experimental design and survey operations. It is a considerable tribute to their skills and ingenuity that the experiment was as well conducted as it was. Although there are few previous, comparable research endeavors with which the experiment can be compared, it is clear at least to this writer that most social researchers would have done a great deal worse and few would have carried off the experiment as well as the combination of Mathematica and Wisconsin.

The participation of sociologists and psychologists remained largely peripheral throughout the experiment. At the core of the research staff was a relatively close-knit group of economists who had a high regard for each other's abilities and who shared a common concern for the undertaking. Clearly, these economists were at best skeptical that the sociologists and psychologists could add anything substantial to the experiment and at worst held disparaging views of their collaborators from these two disciplines. One of the major economists told us that had the OEO not specifically required that sociologists and psychologists be involved in the experiment, he would not have recruited any to participate.

As a consequence, the sociologists and psychologists were given a "piece of the action" in the form of a limited license to add variables of interest to the data collection, but they were not invited into close collaboration with the economists. Nor did the noneconomists form a tightly knit group among themselves: individual sociologists and social psychologists complained to us that it was a constant struggle to get their colleagues to pay enough attention to the tasks of designing questionnaires and taking responsibility for portions of the analysis.

In short, this was not an interdisciplinary venture, but rather one in which the economists apparently acted more or less in concert while the sociologists and psychologists were proceeding on parallel paths as individuals. Decisions had to be made, of course, about what should be included

9. Experienced sociologists and statisticians at both places were consulted. In particular, Frederick Stephan and Charles Westoff of Princeton were consulted on the selection of an initial survey organization.

in data collection, but these decisions were made more on the basis of such considerations as the length of the questionnaires rather than whether the content of the proposed measures made any substantial contributions to the common themes of the experiment.

The consequences of this form of collaboration are important to consider. First, the low professional investment in the project by sociologists and social psychologists probably stemmed in part from their position as tolerated contributors. Second, although it is difficult to specify possible benefits that might have accrued from closer collaboration, any such benefits were lost. The most likely benefit would have been elaboration of the labor force measures to include more data on jobs and occupations. Another area of possible benefit would have been a stronger contribution of sociologists and social psychologists to the field operations of the project. But this obviously is a matter of speculation, and the fact remains that collaboration was minimal.

An Overview of Nonlabor Force Findings

A large number of diverse analyses were made whose main common characteristic is coverage of possible experimental effects on household and individual behavior unrelated to issues of labor. It is impossible to do complete justice to the detailed papers that are reviewed here: the best we can do is to attempt adequate justice. Nothing will replace actual examination of the papers themselves, especially in their final form.[10]

In each of the subsections that follow I will take up three main topics: first, a description and critique of the data series on which the analyses were run; second, a similar review of the analyses of the data series; and, third, a summary of the main findings and an assessment of the extent to which the findings can be regarded as relatively firm.

10. The papers now available from the Institute for Research on Poverty are drafts somewhere between first drafts and final copy for the volumes that are to be issued in 1975. Many of the errors characteristic of intermediate drafts are found in the papers. Some show signs of having been written hastily and hold out promises of extensive prepublication revision. Thus, the summaries in this section to some degree imperfectly represent what will be the final published materials dealing with nonlabor force responses. It seems unlikely, however, given the nature of most of the findings, that extensive revisions will alter these findings materially. Needles may be found in those haystacks, but researchers probably will not run across any overlooked crowbars.

Consumption Behavior

The main objective in the analysis of consumption behavior is to discern any effects of participation in the experiment on the purchase of a variety of goods and services. A common enough theme running through anti-welfare literature—one that might arise as well in arguments against the negative income tax idea—is the possibility that payments may subsidize frivolous consumption, from color television sets to Cadillacs. From the point of view of economic theory, the main issues center around whether payments are to be conceived of as additions to permanent income or as transitory income and whether intertemporal substitution occurs—translated, accelerated acquisition of property.

With the exception of health services, which I cover later, the three papers dealing with consumption behavior have been written by economists.[11] Judith Wooldridge addressed herself almost entirely to experimental effects on housing consumption. Charles Metcalf attempted the difficult task of discerning the possible effects of a permanent negative income tax plan on a wider variety of consumption behaviors. Walter Nicholson's paper dealing with the assessment of experimental effects on the same broad spectrum of consumption is differentiated from Metcalf's work primarily by its lack of concern with estimating the effects of a permanent plan.[12]

DATA SERIES. The data upon which the analyses are based are obtained from a subset of the quarterly interviews. On some quarterly interviews housewives were asked to estimate their expenditures on food for preparation of home-cooked meals, on food consumed outside the home, and on clothing. At the preenrollment interview, questions were asked about the possession of various appliances, automobiles and trucks, insurance policies, assets in savings, cash on hand, and mortgage holdings. All three authors complain in their papers about the inadequacy of this data base.

11. Judith Wooldridge, "Housing Consumption in the New Jersey–Pennsylvania Experiment," Charles E. Metcalf, "Consumption Behavior Under a Permanent Negative Income Tax: Preliminary Evidence," and Walter Nicholson, "Expenditure Patterns in the Graduated Work Incentive Experiment: A Descriptive Survey," in Harold W. Watts and Albert Rees (eds.), *Final Report of the New Jersey Graduated Work Incentive Experiment* (University of Wisconsin—Madison, Institute for Research on Poverty, and Mathematica, 1974), vol. 3, pt. D, chaps. 3(a), 3(c), and 3(b), respectively. (Referred to hereafter as *Final Report of the New Jersey Experiment.*)

12. In practice, this meant that Metcalf used preenrollment income and Nicholson current income in their specifications of experimental effects.

For example, the preenrollment checklist of possessions held did not ask for prices or time of acquisition, and the items on mortgage holdings do not clearly differentiate between current mortgage balance and original mortgage amount. No questions were asked about amounts spent for a variety of services, including services such as utilities that are connected with housing.

The most clearly defined variable concerns homeownership and monthly rental. For the remainder, researchers had to rely on respondent estimates (for example, for food expenditures) or had to impute the acquisition of durable items and automobiles by comparing inventories made at different times.

Several obvious deficiencies exist in the consumption data series: only certain categories of consumption were covered; heavy reliance was placed on respondent estimates; purchase prices and depreciated values of possessions had to be estimated at most points in time; and no attempt was made until the follow-up, postexperiment interview to determine whether families treated benefits separately in their budgeting or lumped them with other sources of income.[13]

Why the data series was so poorly designed is difficult to understand. The initial interest in consumption may have been so low that little attention was paid to devising good measures. Whatever the reason, it is clear that the measures used leave a great deal—if not everything—to be desired.

ANALYSES. Although the base number of families used varies somewhat from paper to paper depending on the number of cases that must be left out because of missing information, all use that set of families that participated in the experiment from beginning to end.

Data are analyzed in all three papers by means of multiple regression techniques, with some additional work in Wooldridge's paper using probit analysis. The differences among the papers lie mainly in the dependent variables and in the definition of control variables to be employed. Thus, Wooldridge confines her analysis entirely to the purchase of housing, the payment of rent in private housing, and moves from public to private housing. In an effort to obtain estimates of effects on consumption that are free from labor force experimental effects, Metcalf uses preenrollment earnings and corresponding payments as a measure of permanent income and experimental effects. In contrast, Nicholson uses actual income disaggregated into earnings, other income, and payments.

13. No analyses have yet been made—and made available to me—of the postexperimental interviews dealing with this topic.

FINDINGS. Perhaps the most dramatic experimental effects were shown in Wooldridge's paper. Families in the experimental group were more likely to purchase a home during the experimental period, renters increased the amount of rent they paid (and presumably achieved better housing thereby), and experimental families living in public housing at the time of enrollment were slightly more likely to move out of it. Even more startling was the fact that experimental families who were not receiving payments— that is, who were above the breakeven levels—showed experimental effects, indicating that being on the experiment either may have given them the security to risk expending more of their income on housing or may have made lending institutions more willing to provide mortgage money.

Unfortunately, the amounts of money spent for housing by homeowners and families in public housing are difficult to estimate with the best of data; without these data, homeowner costs and housing costs for households in public housing are impossible to estimate. Thus, although we know that renters in the private market ended up spending more money on housing if they were in the experimental group, we do not know whether the same can be said with certainty for the other two groups.

Of course, the households participating in the experiment tended to be younger, have a lower proportion of homeowners, and have larger families than is characteristic of households in the tracts from which they were selected. Hence, these are households starting out initially with a depressed rate of homeownership at a point in their life cycles at which families ordinarily acquire homes. Experimental families well may have accelerated their home buying as a result of participation in the experiment.

The experimental effects on other types of consumption are not as clear or dramatic. Both Metcalf and Nicholson find that experimental families are more likely to acquire durable goods, particularly such appliances as washing machines and refrigerators. But other forms of consumption such as food, other durables, and clothing show inconsistent patterns: black families, for example, were less likely than whites to increase their consumption expenditures for food (eaten at home), according to Nicholson's analysis, but Metcalf could not substantiate such a finding in his analysis.[14]

The evaluation of these findings hinges upon two issues. First, because the data bases vary in quality, some of the findings are less plausible than others. A home purchase seems more solid a fact than, for example, house-

14. Not one of the authors directly addressed himself or herself to the issue of frivolous consumption. We do not know from the papers whether the appliances bought were more likely to be color television sets or washing machines, since durable goods were not specified in detail.

wives' estimates of amount spent on food consumption outside the home, so the home purchase behavior probably is more real. A second issue centers around whether these findings are in some sense artifacts to be found only in experiments. Here the main question seems to be whether similar behavior could be expected under a permanent negative income tax plan. Despite Metcalf's heroic attempts to solve this problem with a theoretical model of the relation between short-run experiments and long-range programs, it still remains to be settled in practice.

Another problem is the degree to which such effects are overestimated because of the particular characteristics of the families enlisted in the experiment in New Jersey and Pennsylvania. As noted earlier, these are large families headed by young parents, a group whose housing needs may have been especially poorly met by their preexperimental housing. A permanent nationwide program probably would contain higher proportions of older and smaller families, for whom improvement in housing might not enjoy as high a budget priority. Therefore, the dramatic responses shown in the experiment may be diluted considerably.

The findings concerning housing expenditures and durable purchases are among the firmest positive experimental effects to be found in the entire set of papers coming from the experiment. Assuming that such effects are both firm and characteristic of behavior under permanent plans, the policy implications are considerable. They indicate that a general income strategy might substantially improve the housing situations of the poor—assuming, of course, no compensating price effects that simply would raise the price of low-cost housing without providing material improvement.

Family Composition and Family Relationships

The family life of the poor has been brought into the limelight of public policy discussions by the considerable growth in a major social welfare program, Aid to Dependent Children, which was authorized in the original social security legislation of the 1930s. The ADC program, originally envisioned primarily for the support of orphans and children whose mothers had been deserted or divorced, provided categorical grants to fatherless family units. The rising number of female-headed households after World War II made this program—which became AFDC when support for the mother or caretaker was added—one of the major welfare programs in terms of coverage and funds expended.

Why such a growth in AFDC occurred in the postwar period is not at all clear. Some part of the reason was an increased ability of welfare departments to obtain better and more complete coverage of the eligible population. Some persons had claimed that the program offered a perverse incentive to family dissolution by restricting eligibility to fatherless households, but relaxation of this standard in the 1960s, in the AFDC-UP program, did not seem to halt the proliferation of fatherless households.

The issue of the perverse trends among poor families was injected into the politics of race relations by Daniel Patrick Moynihan's analysis of trends in family composition among blacks, a publication that made its author at once famous and infamous.[15] Moynihan's analysis of postwar trends suggested that the fragility of black families was an inheritance from slavery days augmented by the job and income insecurities of urban living.

In contrast to other areas of behavior discussed in this paper, there was no dearth of hard data on the characteristics of the poor in these respects. The rates of divorce, desertion, separation, and incomplete households clearly were inversely related to household income, occupational level, and educational attainment. Fertility data also have shown an inverse relation to socioeconomic levels, although this has been declining in recent decades.

It could be argued that a negative income tax program would have some impact upon these trends. On the one hand, because payments were not tied to qualitative aspects of family composition, the perverse incentives of some welfare programs would not operate.[16] Thus, participation in the plan could lessen the incidence of family dissolution. On the other hand, the plan had a possible natalist bias because the addition of children to a household raised its breakeven point and payments.

But the design of the New Jersey–Pennsylvania negative income tax experiment failed to provide a good test of either possibility. Eligibility requirements stipulated that families be intact at the beginning, and they were tied to household size. Newly formed households, by virtue of small size, were not likely to be eligible; and thus those families most subject to dissolution under normal circumstances were underrepresented. The households most likely to be eligible were those which already had survived the

15. Daniel P. Moynihan, *The Negro Family: The Case for National Action* (U.S. Department of Labor, Office of Policy Planning and Research, 1965).

16. Neither New Jersey nor Pennsylvania tied welfare eligibility to family composition. At the start of the experiment, New Jersey's welfare program rendered intact families ineligible, a rule that was relaxed shortly after the experiment got under way.

The rules under which experimental payments were divided in cases of family dissolution were set up to provide a continuity of support for individuals but did not recognize a reorganized household as eligible for payments on the same basis as other families of similar composition. Thus, a husband separating from his wife would take some part of the payments with him, but if he or his wife remarried, the newly constituted household would not be eligible for the purpose of payments.

early period of marital instability and had grown large enough to be poor—but were not yet old enough to undergo contraction as children left.

It can be argued that the rules of eligibility provided a set of families that were more stable than a more ecumenical selection would have provided, and also were families that tended to have completed their childbearing years.

DATA BASES. Changes in family composition were among the best measured of the variables. Each quarterly interview reviewed household membership, noting additions and subtractions. Interviews with housewives at the second quarter and each quarter thereafter asked about pregnancies and outcomes of terminated pregnancies.

On the more qualitative aspects of family life, the data bases are less extensive. A single item asked at preenrollment and in the fifth quarterly interview was designed to measure "husband and wife togetherness." A four-item family togetherness scale also administered at preenrollment and the fifth quarterly interview was constructed of such items as how often parents played with their children and took their children places and how often the family sat down to meals together. Finally, a family leisure scale—administered at the third, seventh, and eleventh quarters—measured whether family members went to the park or to the zoo, a restaurant, a movie, or a bar within two weeks prior to interviewing.

These scales hardly exhaust the measurement of family relationships. There is certainly more to family life than "doing things" together, even though "things" is a term vague enough to cover patchwork quilting or bizarre sexual practices. The considerable research tradition of family sociology is completely unrepresented both in the items used and in the bibliography of the paper in which these data were analyzed. Family sociology may not be a field that has attracted the best of empirically oriented sociologists, but a lot more is known about family cohesion than is represented in these items.

ANALYSES.[17] Two of the papers dealing with these issues employ familiar multiple regression techniques. Glen Cain's paper on fertility regresses pregnancy, newborn children, or both on a set of demographic variables and a set of experimental variables for second, sixth, and tenth

17. The papers reviewed are Jon Helge Knudsen, Robert A. Scott, and Arnold R. Shore, "Changes in Household Composition," Jack Ladinsky and Anna Wells, "Social Integration, Leisure Activity, Media Exposure, and Life Style Enhancement," and Glen G. Cain, "The Effect of Income Maintenance Laws on Fertility: Results from the New Jersey–Pennsylvania Experiment" (described as a preliminary analysis), in *Final Report of the New Jersey Experiment*, vol. 3, pt. D, chaps. 8, 6, and 7, respectively.

quarterly interview data. Jack Ladinsky and Anna Wells do much the same with respect to the measures of family integration.

The paper by Jon Helge Knudsen, Robert Scott, and Arnold Shore stands out among all the papers in the entire set by employing a very different mode of analysis. Having characterized each family unit as in one or another of several states of household composition—for example, nuclear family, extended family, female headed with children, and so on—the authors undertake a Markov chain analysis contrasting experimental and control families by the transition probabilities computed to account for changes from one household state to another over various periods of time. Households are disaggregated into subclasses on the basis of demographic characteristics: for example, race, educational attainment, preenrollment income, husband's age, generosity of plan, and the like.

It is difficult, at least for this reader, to discern what is going on in the Markov chain analysis presented in this paper. The parameters computed, being ratios of transition probabilities, have little directly interpretable meaning, and no tests of statistical significance are presented (although computed), a deficiency that makes it hard to know when to pay attention to a finding. More important, however, the necessity to form subclasses by the polytomization of continuous variables—for example, age of husband is divided into above and below age thirty-five—means that much information is thrown away and few stratifying classes can be used without running out of cases. Therefore, the effects shown are not the usual ones that are the net of a more or less uniformly employed set of background variables; rather, they are only the net of some subset treated crudely.

FINDINGS. None of these papers found significant and consistent experimental effects. Experimental treatments neither increased nor decreased fertility; nor did they affect probabilities of transition in family state; nor was family togetherness increased or decreased. Whatever variance was found is accounted for mainly by interindividual differences rather than as treatment effects.

Additional and more sophisticated analyses of these data—especially those relating to changes in family composition—might bring to light some experimental effect, although the likelihood of so doing is quite small. Especially unlikely are experimental effects on family togetherness measures, variables whose measurement leaves so much to be desired.[18]

18. It is difficult to judge whether the levels measured—fertility, family togetherness, probability of family composition change, and so on—are particularly high or low in relation to those of comparable groups. Ladinsky and Wells express surprise that these

Educational Effort of Adolescents

Because payments were tied to total family income and to household size in the New Jersey–Pennsylvania experiment, the labor force participation of young people could be expected to be affected by experimental treatments. From one point of view, young people whose wage rates are low may be especially affected by tax rates making leisure more attractive, assuming that their earned income is pooled with other sources of household income. From another point of view, young persons have the option of remaining or continuing in school, a leisure activity not immediately productive of income but one that can have some impact on future earnings. Experimental treatments therefore should make staying in school or resuming schooling more attractive to those youth in families receiving experimental treatments.

Sample selection and experimental design should provide a larger-than-usual proportion of adolescents in the experiment. The bias toward large families creates a higher probability of older children in the household, and actually about 20 percent of the households had at least one adolescent between sixteen and eighteen.[19] It is not clear what the impact of this factor is, but if we take seriously the findings in several researches that an increase in number of siblings has a steady, although minor, depressing effect on educational attainment,[20] then this is a group that is especially likely to discontinue its schooling early.

A person usually may leave school without being declared a truant at sixteen, but most young people remain in school beyond that point. A majority of most subgroups in the United States today completes high school, and a large minority goes on to some kind of postsecondary education. Therefore, although a sharp drop in school attendance occurs at

couples seem to be high on togetherness. Knudsen and others never present marginal frequencies on amount of family composition changes, nor does Cain compare his fertility data with those of some possible comparable group that is not in the experiment. If the experimental design did bias selection toward more stable families, the findings of Ladinsky and Wells are consistent with the interpretation, and we should also expect to find lower than expected rates of fertility and change in composition.

19. This statistic is calculated from the paper on which this subsection is based—Charles Mallar, "School Enrollment and Labor-Force Participation among Young Adults," in *Final Report of the New Jersey Experiment*, vol. 1, sec. 1, pt. B, chap. 4—and may be off base if many of the households had more than one adolescent in this age range.

20. James S. Coleman, Z. D. Blum, and P. H. Rossi, "Intra-Generational Occupational Mobility" (processed).

eighteen, when the largest proportion finishes high school, significant degrees of school attendance persist into the early twenties.

Given this pattern of school attendance, the critical years to observe for experimental effects encompass the age period from sixteen through at least twenty-one. In the first quarter of the experiment, 16 percent of the sixteen- to eighteen-year-olds are neither working nor in school, another 20 percent are working, and the remaining 64 percent are in school. In short, nearly two-thirds are continuing their educational effort during this age interval, presumably to move into the labor force at or after age eighteen.

I have emphasized this pattern of school attendance because the paper by Charles Mallar is based upon an analysis only of sixteen- to eighteen-year-olds, a group whose responses can be expected to be less sensitive to choices than the eighteen- to twenty-one-year-old group. Thus, the analysis presented represents a very conservative estimate of the effect of experimental treatments upon the labor force participation and school enrollment of young persons.[21]

DATA BASE. School attendance of young persons probably is underestimated because questions in the quarterly interviews directed at adults over sixteen in the household focused mainly on labor force participation and failed to include going to school full time as one of the several alternative responses. School attendance thus had to be volunteered as a special response category, and some or even many respondents may not have realized that going to school was an acceptable alternative response. (In addition, no follow-up question was asked on what sort of school was attended.)

ANALYSIS. Mallar assumes that the young people make two decisions: first, they decide whether or not they will participate in the labor force, go to school, or do neither; and, second, once they have decided that they will either go to school or work, they then decide between those two activities. This decision model leads him to present two forms of analysis: one attempts to discern experimental effects on the first decision; the other form is concerned with the second decision. The data are analyzed separately for each of three quarters by ordinary least squares as well as by probit analysis.

FINDINGS. Although experimental effects can be discerned for some subgroups during some quarters, no clear-cut patterns emerge for either nonlabor force participation or school enrollment. A possible slight effect

21. Mallar has reported that subsequent analyses beyond age eighteen indicate strong experimental effects.

appears for older young men, who are slightly more likely to stay in school. Thus, experimental treatments do not lead young people to drop out of the labor force nor do they bolster the retention ability of schools.

Again, it is difficult to interpret the findings. There are good reasons to suspect that analysis is conservatively biased and possibly applied to the wrong age group. Certainly, no drastic effects are perceived for young people who ordinarily would be in school.

Job Turnover, Duration of Unemployment, and Job Characteristics

The experimental effects on the earnings and work effort aspects of labor force participation are treated in another paper in this volume, but some effects can be expected in other aspects of work. In particular, experimental effects might be discerned in job turnover, with guarantees lessening the risks of temporary unemployment and perhaps subsidizing more productive job searches. In addition, qualitative aspects of the occupations and jobs are involved. Some jobs are more satisfying or provide more prestige than others having the same earnings.

The job turnover among participants in the experiment was quite high: at least 47 percent of the male household heads changed employers during the two-year span between preenrollment and the eighth quarterly interview.[22] Compared with the change of 38 percent over five years shown in the 1970 census for the New York–Newark combined standard metropolitan statistical areas, the experimental turnover rate of 47 percent is high.[23]

DATA BASES. At preenrollment and each subsequent quarter the job title and employer were ascertained for each adult sixteen or over. Respondents also were questioned about periods of unemployment in the three-month period covered by each quarter. In the paper by Seymour Spilerman and Richard Miller,[24] job turnover is measured by comparing the employer

22. This proportion refers to net change arrived at by comparing employers at the two periods and noting whether they were the same or different. If a person had changed employers several times in that period, the additional changes were not counted. Thus, the 47 percent turnover figure is a conservative lower limit.

23. The earnings of participants are considerably below the average for persons occupying the same occupations in the New York–Newark combined SMSAs, suggesting that participants may be holding marginal jobs in marginal occupations, and for these reasons are subject to greater job instability.

24. Seymour Spilerman and Richard E. Miller, "The Effect of Negative Tax Payments on Job Turnover and Job Selection," in *Final Report of the New Jersey Experiment*, vol. 1, sec. 2, pt. B, chap. 7.

at preenrollment with the employer at the eighth quarter. Extremely limited coding of occupational data unfortunately precluded the use of alternative definitions: for example, all job transitions for all quarterly periods might have been used.

In addition, Spilerman and Miller used outside sources of data to characterize the occupations held at both times. Data from Parnes's 1966 national longitudinal study of males were used to construct Duncan occupational status scores[25] and aggregate measures of job satisfaction in two dimensions—job content and financial rewards—for each occupational title. The 1 percent sample tape of the 1970 Census of Population yielded average earnings for each occupational title for job holders in the New York–Newark combined SMSAs and thus provides expected earnings for persons in roughly the same geographical region as participants in the sample.

These two outside data sets provided measures that were independent of the data set generated by the experiment and, thereby, variables that represent what Spilerman and Miller call the expected job characteristics of occupations held by participants. Comparison of participants with expected variables produced some surprising results. The most striking contrast is between participants' earnings and the expected earnings for persons holding those occupational titles among participants. The Census average earnings for persons in those occupations is $7,573, whereas earnings of participants in the experiment were only $4,001, or about 53 percent as large. Although participants may be younger than their fellow workers, the age difference and associated age-related earnings differentials cannot be large enough to account for this great disparity. Participants were on the bottom of the occupational structure in terms of the job titles they held, and even for those poor jobs they were being paid considerably less than was customary at the time.[26] Obviously, participants in the sample were very marginal indeed.

ANALYSIS. Regressions were run with job turnover, weeks unemployed, Duncan occupational status score, expected earnings, and expected job satisfaction levels as dependent variables. Experimental treatments were expressed in the regressions both in the spline formulation and as benefits

25. See the chapters by Otis Dudley Duncan in Albert J. Reiss, Jr., *Occupations and Social Status* (Free Press, 1961), pp. 109–61.

26. Of course, labor market differentials also are at work. Trenton, New Jersey, and Scranton, Pennsylvania, lie outside the New York–Newark combined SMSAs, but even within that SMSA, workers in New York City count more toward these SMSA averages than workers in the New Jersey experimental sites. It seems highly unlikely, however, that such area differences alone can account for the discrepancy.

defined as payments anticipated on the basis of the previous year's earnings—and, in the case of unemployment, as wife's earnings in the previous year.

FINDINGS. The authors find some of the few relatively strong occupational effects that have yet been uncovered in the reports. They find that the more generous the plan experienced, the less the probability of job turnover. Furthermore, occupations that have good expected job characteristics—earnings, occupational status, and job satisfaction—tend to retain their employees. These findings, taken together, suggest that the generous plans act as wage subsidies, elevating the ability of poorer jobs to retain their employees.

Regressing duration of unemployment in 1969–70 Spilerman and Miller find a slight tendency for persons in lower-earning occupations on generous support plans to have a shorter period of unemployment if they change jobs. They argue that this finding is consistent with the wage subsidy effect.

The experimental effects on expected job characteristics are complicated and not entirely clear.[27] The authors claim, however, that they discern two tendencies: first, younger persons tend to move to better jobs the more generous the treatment given to them; and, second, older persons tend to stay on in their jobs the more generous the experimental treatment. Perhaps young persons were using the payments to subsidize job transfers that improve their status and earnings, whereas older persons were using payments to fill out the deficiencies in their earnings.

The Spilerman-Miller paper points in some potentially quite productive directions. Their findings concerning job turnover and its functions for young and old workers are intriguing. The full data set, however, has been far from exhausted: many more job changes can be analyzed and other job characteristics might be looked into. The interpretations of the findings will be more plausible if they hold up under replication in the general set of job changes provided by the data.

Health

Health was viewed in the experiment from two perspectives: the impact of the health status of household members on their labor force efforts under

27. For example, comparisons between preenrollment and eighth quarterly expected earnings show that whites are reducing earnings whereas blacks are doing the opposite. But, when analysis is restricted to those persons present at both preenrollment and eighth quarter, the results are the opposite.

experimental treatment; and the impact of experimental treatments on health status. From the first perspective, leisure might be regarded as a more desirable good by those who are suffering from ill health, and the experimental treatment thus may decrease their work effort. From the second perspective, health may be affected by various changes in way of life afforded by experimental treatments, and health care may be regarded as another item of consumption.[28]

In the first case, the health status of an individual is a variable that changes the price of both leisure and work. In the second case, health care is conceived of as an effect similar to the consumption of housing and durables.

DATA BASES. The data used in both analyses[29] come from questions adapted from National Health Survey questionnaires. They ask—retrospectively over the previous period—about chronic conditions, number of days lost from work, number of days spent in hospital, number of physician visits, and the like.

For the analysis of the impact of health conditions on labor effort, a respondent was characterized as unhealthy if he or she claimed at least two chronic illnesses or was absent from work at least seven days in the year prior to the interview. By this definition, 32 percent of the sample were classified as unhealthy. It should be noted that this definition is contaminated by incorporating within itself labor force effort in the form of days lost from work.[30] Although this contamination may not be serious in the analysis of male household heads, it becomes quite serious in the analysis of wife's work effort. Because wives worked an average of about four weeks a year, the use of days lost from work as part of the definition of "unhealthy" leads to the anomalous finding that unhealthy wives work more than healthy wives.

Data on health and health care consist of simple counts of number of reported chronic conditions, days lost from work, physician visits, and so on.

28. Although asked for in some of the quarterly interviews, money spent on health care exclusive of insurance repayments was not used in the analyses reviewed here.

29. David Elesh and M. J. Lefcowitz, "The Effects of Health on the Supply of and Returns to Labor," and Lefcowitz and Elesh, "Experimental Effects on Health and Health Care Utilization," in *Final Report of the New Jersey Experiment*, vol. 1, sec. 2, pt. B, chap. 8, and vol. 3, pt. D, chap. 4, respectively.

30. The extent to which work effort and the definition of ill-health overlap is not clear. The authors report a correlation (gamma) of 0.575 between the number of chronic illnesses reported and the number of days lost from work, but this index does not provide a sufficiently specific measure of the degree of overlap between the two components of the definition. The seriousness of the contamination obviously depends on the degree of overlap.

ANALYSIS. For each of the three years of the experiment, earnings, number of hours worked, and hourly wages were regressed on the health parameters and a set of usual background factors. The experimental effects on health were studied by regressing the health parameter on each of the indexes referred to above and on the background factors.

FINDINGS. There is a decided effect on work effort of being healthy or unhealthy. Healthier persons earn more and work more hours than unhealthy persons. Three major experimental effects were found. First, the experimental effects were strongest during the first year of the experiment. Second, the lower the guarantee, the greater the difference in earnings between healthy and unhealthy household heads. Third, the higher the tax rate, the smaller the earnings difference between healthy and unhealthy household heads. Thus, the less generous the guarantee, the greater the divergence between healthy and unhealthy persons in the labor supply and work effort; but the less generous the tax rate, the more the two groups converge.

To make any sense out of these findings, to think of mechanisms— economic, sociological, or psychological—that would lead unhealthy individuals to work as much as healthy individuals under these conflicting circumstances, is indeed difficult.

The findings with respect to experimental effects on health status and health care utilization can be summed up in one word: nothing. There are no significant effects of experimental treatment on any of the indexes for household heads, their spouses, or the children.

The analyses and findings in these two papers leave much to be desired. One of the major problems is to define health conditions that are uncontaminated by work effort. It would seem to me that had the authors chosen to use only the number of chronic conditions as the definition of health, they would have been much better off when it came to the interpretation of effects.

Social Psychological Variables

Perhaps the most uniquely sociological and social psychological contribution to the data of the experiment was a set of scales designed to measure variables of a more purely sociological and social psychological type. Some of the measures refer to social bonds between the respondent and other people, others refer mainly to states of morale, and still others are counts of common psychosomatic symptoms.

Nothing seems more firmly established in the nearly half century of field surveys than the ever present but modest correlations between measures of socioeconomic status—income, occupation status, educational attainment—and a large number of such sociological and social psychological measures. The higher the social status of the individual, the more he reports he is happy and feels contented with the political system; he exhibits fewer psychosomatic symptoms, worries less, has higher self-esteem, experiences less anomy,[31] has a higher sense of being in control of his fate and destiny, is more satisfied with his job, income, and life in general, has more friends, belongs to more organizations, and even sees more of his relatives.

The literature upon which this generalization is based often shows only that poor people are worse off in one or more of these respects than the more affluent. The size of the relation and its ability to withstand testing for spuriousness often is not shown in detail. The zero-order correlations involved appear to be 0.2 to 0.3, computed over a fairly wide range of socioeconomic status. Of course, the relation would be considerably lowered were one to compute over a restricted range of socioeconomic status, either on the high or low side of the status distribution. Therefore, there is every reason to expect that, within the narrow range of socioeconomic status represented among families selected for eligibility under the experiment, relations of these variables to socioeconomic status are likely to hover around zero. Shifting families around within this range by experimental treatments probably would not produce noticeable effects.

More important, these variables are supposed to measure relatively steady states of individuals. Psychosomatic symptoms, for example, are supposed to reflect psychic conditions of neurosis or even psychosis, which supposedly are characteristics that are difficult to change and not subject to easy manipulation through any sort of therapy. To expect that experimental treatments would affect such states is to violate such a view of what these conditions are supposed to represent.[32]

Two of the three relevant papers[33] regard these variables as possibly

31. Anomy is characterized by a feeling that norms and standards are in a state of great flux.

32. Of course, empirical evidence on the correlations across quarterly interviews indicates that they are far from steady states. For example, Ladinsky and Wells report inter-quarterly correlations ranging from 0.02 to 0.203 for measures of sociability. Jack Ladinsky and Anna Wells, "Social Integration, Leisure Activity, Media Exposure, and Life Style Enhancement," in *Final Report of the New Jersey Experiment*, vol. 3, pt. D, chap. 6, p. D-VI-13.

33. Ladinsky and Wells, "Social Integration," Russell Middleton and Vernon L. Allen, "Social Psychological Consequences of the Graduated Work Incentive Experiment," and Sonia Wright, "Social Psychological Characteristics and Labor-Force

being affected by experimental treatments, while one considers the social psychological variables as mediating between experimental treatments and labor force response.

DATA BASES. The data are derived mainly from short scales posed to male household heads in the form of attitudinal questions. A few examples probably can best capture the flavor of these questions:

—How much do you worry about the possibility of losing your job? (Worry a lot, worry a little, or don't worry?)

—I feel that I have a number of good qualities. (Agree strongly, agree, disagree, or disagree strongly?)

—Have you felt irritable, nervous, or fidgety (in the last month)? (Often, a few times, once or twice, or never?)

—What is lacking in the world today is the old kind of friendship that lasted for a lifetime. (Agree strongly, agree slightly, disagree slightly, or disagree strongly?)

—How often do you see relatives? (Nearly every day, once a week, every couple of weeks, monthly or less?)

The scales have been used principally by other investigators and have some standing in the literature of social psychology. Some have had considerable practical use: for example, the psychosomatic symptom list was developed during World War II as a screening device to detect soldiers who were likely to break down under battlefield conditions, and it has been used in several major epidemiological studies of mental health. Middleton and Allen and Wright further refined some of the scales by factor analysis of items from a number of different scales, using as final scales only those which showed up as distinctly different from others in the final rotated factor matrix.

Used with the participant population, most of these scales had very low reliability from one interview to the next, with correlations of about 0.20 (according to Middleton and Allen). Reliability measures constructed on the basis of internal consistency among items belonging to each scale also yielded low coefficients for most scales.

It is difficult to take these measures seriously, especially when they are used with a very poor population of low educational attainment.[34] Often the scales used were shortened versions of the scales originally developed.

Response of Male Heads," in *Final Report of the New Jersey Experiment*, vol. 3, pt. D, chap. 6, pt. D, chap. 5, and vol. 1, sec. 2, pt. B, chap. 9, respectively.

34. Average educational attainment for male household heads participating was about ten years, indicating that the typical participant was a high school dropout.

Response categories were crude. Face validity, although viewed as sufficient by Middleton and Allen, since the questions generally were direct and straightforward, seems to this author to be less than obvious.

ANALYSIS. Scale scores used were simple summations of answers to items in each scale. More sophisticated scoring schemes correlate very highly with the procedure used, according to Middleton and Allen.

Each of the papers used a slightly different approach. Perhaps the most elaborate was that used by Middleton and Allen, who first factor analyzed the items to purify scales, then regressed experimental variables and background factors on the purified scale scores. They also attempted several path analyses, the most elaborate of which used canonical correlation techniques to compute path coefficients for unmeasured variables.

Wright's paper also began with a factor analysis of items, using the purified scales as regressors on labor force measures, along with experimental parameters and background factors.

Jack Ladinsky and Anna Wells simply regressed their scale scores on experimental parameters and background factors.

FINDINGS. All three papers found that these variables had no discernible consistent effect on earnings and work effort, and they were unaffected by experimental treatments. Middleton and Allen end their paper on a slightly upbeat note, stating that the results of the analysis indicated that experimental treatments neither improved those who were subjected to them nor worsened their social psychological states.

It is difficult to take these analyses seriously. The measures used are simply bad measures of anything, as indicated by their low internal consistency reliabilities and low correlations between interviews. In addition, there was no particular reason to expect that the experimental treatments would affect such outcomes, even if measured well, since previous literature contains little evidence that such variables are sensitive to income differentials in a narrow range of incomes. Finally, although I am certain that such concepts as self-esteem and anomy have some utility, I have strong doubts that they are tapped by the measurement devices used here.

Whither?

Although many of the papers reviewed here are characterized explicitly by their authors as intermediate drafts, further analyses probably will change the results very little. The marginal returns from additional work on such analyses decline steeply: the main results of surveys usually can be obtained very quickly; additional work may clarify relations found initially but are unlikely to turn findings around. Moreover, there are serious problems with the basic measurement of many of the variables treated in the experiment.

Three of the analyses can be improved by reworking the existing data set. The analysis of educational effort of young people ought to be extended to those critical years beyond age eighteen during which additional schooling is more problematic than finishing high school. Perhaps experimental treatments did allow more of the young people in the experimental families to pursue vocational education, attend community colleges, or go on to four-year colleges and universities. The Markov chain analysis of family composition changes appears to ignore much of the richness in the data for outcome variables that are probably very well measured. Finally, purging the definition of health from contamination with work effort might help to resolve the seemingly contradictory findings concerning the work effort and earnings of healthy as against unhealthy male household heads.

Aside from complaints and misgivings about the data analyzed in these papers, are there some lessons to be learned? It seems to me that in this regard three major sets of statements can be made.

First, interdisciplinary research is not accomplished by hiring persons from diverse disciplinary backgrounds. Despite the less than striking performance of the sociologists and social psychologists on the experiment, as evidenced in some of the papers reviewed here, these disciplines could have been used more fruitfully in a condition of close collaboration rather than one of semi-independence. Particularly important would have been the collaboration on the further elaboration of the measurement of work, jobs, and occupations. The Spilerman-Miller paper on job turnover provides some evidence of the potential productivity of such a collaboration for economists.

Second, some of the analyses throw light on possibly unanticipated consequences and attendant limitations of the experimental design. For example, how typical of families that would be eligible under a national program are those made eligible for this experiment? Persistent and unexplainable intersite differences raise questions about an experimental strategy that opted for test bores in a very small number of sites as opposed to broader coverage of a state or region or even of the country as a whole. The rules of eligibility yielded a sample of participants who held jobs paying wages far below those typical of comparable jobs in the New York–Newark combined SMSAs, and the sample contained relatively young household heads and rather large households. The levels of home and car ownership were much lower than was characteristic of the Census tracts from which the households were drawn. In short, it appears that participants were unusually marginal families who managed to remain intact—and therefore eligible—despite their marginality.

Third, there are several positive findings. Little evidence emerged that the experimental treatments had any perverse effects. In many instances, there were no differences in presumed effects between experimental and control groups. As Middleton and Allen put it, experimental treatments did not raise the participants' levels of self-esteem, but neither did they lower such levels. Where effects were shown, as in the case of housing, job turnover, and consumption of durables, participants apparently used benefits in ways that raised their levels of living, at least as far as housing and home amenities were concerned.

BETTE S. MAHONEY

W. MICHAEL MAHONEY

Policy Implications:
A Skeptical View

The New Jersey–Pennsylvania income maintenance experiment was conceived, designed, and conducted by people who tend to favor a negative income tax. This is not to say that the design, conduct, or analysis was in any way tailored to favor such a tax. The experiment was conducted with a remarkable degree of objectivity and there is no doubt that, had the results not confirmed prior expectations, they would have been treated in much the same manner as in fact the favorable results have been.

The two principal objectives of the experiment were to explore the issues related to labor supply that are posed by a negative income tax and to demonstrate scientifically that a negative income tax would not produce a large-scale reduction in the labor force. The direct policy implications of the experiment relate to issues of work incentives and the question of the probable cost of a negative income tax. But although the importance of the labor supply effects of a negative income tax has been stressed repeatedly, little attention has been paid to the way in which such knowledge could be incorporated into policy. The first section of this paper is an attempt to remedy this deficiency. The second is a discussion of what the experiment tells us about the design of a negative income tax program.

No single experiment or research effort could hope to address all issues relevant to income maintenance policy. But the concentration on one aspect of the income maintenance policy debate—labor supply—will limit the impact of the experiment. In this context, the third section of this paper examines the New Jersey experiment as an example of research in social policy.

The Optimal Tax Rate

From the time a negative income tax was first seriously proposed, the appropriate marginal tax rate has been considered a critical feature. The lower the rate, the greater the number who will be eligible for benefits and, other things constant, the greater will be the cost. The lower the rate, however, the more also financial disincentives for work are minimized, and the less likely it is that higher payments will result from reduced earnings. The first part of this section discusses what the appropriate tax rate would be if only work effort and program cost are considerations; the second part, whether other considerations, especially equity, also should play a part.

Guarantees and Tax Rates, Labor Supply and Cost

Both the level of the guarantee and the marginal tax rate—that is, the tax in cents deducted from the guarantee for each dollar of additional income—may affect work effort, but the tax rates have received the most attention—from the conservative Milton Friedman and the liberal James Tobin alike. Tobin argues for minimal standards of assistance to keep families from falling below the poverty line; that "the schedule of benefits . . . must provide incentives to work" is another and separate principle.[1] Friedman says about the marginal tax rate that "fifty percent is too high. I should prefer less."[2] Throughout the professional literature on income maintenance policy the pattern is the same: it is through marginal tax rates that the issue of work disincentive is addressed.[3] In contrast, most of the concern of politicians has been over the incentive effect of guarantees.

From the mid-1960s to date, proponents of the negative income tax have stressed the importance of low tax rates by highlighting the presumed 100 percent rate in existing welfare programs. They also stressed the universal coverage of their proposal by highlighting the presumed exclusion from

1. James Tobin, "First Lecture," *Welfare Programs: An Economic Appraisal*, Rational Debate Seminar Series (American Enterprise Institute for Public Policy Research, 1968), p. 16.

2. Milton Friedman, "The Case for a Negative Income Tax: A View from the Right" (paper prepared for the National Symposium on Guaranteed Income, Chamber of Commerce of the United States, December 1966; processed). Friedman nonetheless opted for a 50 percent rate because, in the logic of his form of negative income tax, lower rates would have meant inadequate benefits for families without income.

3. This is a reference to the policy discussions; the New Jersey experiment had greater variation in guarantee levels than in marginal tax rates.

assistance of the working poor. In fact, neither of these views of the existing welfare system was completely correct. Nonetheless, the hallmark features of the negative income tax came to be that it provides for a marginal tax rate of less than 100 percent and for coverage of the working poor.

The perceived need to have low marginal tax rates is evident in the design of the New Jersey experiment: no treatment group was subject to a marginal rate higher than 70 percent, and in determining the number of recipients to be assigned to the various plans, it was assumed that policy interest in 50 percent rates was more than three times greater than in 70 percent rates.[4] Thus, the design of an experiment to determine the labor supply response to different marginal tax rates incorporated the assumption that a 50 percent rate was likely to be preferable from the standpoint of social policy. The basis for this assumption is not clear.

The problem of the tax rate has been posed by many critics as one of providing work incentives. Work incentives would be as cheaply provided by a low guarantee or by having no program at all. A program that gives people income for which they do not work necessarily discourages work and does not encourage it. Thus, the real problem is how to mitigate or offset the disincentives that are inherent in the very nature of assistance programs. Further, what we are really concerned with is not disincentives or incentives as such but the behavior they induce—in this case, work. Whether or not the economic disincentives present in varying degrees in different income maintenance plans are offset by psychological, sociological, or other incentives is an empirical question that the experiment, the cross-sectional studies, and other research have attempted to answer. The constant references to the need for low tax rates have obscured this important point.

But why all the concern about work? Beyond the fact that this is a major concern of politicians, there are two main reasons. The first is because of an interest in program cost; the second is because of the common view that it is better for most people to work than not to.

EFFICIENCY AND COST. A basic objective of income transfer programs for workers is to raise their income, not relieve the necessity for work. If guaranteeing a worker a minimal income means that he will quit and be no better off, why bother? But when the program covers a large group of people, some of whom are expected to work and some not, but between whom there is no easy dividing line, the problem is more complicated. The

4. See the paper by Felicity Skidmore, "Operational Design of the Experiment," in this volume.

possibility of paying somebody more than he deserves—in the sense that the person should be working and receiving less subsidy—is unavoidable. If workers do quit or reduce their work effort, then either the program will cost more than otherwise would be the case or the guarantee will be less.

Because funds available for alleviating poverty or for other public purposes are limited, it is appropriate to consider ways of reducing unintended side effects that make the program less efficient than it could be. Relatively low marginal tax rates have been the generally recommended method of keeping workers from quitting. If the objective of the program is simply to raise the incomes of the poor, then the marginal tax rate should be set at that level which for a given cost would produce the highest possible guarantee. This objective may not imply lower rates. Lowering marginal tax rates might not produce sufficiently greater work effort to make transfer costs go down: for this to happen, work effort has to be fairly sensitive to the tax rate. In this sense, efficiency in a negative income tax is more likely to require a high rather than a low rate; and to determine the optimal rate would require knowledge about both the income distribution and the labor supply response.

WORK AS AN INTRINSIC GOOD. Though efficiency criteria imply high marginal tax rates—even as high as 100 percent—a desire to maximize work effort may prompt lower ones.

Increases and decreases in the gross national product traditionally have been regarded as net gains or losses for society at large: if someone works, it is good for us all. But for the individual taxpayer, the total national product is not of interest, only his share in it. Those who must pay taxes so that the earnings of others may be supplemented have the right to ask what they gain from any work that is thereby induced. If the individual whose income is supplemented works more but also consumes more, no direct benefit may accrue to the taxpayer.

A fear also may exist that the supply of low-wage, unskilled workers and the relatively cheap goods and services they produce will be diminished. To the extent that this fear actually is realized, a true economic loss occurs. The extent of the loss is difficult to measure, however, because people's consumption patterns will change as prices and income change. On the other hand, to the extent that people with higher incomes pay more to employ the lowest paid under a negative income tax, the income distribution will change in a progressive fashion.

It may be that work effort is viewed as a good in its own right for a complex set of reasons, including the puritan ethic and other philosophies of life that hold idleness to be immoral and offensive. But society has not found idleness so offensive that it discourages it with methods beyond economic sanctions and peer-group pressure. It may be that society is willing to accept the degree of idleness that now prevails—but would be unwilling to accept more.

Moral and ethical concern about people who seek to live at the expense of others focuses primarily on a dichotomy of work versus no work. Programs designed to induce more work from those already working might not be considered as attractive as those which produce more workers. Few persons would argue for expensive incentive features solely on the basis that less expensive schemes would discourage overtime and dual job holding. This means that, in examining the sensitivity of labor supply to marginal tax rates and guarantee levels, it is essential, first, to distinguish between outright entries into, or withdrawals from, the labor force and mere additions or reductions in effort; and, second, to specify precisely what kinds of additional work effort are being sought.

This issue is even more complex when the question of secondary workers, part-time workers, and length of job searches is considered. It seems unlikely that many persons would wish to commit funds for the sole purpose of inducing more work effort from secondary workers.

In brief, we do not know how or even whether work as an intrinsic good is preferred by a majority in society. Society clearly should not spend beyond the level at which no additional work is induced: paying for expensive incentive features that do not affect behavior makes no sense. That lower marginal tax rates will bring about a greater total work effort is not at all clear. Modest reductions in the marginal rate faced by people below the original breakeven point will require larger increases in the rate for the newly eligible above it, who previously had been subject only to the positive income tax. Suppose that it is proposed that 80 percent tax rates in a plan with a $4,000 guarantee be reduced to 50 percent. This would represent a 38 percent reduction in the rate faced by those originally eligible. But if the rate above the breakeven point had been 20 percent, there would be a 150 percent increase for the newly eligible.

Marginal Tax Rates and Tax Equity

In recent years, two reasons unrelated to labor supply have been suggested for preferring low tax rates in a negative income tax: first, that high rates conflict with the requirements of vertical equity; and, second, that it is unfair to tax the earnings of the poor. Both are intuitively appealing arguments; both are wrong.

The concept of vertical equity developed out of taxation theory and is generally expressed as "those who earn more should end up with more." But there is nothing in this concept that serves as a guide to how much more. Thus, a marginal tax rate of 99 percent would satisfy the requirements of vertical equity. The concept is more correctly expressed as "those who earn more should not end up with less." The word "equity" connotes fairness and justice, concepts that are deeply embedded in the fabric of our society but that nonetheless are ambiguous.[5]

The meaning of the term "tax rate" also has become troublesome during the debate over welfare reform. The term can refer to average or marginal taxes. In the context of a negative income tax, families have usually been viewed as paying a positive tax if they were above the breakeven point, nothing if they were at that point, and a negative tax if they were below. This view refers to average taxes; the family faces positive marginal tax rates below, at, and above the breakeven point, rates that were regarded as high below the breakeven and low above it. We believe more attention should be given to average tax rates, which show who pays and who receives and thus provide a more comprehensive picture of the nation's tax and transfer system. This also would clarify certain of the equity issues associated with tax rates in the welfare reform debate.

In this debate, it has been argued that only the rich and the poor face high marginal tax rates and that this is unfair to the poor. But in terms of average tax rates, the poor are net recipients of transfers and their average tax rate is negative, which by definition is not high. People who complain that the poor face high marginal tax rates under a benefit program are, in effect, taking the program's guarantee for granted. When a recipient works, the welfare benefits he forgoes as his payments are reduced are tantamount to taxes paid. But all families, not just those receiving reduced benefits, must be considered to have forgone welfare benefits—in effect, to have been subject to a tax. In this view, families from just above the breakeven point to quite far up the scale of income distribution also face high average tax rates.[6]

5. See Martin Bronfenbrenner, "Equality and Equity," *Annals of the American Academy of Political and Social Science*, vol. 409 (September 1973), pp. 9–23; and John Rawls, *A Theory of Justice* (Harvard University Press, 1971).

6. Consider a negative income tax with a $4,000 guarantee and a 50 percent marginal tax rate. At the breakeven point of $8,000, the net additional disposable income over and above the guarantee is only $4,000. Similarly, if the marginal rate of taxation were 20 percent, a family with $10,000 of earnings will have only $6,000 more disposable income *less* the $400 it would pay in positive taxes. Thus, in terms of disposable income, a family with

The problem of taxing the earnings of the poor is a sensitive matter, it being perhaps the mark of civilized society that income taxes are not to be imposed on the destitute. Surely in our wealthy society there is no need to require the poor to share in the cost of public programs. It is a virtue of an income tax over other forms of taxes that the poor can be exempted. But there is no similar virtue in a negative income tax; a positive marginal tax is a necessary condition thereto. In fact, high rates concentrate expenditures on the poorest of the poor, whereas low rates mean that funds will go to the less poor—sometimes to those who clearly are not poor. If fairness is measured by the proportion of the expenditures received by the poor, high tax rates are fair, and low tax rates may be viewed as part of a policy to alter the shape of income distribution considerably beyond the poverty level.

If there are no arguments in equity or in efficiency for low tax rates, are there any others? It has been suggested that marginal tax rates may cause such other behavior as welfare cheating or marital instability. If society wants more or less of such behavior, that fact certainly can be considered in setting marginal tax rates, provided the incentive has some empirical, as well as theoretical, substance.

Implications for the Design of a Negative Income Tax

The New Jersey experiment was a partial simulation of a negative income tax. From its results can be drawn inferences about the appropriate tax rate for a negative income tax. Inferences also can be drawn about other aspects of income maintenance policy. There are some things the experiment can tell us about welfare policy and some that it cannot.

The Marginal Tax Rate

Suppose that the information generated by the New Jersey experiment provides the basis for the design of a negative income tax. Setting aside the need for information on other issues and the important question of whether the results truly reflect the impact of a full-scale, permanent program, the New Jersey results can be summarized in this manner: A negative

---

$10,000 of earnings has only $5,600 more than another family with no earnings. On this basis, the $10,000 family may be regarded as having been subject to a 44 percent average tax rate.

income tax with guarantees at or near the poverty level and marginal tax rates between 30 percent and 50 percent will cause a reduction in the amount of labor supplied by low-income households of about 5 percent, certainly no more than 10 percent. Within the stipulated range, differences in the marginal tax rate do not cause different labor supply response. Secondary workers will reduce their work effort more than primary workers. Overall, reductions in work effort do not come from outright withdrawal from the labor force but through reduced hours of work, dual job holding, and to some extent slightly longer periods of unemployment.

In line with the arguments of the preceding section, these results clearly suggest that the marginal tax rate should be at least 50 percent—presuming, of course, that the income of eligibles would not be subject to other taxes. This conclusion can be reached without reference to income distribution data for both objectives of efficiency and work inducement; it follows from the finding that different tax rates produce no differences in labor supply.

Could the tax rate be higher than 50 percent? Unfortunately, because of contamination of the 70 percent treatment by other welfare programs and failure to include treatments at even higher tax levels, the experiment provides little basis for inferences about the labor supply responses to rates higher than 50 percent. Nonetheless, to oppose a higher tax rate, one would have to believe that it would cause a sharp increase in labor supply withdrawal.

Tax rates higher than 50 percent might produce some cost savings and some further reductions in work effort among eligibles, although perhaps not a net reduction in work effort. In any event, so long as additional reductions were to manifest themselves as modest reductions in hours worked and dual job holding and not in withdrawal from the labor force by primary workers, they probably would not be considered socially undesirable.

The Work Requirement

In the traditional form of a negative income tax there would be no such thing as a work requirement: that is, benefits would depend solely on income and not on work status. This controversial feature of the negative income tax is deemed essential by proponents but provides the basis for opposition from others. The experiment was not designed to illuminate discussions of the feasibility or desirability of a work requirement. Nonetheless, its findings that the poor have relatively strong labor force attachment, like similar findings in the past, have been used to support the view that work requirements are not necessary, thus perpetuating a misconception of the role and possible effectiveness of a work requirement.[7]

Surely, if an income assistance program produced large-scale withdrawal from the labor force and efforts to beat the system were widespread, no army of bureaucrats could enforce a work requirement. If the reverse were true—that is, if there were few efforts to get away with something—a work requirement very well could be designed and administered in a manner that was equitable and firm and preserved public faith in the program. The New Jersey results strongly suggest this possibility.

To maintain program integrity, a work requirement may be considered essential regardless of the rate of marginal tax. A work requirement also may offset some disincentive effects of higher marginal tax rates. If the real policy alternatives lay between, first, a modest guarantee, a relatively low tax rate, and no work requirement and, second, a generous guarantee, a high tax rate, and a work requirement, the not-so-poor, who would receive income supplements with a low tax rate, might side with those who oppose the work requirement. But it seems likely that the very poor would agree with the general public and endorse a work requirement.[8]

Compound Marginal Tax Rates

Much has been written recently about the high marginal tax rates that can result when several programs condition their benefits on income. There is no reason to assume, however, that the disincentive effects of an all-cash program would be the same as a combination of cash and in-kind programs, even where the apparent marginal rates are the same. There is, in fact, some reason to believe that the disincentives from a combination program might be less. For example, if a family's income increases to the point at which the family felt it could afford better housing than is available in public housing programs, it might disregard the loss in housing benefits. An individual going to work where he would participate in an employer-subsidized health insurance program may substantially discount his loss of medicaid benefits.

7. See U.S. Department of Health, Education, and Welfare, "Summary Report: New Jersey Graduated Work Incentive Experiment" (1973; processed), p. 45.

8. The level of guarantee constitutes the actual work requirement. An administrative work requirement is only a device to lower or eliminate the guarantee when an able-bodied individual refuses to work.

Enough of this kind of reasoning can be developed to suggest that the very attempt to calculate arithmetically the compound rate of in-cash and in-kind programs is futile. The differing participation rates associated with in-kind programs also are important. "Selection-out" by participants at higher levels of income generally is thought to be more commonly associated with in-kind than with in-cash programs. If this is true, programs otherwise similarly designed will differ in the degree to which their benefits are distributed to the poorest households.

Discussions of the advantages of cash benefits over in-kind benefits have focused on maximizing utility to the recipients and, more recently, on maximizing the utility to both taxpayers and recipients taken together. The political attractiveness of in-kind programs is well known, of course, and many have acknowledged that they would prefer having in-kind programs to assist the poor rather than having no program at all. The point here is somewhat different: in-kind benefits may provide greater total benefits to the poorest households because the nonparticipation of those with higher incomes will allow more generous benefits to the poor. This important area of debate is one to which the experiment contributes little. It is, in fact, an area that has become much more important since the experiment was launched.

Cost of a Negative Income Tax

A third and final topic that the experiment tells us little about is the increase in transfer cost that would be associated with the adoption of a negative income tax. This is the result in part of the existence of a nearly universal food stamp program that already may have caused some of the labor supply effects that would be associated with a negative income tax, and in part of the ambiguity of the results. In addition, a nationwide negative income tax would include numerous groups that were not eligible under the experiment. Moreover, shifting from a food stamp program to a cash program might increase participation, but the results of the New Jersey experiment cannot be used to estimate the extent of the increase.

The New Jersey Experiment as Policy Research

At the time it was undertaken, the New Jersey experiment was among the government's most ambitious and expensive projects in social policy research. With the advantage of hindsight, the experiment now provides us some important information about experiments in particular and about policy research in general. The following paragraphs contain a discussion of some of what has been learned.

Some Lessons for Planning

In their overview of the New Jersey results, Rees and Watts say: "If there were people who expected our experimental treatment to cause large declines in the [labor force] participation rates of male heads of households, they were not in our research group."[9] It seems likely that neither were they in the HEW or OEO offices sponsoring the experiment. Why, then, was an expensive program of experimentation in income maintenance programs undertaken?

First, those persons who were urging the enactment of a negative income tax felt that it was necessary to obtain better proof that the labor force effects would be acceptable; but "how much" would be considered acceptable was never defined.[10] Moreover, whatever the anticipated levels, they were expected to vary from one marginal tax rate to another—but just how they would vary was not set forth. Why 100, 90, and 80 percent marginal tax rates were expected to produce unacceptable levels of withdrawal, whereas a 50 percent rate would not, is unclear.

If the arguments of the first section have any merit, relatively high marginal tax rates might be preferable to low rates. Both by design and by accident, the New Jersey experiment provides little information about the impact of higher tax rates. The impact of the experiment may be limited because policymakers may choose to defer decisions until such information does become available. Certainly, one requirement for an effective experiment must be a thorough examination of all the policy alternatives and issues.

Second, in the view of its advocates, the proof that disincentive effects of a negative income tax were small had to be rigorous. This implied careful use of controls rather than the less formal and less expensive demonstrations and analyses of program data. Moreover, the results had to be quan-

9. See Albert Rees and Harold W. Watts, "An Overview of the Labor Supply Results," in this volume.
10. It would be ironic if those who opposed the negative income tax because of fear about work effort actually expected the same amount of labor force withdrawal as those who supported it.

titative: it was essential to measure the disincentive effects as well as to make a judgment as to whether they were large or small. Finally, the results had to show the impact of variations in guarantees and tax rate.

The failure to exploit the research potential inherent in existing programs is in part attributable to this preference for the "rigorous proof of experimentation" and in part to ignorance about such programs. To our knowledge, neither the AFDC-UP program nor the state-run working-poor programs—some of which have 100 percent marginal tax rates and some of which do not—have received anything remotely approaching the investment of funds, talent, and effort that have been expended on the experiments and cross-sectional analyses in the negative income tax program. Ignorance about these programs also may have contributed to undue concern about labor supply response. Much of the information about how existing programs actually operate, which the experiment was to reveal, was and is readily available without resorting to experimentation. Certainly, before experimentation is undertaken, other potential sources of information should be fully explored and analyzed.

As to the rigor of experimentation, rigor may have been unattainable or unnecessary. Questions about the feasibility of simulating a full-scale, permanent national program with a short-term, random, local experiment were raised from the very beginning. These questions never were answered and have been reinforced by the ambiguities and paradoxes of the experimental results. Moreover, if small declines in labor supply are expected, small differences among different treatments also must be expected. For policy purposes, once it is known that the differences will be small, there is no great value in knowing exactly how small. For firm evidence that the decline would be small, analysis of existing programs, coupled with a set of demonstrations, could have been performed more quickly and less expensively.

Third, recent research suggests that the costs of a negative income tax are not sensitive to changes in labor supply.[11] At least for the types of plans that generally have been advocated, greater precision in cost estimates than is offered by the experiment could be obtained by improving data sources and exploring other factors affecting cost, such as the propensity of program eligibles to participate. For example, the supplementary security in-

11. Ralph D. Husby, "Work Incentives and the Cost Effectiveness of Income Maintenance Programs," *Quarterly Review of Economics and Business*, vol. 13 (Spring 1973), pp. 7–13.

come program has had fewer applicants than were estimated: either its data bases, the participation rate assumptions, or both were in error.

The Contribution of the New Jersey Experiment

The New Jersey experiment already has had an impact. It has made experimentation in the social sciences respectable and has helped spawn not only three other income maintenance experiments but also an elaborate program of experiments in housing allowances and in health insurance. It has had other impact as well. During the first round of hearings on the family assistance plan, the House Ways and Means Committee invited Harold Watts, Lee Bawden, and David Kershaw to testify in executive session. One of the authors was present throughout the hearings, and it seemed to him that their testimony was an invaluable contribution: a program similar to the family assistance plan, although on a much smaller scale, actually was being run, and no abrupt withdrawals from the labor force had been observed; possibly the concern about work incentive was misplaced.

The experiment demonstrated another value of experimenting before implementing: the opportunity to think through the multitude of administrative and definitional problems associated with turning an idea into an actuality. The experience of the New Jersey experiment, augmented by the experience of the states in operating existing welfare programs, will furnish the basis for the administrative features of any new program.

What about the future impact? Unfortunately, the program of experiments concentrated on negative income tax programs to the virtual exclusion of alternative approaches to income maintenance. Therefore, although we now have a great deal more information about the operation and labor supply effects of a negative income tax, we have little additional information about alternatives. Proponents of programs as diverse as wage subsidies, guaranteed employment, family or children's allowances, and expanded social insurance may feel that it would be appropriate to have more information available about such proposals before this country selects its course on an income maintenance policy. This fact alone will temper the impact of the experiment.

Moreover, additional information is needed about negative income tax programs, including data regarding:

—The employability of female heads of families

—The design and potential effectiveness of work requirements
—The programmatic impact and equity implications of alternative accounting periods
—The effect of compound marginal tax rates, especially where they result from in-kind transfer programs
—The effect of taxing income aside from wages and salaries
—Ways to vary guarantee levels by family size
—How and whether to supplement a negative income tax or its alternatives with a program to meet emergency and special needs

What these additional needs clearly suggest is that for a social experiment to have a truly significant impact on the policy development process, it must be part of comprehensive and balanced programs of research and analysis.

But in terms of what it set out to do—to illuminate labor supply effects—what has the experiment accomplished? That cash assistance will encourage the poor not to work is a deep-seated fear, a depressingly constant theme of discussions of welfare policy stretching back beyond Elizabethan poor law. For all practical purposes, the statement that the able-bodied poor should not be given welfare can be as much a moral dictum as it is a corollary to an economic prediction. It seems unlikely that the New Jersey results will still such fears: too many questions can be raised about the validity of the experiment. In 1968, Guy Orcutt and Alice Orcutt suggested that the successes of experimentation in the biological and physical sciences would lead the public to accept experimentation in the social sciences.[12] But accepting experimentation and accepting results as reported by the experimenters are not the same thing. Those persons who originally believed that there would be small disincentive effects may well accept the New Jersey results, whereas many of those who believed otherwise may well remain unconverted.

Conclusion

The New Jersey experiment was undertaken at a time when many economists assumed a priori that low marginal tax rates were preferable to high and had favorable implications for labor supply. With respect to program

12. Guy H. Orcutt and Alice G. Orcutt, "Incentive and Disincentive Experimentation for Income Maintenance Policy Purposes," *American Economic Review*, vol. 58 (September 1968), pp. 754–72.

cost, however, high tax rates may be preferable. Moreover, low tax rates do not lead unambiguously to increases in labor supply. But unfortunately, the design of the experiment was dictated by the assumption of the times.

The experiment was undertaken to prove that a negative income tax would not induce large-scale withdrawal from the labor force; to measure the difference in responses to different combinations of guarantees and marginal tax rates; and to provide the basis for estimating the cost of a national program. But for purposes of policy formulation, existing programs or demonstrations could be just as suitable for stilling unwarranted fears about labor supply; small differences in response do not have important policy implications; and other factors contribute more to uncertainty about program cost than does labor supply.

Experiments in social policy should be considered in relation to their cost and to the likelihood that some spectrum of opinion will be shifted—and how far. In our view the New Jersey experiment does not stand up well to these measures. It was conducted with intelligence, perseverance, objectivity, and wit, and yet it produced something less than overwhelming evidence.

Sunk costs are sunk. But it is not too late to consider whether the continuation or expansion of the current experiments is worthwhile. The cost of all the income maintenance experiments is approaching $70 million; the many permutations of labor supply response to negative income taxes that these experiments will test are not worth the cost. Although ethics require that promises to existing participants be kept, expansion to explore other issues should be seriously questioned.

None of the foregoing should be construed as implying that the New Jersey experiment was a failure or a waste of time and money. Among other things, it was an experiment in experimentation. The experiment produced extensive data about labor force behavior at a cost of $8 million, which seems quite reasonable when compared with the costs of such other research information as the Survey of Economic Opportunity of the U.S. Bureau of the Census or the Panel Study of Income Dynamics, the longitudinal survey of the Survey Research Center of the University of Michigan. It also produced information about the design and administration of welfare programs, which, although not an argument for experimentation, is valuable nonetheless. Finally, the experiment did generate another and unique observation: that for relatively low levels of welfare, the poor will not opt for leisure. This, and the other observations available, eventually may convince the doubters.

Comment by Richard P. Nathan

As a practitioner in welfare policymaking, I was asked to comment on the Mahoneys' paper. I was a member of that group of welfare planners who, in Gilbert Steiner's words, went blithely ahead on the family assistance plan in 1969 despite the fact that the New Jersey experiment was well under way and presumably would produce findings pertinent to these decisions.

The Mahoneys make an important contribution by their thoughtful treatment of the principal question of the New Jersey experiment: namely, the role of the marginal tax rate in income support programs. We learned such lessons the hard way in designing the family assistance plan: the lower the marginal tax rate, the more resources are shifted from the poor to the near poor or nonpoor. If insufficient resources are available to allow income support programs to eliminate poverty fully, the issue becomes how much poverty should be retained in the interest of maintaining strong work incentives.

I was pleased also that the Mahoneys included in their paper a discussion of the role and efficiency of in-kind transfers. As a proponent of a strategy of incremental reform for income support programs at this time, I believe we should devote more attention to this subject. The food stamp program now provides benefits to most poor working families at a higher level than would have been the case under the family assistance plan.

I want to distinguish between design problems in the New Jersey experiment and what I shall call questions of policy relevance. Henry Aaron's paper provides the framework for looking at this distinction. Aaron lists what he calls the "acknowledged problems" of the New Jersey experiment. The first two of these—the brevity of the experiment and the introduction of an AFDC-UP program—are design problems that make extrapolation of the results hazardous; both presumably could be corrected in the design and implementation of future or current experiments.

But Aaron's third acknowledged problem gets at what I define as the larger question of policy relevance. He states that "the thinness of the sample and the brevity of the experiment make it impossible to observe the impact of a negative income tax on the *mores* of entire groups" (emphasis added). The use of the word "mores" raises for me the question of whether the kind of a prolonged and emotional debate that would be necessary to pass a negative income tax would result in changes in behavior in terms of the choices between work and leisure that will be made by eligible or potentially eligible persons. Put another way, even if all the design problems of the New Jersey experiment were resolved—and this is no easy task—the basic question remains as to whether the findings from such an experiment would apply after a national and highly visible shift in policy— such as adoption of a negative income tax would represent—had occurred. Bluntly stated, is it not possible that adoption of a so-called "guaranteed-income" program would be interpreted by the eligible population as a congressional sanction for leisure?

What are the answers to this criticism of the New Jersey experiment in terms of its relevance for national policymaking?

One answer is that in Seattle an attempt is being made to advertise the availability of the new income maintenance program. This, it is suggested, will allow the researcher to claim that people understood the policy change and therefore that the experiment has taken into account the full impact of the new program on public opinion. I do not consider this an adequate answer to my suggestion that a change in mores could take place after a negative income tax had been enacted. We are not interested in how people's attitudes change in one locale in response to a program of limited duration. We are interested in how attitudes would change nationally after a long and emotional debate—as part of the broader debate over the adoption of a nationwide negative income tax program—has taken place on the fundamental question of the employment obligations of the poor.

A second answer is simply that this line of criticism could be directed against all social experimentation and that I am overstating its importance. Again, I am not satisfied. If we assume limited resources for social experimentation, as we must, my argument is that we should select areas for experimentation in which our findings are most likely to be relevant to policy and used accordingly. We could experiment in many social program areas. Generally, however, we should hold off experimenting in areas in which policy change is apt to be of so fundamental a nature and so emotionally charged that concern must necessarily exist about the effect on behavior of the policy changes being studied—and hence about whether the findings will remain relevant once the policy has been adopted and put into operation. Experiments in such areas are less useful than those which we judge will not involve policy changes likely to affect behavior on a broad scale: for example, new types of manpower, child-care, educational, and health-financing programs.

I conclude, therefore, that at the very least we must give more attention to efficient use of the resources available for social experimentation, and that we must develop strategies that weigh the potential payoffs of different types of social experimentation.

Comment by Alair A. Townsend and James R. Storey

We applaud the Mahoneys for reminding us that tax rates are only one parameter in the highly complex structure of an income maintenance system. Analysts probably have overindulged themselves in the study of tax rates, perhaps because they prefer to study problems that are well structured and quantitative and to which high-powered analytical tools can be applied. In addition, many of the analysts are economists, who naturally focus on policy issues related to labor markets.

The Mahoney paper, however, overreacts to the tax-rate focus. The tax rate is, after all, the single most significant factor in most income maintenance programs. It not only affects work incentives and program costs but also is a primary determinant of income adequacy for recipients with income—as well as of equity, both among recipients and between recipients and nonrecipients. Because the tax rate represents the marginal response of the system to any marginal change affecting income, the rate level and structure are crucial in many ways.

But although analysts may have been preoccupied with tax rates, politicians have not—at least not in the broad context just outlined. As a result, many programs of the negative income tax type are operating at all levels of government, with tax rates ranging from 25 percent to 100 percent—or even higher if one includes notches. The present conglomeration of programs includes such bizarre contrasts as states applying 100 percent tax rates to working men in general assistance programs, while the federal government taxes at 50 percent the wages of aged, blind, and disabled recipients of supplemental security income and social security.

The Mahoneys suggest that, in the compromise among adequacy, costs, coverage, work incentives, and equity, the greatest weight should be given to raising guarantees while minimizing costs. On these grounds, many current programs come remarkably close to meeting their objectives. We disagree that the balance should be struck in this way. Our view of the problems to be addressed by income maintenance reform leads us to urge moderate guarantees and tax rates.

In our view, a negative income tax or other income-related reform plan must accomplish three financial tasks:[13]

—Higher incomes for persons with little or no income or income-producing opportunities who either are currently excluded from categorical coverage or live in states paying well below average benefits

—Higher incomes for persons with income that is inadequate

—Constraining to reasonable levels combined benefits and tax rates that result from multiple programs

Given these priority objectives, it is difficult to see how high tax rates could supplement modest wages or facilitate program coordination.

Exploring Equity

The concepts of equity applied by the Mahoneys seem to be only straw men. Extreme positions have been taken along dimensions on which there is great room for compromise.

They have taken a restrictive view of vertical equity—that it forbids only a reversal of income positions. By this definition, programs that equalize or nearly equalize unequal pretransfer income positions meet the criteria for vertical equity. The definition of vertical equity with which we are familiar and comfortable requires some degree of posttransfer differentiation among former unequals. We expect popular acceptance of this view to be manifested by increasing concern over the fact that millions of social security beneficiaries who receive added income from the supplemental security income program or supplemental state programs received only $20 per month as a bonus for their social security contributions. A further result is that persons with markedly different previous earnings levels and social security benefits will receive identical posttransfer income.

Another straw-man concept of equity is that the poor should not pay taxes out of funds that were rightfully theirs. We do not know of serious analysis in which this argument has been advanced. Rather, we believe the argument is that people should not be made worse off for having worked.

It seems to us that there would be wide agreement in Congress—if the proposition were phrased in straightforward terms—that those who earn more should have more income. That the Congress does not always act this

13. The tasks noted here relate only to financial parameters. Other important targets of reform are improved administration and more standardized treatment of recipients.

way is another matter. We believe that these considerations are only now becoming understood, and that the legislative results may change as a consequence.

The Mahoneys' willingness to level incomes with 100 percent tax rates disturbs us and no doubt would disturb many members of Congress as well. Furthermore, implicit in their own questioning of the New Jersey income maintenance experiment seems to be a thread of doubt that they can state so categorically that tax rates do not matter. Finally, it seems to us to be socially destructive to apply a 100 percent or nearly 100 percent tax rate to the very bottom end of the income distribution. Such a policy in effect says that the work efforts of recipients are meaningless.

Equity is a slippery concept, especially because it is virtually impossible to separate out equal opportunities from equal outcomes. That is, do people have low pretransfer income because they have had unequal opportunities or because they have applied unequal efforts? If in part the answer is unequal opportunity, is it fair to treat such people as if they had an equal chance? It seems virtually impossible to make such determinations. Thus, a moderate guarantee for those who have had unequal opportunities provides something in the way of recompense, and a moderate tax rate then helps to differentiate among people on the presumption of unequal efforts.

To us, the equity issue revolves in large part around the bases for benefit distribution. The primary question is how far one wants to deviate from market rewards rather than build on them in the absence of any other clear basis for distribution. In practice, decisions about whom to aid and how much to aid them become decisions about whom and what behavior to reward.

Guarantee Levels and Adequacy

The Mahoneys stress their view that the role of tax rates is apparently to keep costs low and the role of the guarantee is to give people adequate incomes. We disagree. We would state the objective of both tax rates and guarantees as the maximization of recipients' total incomes in a fair way. This focus on goals is important.

The Mahoneys neglect the role of tax rates in reducing poverty and raising incomes. High tax rates essentially prevent people from raising their incomes except through very large jumps in earnings. It should be clear that in determining total income the tax rate is as important or more important for many people than the guarantee. Achieving income adequacy is nowhere nearly as simple as the Mahoneys present the matter. Because federal guarantees are unlikely ever to achieve levels that are accepted by everyone as adequate, helping the poor means building on their own efforts by applying a relatively low tax rate to their earnings.

Moreover, it can be argued legitimately that guarantee levels—at least in a federal program—should not be set at adequate levels, where adequacy is defined as benefits sufficiently high that supplementation from private sources is not required. First, there is the concern about the impact of such benefit levels on labor force participation. Only by ignoring the potential work-reduction effects of high guarantees can one argue wholeheartedly in favor of putting most of the dollars into the guarantee. There is disquieting research on AFDC that suggests that guarantees have a greater impact on work than do tax rates. Second, relatively few persons under sixty-five have no private income or income-producing opportunities. Most persons and families thus require income supplementation, not total income support. Therefore, to construct a federal program oriented largely to the few truly destitute seems misguided. The needs of special cases are better met under more subjectively operated state-operated supplemental programs.

The Mahoneys properly stress that the negative income tax can only reduce hours of work, not increase them. They argue that analysts and others have focused too much on the tax rate, to the exclusion of the guarantee. This statement certainly does not hold for most politicians, who seem to worry about one of two things: either the impact of giving aid to employables or how to raise benefits to high levels for groups that arouse sympathy. And with respect to the family assistance plan, the tax-rate issue was merely a convenient way to scuttle a plan that was objectionable largely because it offered an income guarantee to male-headed families. Within weeks of the plan's demise, the Senate Finance Committee reported out a provision that would have raised the AFDC tax rate on working women. We find little evidence that policymakers are excessively concerned about tax rates. Indeed, there is room for much greater concern about tax rates, especially from combined programs.

Of course, one factor pushing up the guarantee level is the problem of integrating a negative income tax with existing programs. The Mahoneys' paper gives little attention to program integration, but the vested interests of old programs and the objectives of new programs dictate some kind of integration. The Mahoneys hold that to compare benefits and tax rates from combined programs is a misleading and irrelevant exercise. They quite properly point out the technical difficulties and the extreme assumptions one has to make to construct such tables. But they offer no alternative. A look at combined programs is important, whether one looks at combined benefits or combined tax rates.

The tax-free combination of food stamps and AFDC, for example, is reaching astonishing levels: in eleven states it ranges from $3,900 to $4,500 for a penniless family of four and in eleven states, from $4,500 to $5,000; in five states it exceeds $5,000 a year. In the median state the combined benefit of $4,092 is equivalent to $5,360 in gross earnings (after taxes and work expenses of 15 percent of earnings). In New York State, this gross earned income equivalent rises to $7,020. At one time, food stamp tax rates were not significant for most AFDC recipients. In low-benefit states such as Indiana, Mississippi, and Missouri, there was virtually no AFDC tax rate over large ranges of income because of state use of maximums and other methods of computing payment amounts. In such high-benefit states as New Jersey and New York, recipients usually received the minimum food stamp bonus so long as they were eligible for AFDC. But tax-rate additivity is more important now because of increases in the food stamp allotments and breakevens.

Value of the New Jersey Experiment

We agree with many of the technical criticisms the Mahoneys level at the design of the New Jersey experiment. Much of the criticism of the experiment at the policy level clearly comes from years of further knowledge and experience accompanied by 20–20 hindsight. For instance, the Mahoneys continually stress that the experiments are limited to only one type of program. But the experiments followed on the work of a number of government task forces and agencies that analyzed the negative income tax as only one of several alternatives, from which it emerged as the vehicle of choice within government. Why should federal funds have been used to experiment with ideas rejected on the basis of previous analysis?

We think the Mahoneys understate drastically the role that the experiment has played and will play in determining that negative income taxes can be administered and that they will not undermine work efforts. The impact of the experiment will take time because the basic structure of programs and the trade-offs are woefully misunderstood outside a small circle of analysts.

There is no question, of course, that the utility of the experimental data is limited. We have learned much more about this type of research since

1968, and future attempts certainly will resolve some of the problems in the New Jersey experiment.

But the experiment cannot be termed a failure. We think it has proved its worth in the area of program administration alone. The experience in designing administrative systems and the resulting data should aid both administrators of existing programs and those planning future programs. In fact, program administration itself would be a useful subject for future experimentation, and one that should be accorded a high priority.

MICHAEL C. BARTH

LARRY L. ORR

JOHN L. PALMER

Policy Implications:
A Positive View

The New Jersey–Pennsylvania experiment was designed and implemented with the primary objective of determining the labor supply response of able-bodied, prime-age male heads of families to negative income tax types of programs having various tax rates and guarantee levels.[1] For this reason, the labor supply results generally are regarded as the most critical policy aspect of the experiment. But the experiment also has considerable policy significance in two other areas. First, it generated a substantial body of knowledge relating broadly to programs involving cash transfers whose level is scaled according to recipients' income. Second, it enlightened debate on the use and value of social experimentation as a tool of policy research.

We consider the policy impact and implications of the New Jersey experiment from a dual perspective. As economists, we are interested in better estimates of the parameters of labor supply. In addition, our positions provide us a vantage point from which to observe both the development of social experimentation and the utilization of the results of this particular experiment.

We also discuss the choice of a specific tax, or benefit reduction rate, in a

---

1. The labor supply and most of the nonlabor supply findings of the experiment are relevant to more than a negative income tax program. Existing cash welfare programs such as AFDC-UP and supplemental security income also have a structure involving guarantees and a tax imposed on other sources of income—as do such major in-kind welfare programs as food stamps and certain housing programs. Although we will use the term "negative income tax" in this paper, much of our discussion applies equally to any income-related transfer program having the same basic structure.

negative income tax program—and the implication of the experiment for that decision. The criteria for evaluating social experiments also are developed and applied to the New Jersey experiment, along with an exploration of the implications for policy research emerging from this first, successful fielding of a controlled social experiment.

Welfare Policy: Implications and Impact of the Experiment

Policy impact and policy implications, although closely related, are separable. Policy implications are abstract. They emerge from some portrait of reality that is imposed upon a particular policy issue, most often one of program design. Policy impact concerns the actual effect of the experiment on the attitudes and behavior of policymakers and persons who influence them. Such effects are of most interest when they contribute to the promulgation or prevention of policy changes.

Labor Supply

POLICY IMPLICATIONS. We believe that the findings of the New Jersey experiment lend considerable support to the contention that, based upon existing evidence—that is, the results of the experiment viewed in conjunction with, and in relation to, other evidence on this issue—the best estimate of the effects of a national negative income tax type of program, one with tax rates and guarantees in the range tested, on the labor supply of prime-age able-bodied male heads of intact urban families are:
—First, in the aggregate, both in the short and the long run, the reduction in labor supply is likely to be quite modest, less than 10 percent, at worst.
—Second, any reduction will be distributed across many workers rather than concentrated among a few.
—Third, the degree of reduction will not be very sensitive to the particular guarantee and tax rate chosen, at least among the lower tax rates.

These findings contain four important policy implications. First, public opposition to coverage of all intact families by an income-related cash-transfer program—to the extent that such opposition is based on fear of large reductions in work effort—should decrease. Second, the concern of policymakers about the disincentive effects of particular tax rates and guarantee levels should diminish. They can place heavier weight upon other criteria in the selection of an appropriate tax rate and guarantee level in any income-related cash transfer program.

Third, the case for a work test in an income-related cash transfer program covering intact families is weakened. In light of the administrative and other costs of a work test, the smaller the reduction in labor supply that would occur in its absence, the less cost effective it will be. In addition, whether a work test could prevent the small reductions that do occur is questionable. The fact that a work test for male heads of families is likely to be cost ineffective, however, does not necessarily make it undesirable. It may be necessary to preserve the integrity of the program.

Fourth, the very existence of the experiment as well as its results should raise the level of the policy debate surrounding work and welfare in general and the work-disincentive effects of income-related transfer programs in particular. Policy concern should be more explicitly articulated: for example, distinctions among responses of male heads, female heads, and secondary workers are more likely to be made. Debate now may center on acceptable amounts and kinds of labor supply response rather than on its presence or absence.

POLICY IMPACT. Because the final results of the experiment have been available for only a short time, we expect that most of the policy impact is yet to come. We have no way of knowing to what extent preliminary results reported to the House Ways and Means Committee may have influenced its chairman, Wilbur D. Mills, to support the family assistance plan. But it does seem likely that the negative findings at that time—that no abrupt or large reductions will occur in labor supply—might have allayed the concern of those who were not opponents of the program on other grounds.

High-level administration officials have been involved in a detailed examination and an increasingly sophisticated discussion of the major issues involved in potential welfare reform policies and of evidence that could be brought to bear on them. The relation between work and welfare, particularly work disincentives, is among these issues. Many officials who originally believed that there would be large disincentive effects associated with high basic benefits or high benefit reduction rates were willing to revise their beliefs substantially in the face of the New Jersey experimental results and other relevant evidence. As a consequence, their willingness to give serious consideration to a program for which the working poor would be eligible has increased.[2] We see no reason to believe that, once the evidence

2. One lengthy briefing on, and discussion of, the final results of the experiment included the secretary and under secretary of HEW, the under secretary of labor, and at least seven officials at the assistant secretary level from various executive agencies.

has been more widely discussed, most congressmen and the general public would respond very differently.[3]

Nonlabor Supply Policy Implications and Impact

In retrospect, the policy significance of the nonlabor supply aspects of the experiment appears to be at least as valuable as, if not more valuable than, that of the labor supply results. Many of the findings are relevant not only to a new cash program for intact families, but also to any income-related program, including existing welfare programs. Most of these nonlabor supply findings emerge from what Robert Levine terms the "demonstration aspects" of the experiment.[4] They pertain largely to administrative matters, but ones with important policy implications.

ADMINISTRATIVE FEASIBILITY. One apparent fear was whether a negative income tax program—or any other comprehensive federally administered income-related program—could ever be successfully administered. But more important than whether it can be done is how it should be done. The New Jersey experiment has helped to answer both questions.

The administrative lessons of the experiment are also relevant to other types of negative income taxes: for example, to a refundable tax credit that would replace personal exemptions. Administration of a refundable tax credit would involve detailed self-reporting, similar to that developed in the New Jersey experiment, by a population presently having minimal contact with the positive tax system.

THE ACCOUNTING PERIOD. Everyone can agree that an income-related transfer program should treat equally needy people equally. But even if one assumes that income is to be the measure of need, difficult issues are involved in the design of an equitable program. Are people with the same

---

Rarely does a research project receive this much interest from such high-ranking officials. Such exposure cannot help but improve the quality of subsequent discussion of related issues by these decisionmakers.

3. There is already some evidence about Congress. Representative Martha W. Griffiths, in releasing Paper 13 of *Studies in Public Welfare* (prepared for the Subcommittee on Fiscal Policy of the Joint Economic Committee, "How Income Supplements Can Affect Work Behavior," stated: "A key obstacle to extending cash supplements to poor families headed by able-bodied men has been the fear that many will leave their jobs. The bulk of the evidence shows that such fears are unfounded. . . . The studies are in substantial agreement: a broad income supplement plan would add to the incomes of poor fathers, without causing such men to leave full-time work." JEC Press Release, February 18, 1974. The New Jersey experiment was among the studies cited by Griffiths.

4. See Robert Levine's paper, "How and Why the Experiment Came About," in this volume.

income in a given month but very different regularized annual incomes equally in need? Over what time period should equality of need be measured? Because there is no obvious answer to this latter question, the implications of alternative definitions of equal need must be examined.

The income maintenance experiment generated the first longitudinal data bases containing intrayear income flows for the low-income population, thus making possible the analysis of alternative periods of time over which income is to be counted to determine eligibility and benefit levels. Because the income of the low-income population generally fluctuates considerably within a year, both costs and coverage are highly sensitive to the length of the accounting period for a given guarantee. A given number of transfer dollars can be distributed in quite different ways depending on the length of the accounting period. Those with fluctuating, higher-than-average, but occasionally low monthly incomes are aided relatively more by a short accounting period; those with more stable monthly but lower average annual incomes are aided relatively more by a long accounting period.

In addition, there is continuing analysis and discussion of changing the accounting period in AFDC-UP and other income-related programs, most of which have a (nominal) one-month accounting period. Neither the acute awareness of this issue nor the data to permit its analysis would exist in the absence of the experiment.

INCOME REPORTING AND INFORMATION PROCESSING. The experiment generated considerable information on such issues as the trade-off in administrative cost between reporting at regular intervals as against reporting only when significant changes occur or between frequency of reporting and accuracy of the data reported. What is the ability of the population to report on a self-assessment basis, as in the U.S. income tax system? How much and what types of assistance are compatible with self-reporting? These are critical issues in the design of an administrative system for an income-related program. The reporting practices in present programs have not yet been much improved as a result, although evidence from the experiment has been brought to bear on the issue of increased frequency of reporting in the AFDC-UP program. But the experiment's results are having a major impact on the design of an administrative structure under current reform proposals.

Useful information with strong policy implications also was acquired about data processing needs of a regularized reporting and payment system, techniques of audit and verification, and the application of an assets test. As with income reporting, this information is having little impact on current program practices but is important in the design of reform proposals.

BEHAVIORAL RESULTS. Another major portion of the experimental analysis was devoted to exploring the effects of the negative income tax plans on economic, social, and psychological behavior and attitudes beyond the issue of the labor market.[5] With the exception of some aspects of consumption behavior, job search patterns, and educational attainment, the results of these studies were almost uniformly negative: no systematic pattern of significant experimental effect was found.

The policy implications of these results also are negative. If these findings are to be accepted at face value, marginal increments of income—increases in family income of about 25 percent in the experimental plans—will have no major impact on the life style and attitudes of low-income families. By the same token, such payments appear not to produce the deleterious effects sometimes associated with being on "the dole." If these basic propositions were to be accepted by all parties to the welfare reform debate, much extraneous rhetoric and emotional undercurrent could be dispensed with, and policy deliberation focused on more central issues.

Finally, we agree with Levine that, at least with respect to the New Jersey experiment, social experimentation is as much a political process as a detailed scientific one. We, too, think that a major result of the experiment probably will be "to make the negative income tax visible and therefore more feasible than it otherwise would have been."[6]

Choice of a Tax Rate for Policy

The results of measuring the differential effects of various guarantee levels and tax rates on labor supply fail to indicate that the different tax rates studied have significantly different disincentive effects.[7] It has been

5. The paper prepared by Peter Rossi, "A Critical Review of the Analysis of Nonlabor Force Responses," in this volume, contains a discussion of most of these analyses. These effects were not central to the purpose of the experiment and therefore received less attention than the labor supply effects. For this reason, the evidence mentioned below should not be considered definitive.

6. Levine, "How and Why," p. 23.

7. The experimental evidence for the 70 percent tax rate is relatively inconclusive because the benefits of the New Jersey and Pennsylvania AFDC-UP programs tended to dominate those plans with this high tax rate. Unless further analyses of the data are successful in disentangling these effects, the experimental results probably cannot be relied upon to predict the effect of tax rates in excess of 50 percent.

argued that such a finding supports the view that any income-conditioned transfer program for male-headed families should embody high tax rates in order to concentrate benefits among families with the lowest incomes.[8] Such a strategy, it is argued, will maximize the antipoverty efficiency of cash transfers so long as the labor supply response to cash transfers is small. Although we agree that the experimental results have an important bearing on the choice of tax rate for public policy, we do not agree that the results necessarily argue for high tax rates.

The Goal of Transfer Policy

In the absence of any labor supply response, high tax rates certainly reduce the cost of bringing all low-income families up to a specified minimum income level. But it is not clear that the distributional objectives of transfer policy are simply to maximize the portion of total transfers going to the lowest decile of families or to minimize the cost of providing a specified minimum income. Ultimately, the goal of transfer policy is to change the shape of income distribution; thus, the optimal transfer policy is one that achieves the income distribution deemed optimal by policymakers. Viewed in this way, it makes no sense to speak of allocating a fixed transfer budget efficiently or setting transfer policy to minimize net transfers. The size of the transfer budget that policymakers ultimately will approve, large or small, will reflect the pattern of income distribution they prefer.

Distributional Effects of High and Low Tax Rates

What, then, are the distributional implications of the level of the tax rate?

High tax rates would have the effect of drastically compressing income differentials in the lower tail of the income distribution. In the extreme case, a program with 100 percent tax rates would virtually eliminate the gap between families with no private income and those just above the guarantee level.[9] At a minimum, this is certain to offend the sense of equity of those

8. See the paper by Bette S. Mahoney and W. Michael Mahoney, "Policy Implications: A Skeptical View," in this volume.

9. The distributional question on the positive tax side is analogous. A tax policy that imposed 100 percent marginal rates on incomes above a certain level would maximize tax collections from those best able to pay, just as 100 percent tax rates on the transfer side

unaided—and quite possibly poor—families who end up near the bottom of the new income distribution; it may strike policymakers as inequitable as well.

In contrast, low tax rates would allow a much smoother compression of the income distribution over this range. The income differential between any two recipient families would be reduced by a fraction exactly equal to the tax rate—assuming no labor supply response. It seems quite plausible to us that policymakers might wish to preserve some degree of income differentials within the lower tail of the income distribution as a reward for private effort and initiative, even if work effort in itself is unaffected by the tax rate.

Basically, the choice of the tax rate is a question largely of distributional equity between the working poor and near poor whose incomes fall near the poverty line and the nonworking poor. At any reasonable budget level, a transfer program with a high guarantee and high tax rate would exclude from benefits large numbers of full-time, year-round workers whose earnings are low by any standard while providing relatively generous assistance to the families of unemployed or partially employed individuals.

In short, high tax rates are an efficient means of attaining a very specific type of income distribution, one in which all recipients have total incomes close to the guarantee level, and in which the remainder of the income distribution remains unchanged (except for changes caused by taxes required to finance the transfers). Whether this is an optimal distribution is a policy question that cannot be resolved by empirical evidence. What can be said on the basis of the experimental evidence is that, in making this distributional decision, policymakers need not be constrained by an expectation of induced labor supply responses to tax rates in the range for which the experimental evidence is relevant.

Perhaps other adverse behavioral responses to high tax rates must be taken into account. For example, the incentives for divorce and desertion or for individual family members to leave the home may be a function of the tax rate. The abrupt change in marginal tax rates at the breakeven point also would create a variety of incentives for real or apparent shifts in income patterns over time and among sources of income. These incentives are similar to those involved in the infamous tax loopholes of the positive

---

maximize payments to those most in need. Tax policymakers, however, have opted instead for a posttax income distribution that narrows rather than eliminates income differentials.

income tax; in the case of the negative income tax, families can largely escape taxation by clustering their income in periods when it is above the breakeven or switching to sources that are easily underreported.

Potential Effects of Extremes

But in viewing the tax-rate issue, the experimental findings do indicate some overall labor supply reduction in response to negative income tax payments—for secondary workers, a fairly substantial response. True, no clear and systematic variation in response appeared over the range either of tax rates tested or of guarantee levels employed, but the observed labor supply reduction must be in response to changes in one of these parameters, since they uniquely define the experimental treatments. Thus, we cannot say that either or both the tax rate and guarantee effects are zero, only that the experiment was unable to measure their separate effects reliably. Therefore, the potential for extreme values of these parameters to induce labor supply reduction cannot be dismissed out of hand, especially in light of the inconclusive evidence about the 70 percent rates.

As we have been reminded repeatedly, the tax rate that matters is not the rate applicable to a single program but the cumulative benefit reduction rate involved in the combination of program benefits that any individual receives. Even under a negative income tax that is fully integrated with the positive income tax system and replaces existing income-related cash transfers and food stamps, a variety of other income-conditioned tax and transfer programs are likely to remain: for example, the social security payroll tax, sales taxes, public housing, and premium contributions and benefits under national health insurance. If the cumulative benefit reduction or tax rate is to remain below 100 percent, the negative income tax rate must leave room for additional rates.

The Experiment as a Tool for Policy Research

By what criteria should anything as complex as the New Jersey experiment be judged? A nonexhaustive list would include the following:
—The central hypothesis should have been of compelling policy importance at the time the experiment was designed, with good reason to believe that this would continue to be the case.

—At the time of the experiment's design, there should have been no
cheaper or simpler way of obtaining the desired information.[10]
—The experiment should have been competently and honestly managed—
including, of course, the analysis.
—The tracks of the experiment should allow other social scientists, in principle, to replicate the operations and other analysts, in fact, to replicate
the econometrics.
—The results, however complex, should speak directly to the initial hypothesis.

There is, we believe, little dispute that the experiment satisfies the first
four criteria. A strong case for its meeting the fifth criterion also can be
made, but there may be some disagreement. Having written the summary
report of the experiment,[11] we are aware of the complexity of the results
and of the paradoxes and loose ends. Complex results, however, often are
produced by complex investigations of complex social phenomena. Even
the initiators and designers of the New Jersey experiment did not expect it
to provide definitive findings on the labor supply response of the population it covered. It was assumed in advance that no matter how apparently
successful the execution of the experiment and how meticulous the analysis
of the data, issues such as the potential Hawthorne effect and the methodological complexity, short duration, and small scale of the program would
lead many people to question the relevance of its results for a national
program. Nevertheless, it should be clear to everybody that the New Jersey
experiment directly addresses the null hypothesis, that a negative income
tax treatment would have no effect on labor supply.

What is troublesome about the experiment, particularly to those who
must use its results, are precisely the paradoxes and loose ends. Because the
results of the experiment are somewhat clouded at present by such factors
as the AFDC-UP contamination and the inexplicably slow income growth
of black families in the control group, the findings at this point are by no

10. It has been suggested that analysis of data from ongoing federal social programs
could have shed some light on those issues which the experiment was designed to examine. Although we have supported, do support, and will continue to support analyses
of program data, we feel there were compelling reasons to seek better data. First, there is
no control group for persons whose behavior generates the observations reflected in program data, and to a large extent those observations are self-selected. Second, the treatments of greatest interest are defined imperfectly at best and are uncontrolled in operating programs. Third, the cross-sectional data available from program records are grossly
inferior to the longitudinal data obtained by special studies such as the experiment.

11. U.S. Department of Health, Education, and Welfare, "Summary Report: New
Jersey Graduated Work Incentive Experiment" (1973; processed).

means beyond question. Thus, one cannot expect unanimity about the usability of the results in a policy context. Rather, one must rest upon a consensus of experts and consistency with other evidence. But is this really much different from the problems encountered in the utilization of any product of policy research? It is perhaps the costliness of this experiment and the presumed importance of its basic task, as much as the complexity of its results, that—quite rightly, in our view—lead to the calls for caution in generalizing from the results now available.

Usefulness of the Experiment

One evaluative criterion that is certain to be raised is the usefulness of the experiment. The fairness of this criterion deserves comment. Suppose Congress had enacted a universal cash transfer program in 1970. Would the labor supply results of the experiment have been useful? One can always argue that fine tuning of tax and guarantee parameters would always be important. Our guess, however, is that the answer to the question of usefulness would then be negative. But surely this would not have been a fair criterion upon which to judge the experiment. Even though the labor supply results no longer would have been of compelling policy interest, the validation of the initial hypothesis alone suggests that the experiment performed its task.

Congress did not pass a cash transfer bill, but the administration currently is developing a comprehensive proposal for welfare reform, and the results of the experiment already have been useful in policy discourse. The experiment's enduring contribution and its impact on any particular piece of legislation are for historians and journalists to argue.

Current policy developments aside, our model of the policy impact of the experiment runs as follows. In the short run the experiment may have little effect. If its results are not proved incorrect by competent authority, however, a strong presumption of a small disincentive effect probably will begin to prevail, in no small part because of the consistency between the results of the experiment and the cross-sectional studies.[12] Neither alone is sufficient to establish such a presumption. But this presumption is unlikely to produce a rapid change in the public stance of decisionmakers. A more

---

12. See Irwin Garfinkel, "Income Transfer Programs and Work Effort: A Review," in *Studies in Public Welfare*, Paper 13.

probable outcome is that work-incentive effects will be given less weight in decisionmaking about transfer plans.

Longer-term attitudes may be affected in the following manner. Those who understand the methodology, assuming they are convinced of the accuracy of the experimental results, will begin to believe the results, which will represent a subtle shift in the conventional wisdom regarding the labor supply effects of transfer programs. Similarly, assuming professional approval, the results will begin to be accepted by the public.

Others may feel that this is too optimistic a view. But if policy research, which includes social experimentation, does not and cannot change the layman's views, why are we in this business? Our model of the utilization of the experimental results allows a very positive answer.

What the Experiment Did Not Do

To this point, our evaluation of the experiment has considered only errors of commission. This is appropriate for two reasons: first, the criterion of compelling policy importance would not be satisfied if an experiment did not investigate a sufficiently important question; and, second, anything so complex as an experiment in the social sciences really can have only one hypothesis as its driving force.[13] Therefore, we feel that errors of omission are less consequential. Nevertheless, the experiment has been faulted for what it did not do, a criticism that deserves comment.

To expect that the experiment would answer all questions of policy interest regarding cash-transfer plans is to impose an impossible and unjustifiable burden upon it. Research, of whatever type, attacks targets of opportunity. The justification for a policy research project is that the research question be of policy importance and that the research can be done. On this criterion we give the experiment a good grade.

Moreover, the experiment does not and should not decide for policymakers whether to extend cash assistance to the working poor or at what levels and with what benefit-reduction rates. Indeed, no empirical evidence could do so. Research, no matter how relevant and competent, cannot tell us what national policy ought to be. It can provide some hard data as one input to the process that balances competing demands for scarce public resources.

13. Felicity Skidmore's paper in this volume, "Operational Design of the Experiment," supports this point.

Much more analysis of the experimental data certainly must be done. Only relatively simple models have been estimated to date, since the first task was to identify what happened. As time permits, a search for the "why," more explicit use of models of family labor supply, the joint determination of participation and hours, and other refinements will be required. Whether policy will move faster than analysis is a matter about which we can only guess. If the prospect of such an eventuality were to deter research, research would never get done.

Implications for Policy Research

Among the longer-lasting effects of the New Jersey experiment may be those on governmental policy research. If one views policy research as an integral part of the policy process—and we do—then these effects may be regarded as policy implications or impact of the experiment. In the long run, we believe that these will prove to be substantial.

Whatever the technical defects of this particular experiment, it represents a marked departure from traditional techniques of research and evaluation, on the one hand, and, on the other, a monumental advance over demonstrations as a technique for testing behavioral hypotheses. As the first major controlled social experiment, it opened up an entirely new methodology of policy research. Like any other research tool, it must be used judiciously. But we believe that experimentation may be a superior approach whenever knowledge of individual behavioral responses is important to program design. Examples may be found throughout the whole range of consumption subsidies employed or contemplated by the government: in health, housing, social services, education, transport, and other areas. Of course, proposed experiments in any of these areas must be evaluated on their merits, including the degree to which they satisfy the five criteria set forth in the preceding section.

Prototype for Social Experiments

FEASIBILITY. We are only beginning to explore the potential of experimentation as a tool for policy research. It is far too early to assess the ultimate value of the experiments that have followed the New Jersey experiment, but almost certainly they would not have been possible without the pioneering example set in New Jersey. The change in the attitudes of governmental officials toward large-scale field research since 1967 has been striking. As Levine points out,[14] in 1967 HEW expected major political difficulties in the idea of the experiment, yet only three years later the department launched two new experiments in income maintenance—in Seattle-Denver and in Gary—on a scale that dwarfed the New Jersey project. And in 1973, only HEW's support saved a major experimental study of health insurance from being killed on political grounds by new leadership at the OEO.

There was nothing inexorable about the growing acceptance of experimentation as a means of policy research. Rather, it is attributable largely to the success of the experimenters in implementing an extremely difficult administrative undertaking in a manner that preserved fundamental analytical objectives. In the crudest terms, the experiment appeared to work without operational compromises that would have sacrificed its objectives. This reassured researchers that usable data could be obtained from field projects, and it reassured policymakers that such an undertaking need not be a political liability.

METHODOLOGY. The experiment not only demonstrated the feasibility of this new technique but also made major methodological contributions to its development. Perhaps the most basic and important was the notion that at least some social policies can be parameterized and a continuous response function estimated from observations generated in the field. This notion, so common in nonexperimental research, was virtually foreign to the literature of experimental design in the social sciences, which had been dominated by analysis of variance techniques. It was totally absent from the evaluation methodology in previous demonstrations.

The idea of using regression analysis to estimate a continuous response surface as a function of well-defined policy parameters, combined with the recognition of the different costs of the various types of observations and the different policy interest in the various negative income tax plans, led to the development of the Conlisk-Watts sample allocation model. This statistical technique, which has formed the basis for sample design in most subsequent social experiments, offers great economy and flexibility in the design of experimental research—as compared, for example, with a balanced factorial design. It allows policymakers—or their policy research representatives—to focus their interest on specific areas of the policy domain without excluding less central policy options that may prove impor-

14. Levine, "How and Why."

tant in the end. It allows efficient allocation of resources over policy options and population groups with widely different budgetary costs; and it allows interpolation of results to points in the population domain not specifically included in the experimental design.

One can argue about the extent to which the potential of these statistical techniques has been realized in the New Jersey experiment. But it seems clear to us that they provide a focus of research objectives—in fact, an entirely new way of thinking about experimental design—that takes field tests of social policy out of the ill-defined realm of demonstrations and into the scientific realm of behavioral research.

DESIGN. In other important respects quite aside from the statistical contributions of the experiment, this project has formed a model for subsequent social experiments. The administrative and field procedures developed in New Jersey, including the carefully defined rules of operation, are a major contribution to experimental methodology.

We also have learned a great deal from the mistakes made in New Jersey. Among the more important lessons is that the design of social experiments must be robust with respect to exogenous forces and unforeseen events. The experimental treatments must be designed to insulate the participants both from existing programs that the policy under study is designed to replace and from unexpected legislative developments that threaten the integrity of the experimentally defined policy parameters. In the second generation of experimentation, we are taking great care to build in this insulation.[15]

In addition, we now know that the design of the experiment must be robust with respect to analytical exigencies. The possibility of strong interactions between treatment variables and participant characteristics such as ethnicity dictates some tempering of rigid application of sample allocation models based on smoothly continuous response functions. Finally, although we hesitate to term the concentration of this experiment in a single geographical area a mistake, we have become acutely aware of the problem of generalizability of results. Much thought now is being given by govern-

15. In the Seattle and Denver experiment into income maintenance, all treatments are designed to dominate existing welfare benefits. In the health insurance experiment, a rather elaborate set of rules and compensatory cash payments has been developed to preclude receipt of benefits from nonexperimental health insurance plans, both public and private, although still guaranteeing the participants' eligibility for such benefits at the end of the experiment. The use of compensatory cash payments has quite general applicability for insulating experimental treatments involving in-kind benefits and earmarked cash transfers.

ment researchers to the problem of designing experiments that, although necessarily clustered in a small number of sites, yield results that can be confidently extrapolated to large geographical areas and altered market conditions.

Contribution to the Social Data Base

Apart from its importance as the prototype for social experiments, the New Jersey project has generated an exceedingly rich body of data that will be useful for investigation of a wide variety of behavioral issues wholly unrelated to the labor supply response to a negative income tax. It is virtually the only existing set of longitudinal data on the intrayear family-income dynamics of the working poor. Over $2 million of the $8 million cost of the experiment was devoted to the collection and preanalytical processing of the more than 15,000 interviews administered over the course of the experiment. To generate a comparable data base through surveys or collection of program data, even without the experimental variations, would have been equally expensive. Given the uniqueness of this data base and the care with which it was collected, we feel that at least this portion of the experimental expense is defensible on grounds wholly separate from the major purposes of the project.

More generally, the advent of social experimentation has helped to focus more attention on the inadequacies and defects of nonexperimental data. It was, after all, these defects which were a partial impetus to the New Jersey experiment. The biases attributable to self-selection in observations drawn from ongoing programs and private markets are now well recognized—in part because of the very attention they have received in the context of social experiments. Interest is growing in the use of longitudinal data to study dynamic processes, and with it an increased awareness of the dearth of reliable longitudinal surveys. To parse out the contribution of experimentation to these developments is, of course, impossible. Our own judgment is that it has been consequential.

Contribution to Research Talent

Finally, social experimentation in general and the New Jersey experiment in particular have helped to create a community of academic researchers with an abiding interest in the policy issues of income maintenance. It has provided a focus—and, to some extent, funding—for their research efforts, as well as data for their models. In the process of working through the development of a model negative income tax program, theoretical and programmatic issues that otherwise might have remained hidden have been brought into the light for analysis. Conversely, that same process has helped to broaden the perspective of the researchers themselves, to include programmatic considerations that do not emerge naturally from theoretical models. Those of us who mediate between the research community and the policy process are in a position to appreciate both the creation of this reservoir of talent and that active interest in income maintenance policy which its members have maintained.

Summary

The New Jersey experiment has numerous policy implications and already has had significant policy impact. Assuming that the analysis to date is not contradicted, the experiment suggests that the work-disincentive response of prime-age male family heads in the urban Northeast to an income-related cash transfer would be quite modest. In our opinion, this result, together with the results of cross-sectional studies of labor supply behavior, will begin to establish a presumption of a small labor supply response of male family heads under a national program of similar characteristics. If we are correct, then a rather remarkable shift in informed opinion will have taken place since the 1966–68 period during which the experiment was proposed, designed, and begun.

One of the more important findings of this experiment is that no different labor supply response across tax rates was detected. The policy implication of this finding represents a loosening of constraints on program designers: that in making decisions on the desired income distribution, policymakers can select benefit reduction or tax rates to satisfy a broad range of social goals, not only the goal of minimizing reduction of work effort.

Assessing the policy impact of the experiment at this point is at least as hazardous as deriving its policy implications. Still, there seems to be general agreement that the experiment had some impact on the deliberations about the family assistance plan, at least in the House of Representatives. More recently, the final report of the experiment coincided with a substantial effort at the staff and policy levels to reexamine a range of welfare-related issues. Perhaps a cautious policy analyst would have waited a few years for a reanalysis of the data before presenting the results to policy-level officials.

For good or ill, the results of the experiment, together with other relevant information, have been heard and, we believe, have had some impact on policymakers. Precisely how much and whether the experimental results will affect the existence and nature of a new welfare reform proposal are matters for speculation.

The uniqueness of this particular experiment should be noted. It was, of course, the first, and our positive assessment of the policy value of this experiment results in part from this fact. For example, the experiments that quickly followed—the rural, Seattle-Denver, and Gary income maintenance projects and others on housing allowances, performance contracting in education, and health insurance—no matter how successful they may be, may not have the same impact on future policy research.

What seems most important at this time is that a new methodology of policy research was developed successfully and directed to an important question. Answers, however complex, were produced and heard by persons in a position to act on the information. It is very early in the half-life of the knowledge generated by the experiment to say much more.

Conference Participants

with their affiliations at the time of the conference

Henry J. Aaron *Brookings Institution*
Marcus Alexis *Northwestern University*
Jodie T. Allen *Mathematica, Inc.*
Michael C. Barth *U.S. Department of Health, Education, and Welfare*
C. Worth Bateman *Urban Institute*
D. Lee Bawden *University of Wisconsin*
Duran Bell, Jr. *Rand Corporation*
Blanche Bernstein *New School for Social Research*
Michael J. Boskin *Stanford University*
Elizabeth F. Durbin *New York University*
Martin S. Feldstein *Harvard University*
Edward M. Gramlich *Brookings Institution*
Zvi Griliches *Harvard University*
Robert E. Hall *Massachusetts Institute of Technology*
Robert W. Hartman *Brookings Institution*
Robinson G. Hollister, Jr. *Swarthmore College*
David N. Kershaw *Mathematica, Inc.*
Robert A. Levine *New York City Rand Institute*
Irene Lurie *Union College*
James Lyday *Environmental Protection Agency*
Bette S. Mahoney *U.S. Department of Health, Education, and Welfare*
W. Michael Mahoney *U.S. Social Security Administration*
Charles D. Mallar *Johns Hopkins University*

225

Charles E. Metcalf *University of Wisconsin*

Jacob Mincer *Columbia University*

Richard P. Nathan *Brookings Institution*

Guy H. Orcutt *Yale University*

Larry L. Orr *U.S. Department of Health, Education, and Welfare*

John L. Palmer *U.S. Department of Health, Education, and Welfare*

Joseph A. Pechman *Brookings Institution*

John A. Pincus *Rand Corporation*

Fredric Q. Raines *Washington University (St. Louis)*

Albert Rees *Princeton University*

Martin Rein *Massachusetts Institute of Technology*

Alice M. Rivlin *Brookings Institution*

Heather Ross *Urban Institute*

Peter H. Rossi *Johns Hopkins University*

Charles L. Schultze *Brookings Institution*

Felicity Skidmore *University of Wisconsin*

Gilbert Y. Steiner *Brookings Institution*

James R. Storey *Subcommittee on Fiscal Policy of the Joint Economic Committee, U.S. Congress*

P. Michael Timpane *Brookings Institution*

Alair A. Townsend *Subcommittee on Fiscal Policy of the Joint Economic Committee, U.S. Congress*

Harold W. Watts *University of Wisconsin*

Finis Welch *Rand Corporation*

Index

Aaron, Henry J., 5–7, 198; comment on paper by, 110–14

Accounting period: defined, 37–39; significance of, 209–10

Administrative feasibility, of negative income tax, 12–13, 158n, 195, 205, 209–10

Administrative regulations, in the experiment, 23, 34–40, 220

Adolescents (teenagers), 66–68, 70, 113, 171–73, 181

AFDC, 11, 29, 36n, 39, 152–53, 157n, 167, 203–04; in Pennsylvania, 52, 211n

AFDC-UP, 18, 28n, 30, 168, 194, 206n, 210

—in New Jersey, 19, 66, 90, 93; effect on negative income tax experiment, 6–7, 36n, 44–45, 55, 59, 99, 101, 154–55, 211n

Aid to Families with Dependent Children. *See* AFDC

Aid to Families with Dependent Children–Unemployed Parents. *See* AFDC-UP

Allen, Vernon L., 178n, 179–80, 182

Allowances. *See* Housing allowances; Payments to participants

Ashenfelter, Orley, 109

Assistance programs, government. *See* Government assistance programs

Attrition, problem of, 47–49, 59, 74, 116, 130, 132–33, 150–51, 153

Banfield, Edward C., 160n

Barth, Michael C., 11, 13

Baumol, William J., 47

Bawden, D. Lee, 38n, 195

Becker, Gary S., 137

Behavioral responses in participating families, 9–11, 27, 147–48, 157–82, 198–99, 211, 213, 221

Benefits: cash versus in-kind, 191–92; in-kind transfers, 99, 198, 206n; variety of, 214. *See also* Income maintenance; Payments to participants; Transfer programs

Black families: in control group, 71, 215

—in experimental sample, 52, 106, 116, 166, 168, 175n; attrition among, 132, 153; payments to, 75; wage rates of, 106–07

Black labor supply, effects of the experiment on, 5–6, 9, 71, 78–83, 85–87, 129–30

Blum, Zahava D., 160n, 171n

Boskin, Michael, 8, 102n, 109

Bronfenbrenner, Martin, 188n

Brookings Institution, 18, 21

Bundy, McGeorge, 20

Cain, Glen G., 2n, 29n, 30n, 68n, 91n, 103n, 107n, 108n, 109, 153, 169, 171n

Califano, Joseph A., Jr., 17

California, 90n

Camden, 52

Cash allowances. *See* Payments to participants

Cash payments, compensatory, use of, 220n

Census Bureau, 29n, 69

Children's allowance, proposal for, 16, 19–20. *See also* AFDC; AFDC-UP

Christensen, Sandra, 109n, 119n

Coleman, James S., 171n

Color television problem, 157, 164, 166n

Community action programs (CAP), 16, 19–22, 52

Community cooperation, 50

Congress, U.S., 56–57, 201–03, 209n, 222

Conlisk, John, 4n, 103n, 105n, 219

Conlisk-Watts model, 4, 103n, 105n, 219